INSURING THE ESSENTIALS

INSURING THE ESSENTIALS

BOB BALL ON SOCIAL SECURITY

A Selection of Articles and Essays
from 1942 through 2000
by Robert M. Ball

Edited by Thomas N. Bethell

A Century Foundation Book

2000 • The Century Foundation Press • New York

The Century Foundation, formerly the Twentieth Century Fund, sponsors and supervises timely analyses of economic policy, foreign affairs, and domestic political issues. Not-for-profit and nonpartisan, it was founded in 1919 and endowed by Edward A. Filene.

LIBRARY OF CONGRESS CATALOGING-IN-PUBLICATION DATA
Ball, Robert M.
    Insuring the essentials : Bob Ball on Social Security / by Robert M. Ball and Thomas N. Bethell.
      p. cm.
    Includes index.
    ISBN 0-87078-460-9 (acid-free paper) —0-87078-457-9 (pbk. : acid-free paper)
    1. Ball, Robert M. 2. Social security—United States. I. Bethell, Thomas N. II. Title.
    HD7125 .B2787 1999
    368.4'3'00973—dc21

                                                                    00-011377

To
my wife of 64 years,
Doris McCord Ball,
partner in work and play,
with great appreciation
and
deep love

FOREWORD

In 1937, in the midst of the Great Depression, Franklin Delano Roosevelt noted that "the test of our progress is not whether we add more to the abundance of those who have much; it is whether we provide enough for those who have too little." The Depression stunned both the nation's political leaders and business community; it swept aside, temporarily, longstanding peacetime constraints on governmental innovation and the traditional balance of political forces. Roosevelt's new team in Washington was determined to find solutions to the nation's greatest economic downturn. Some felt that the very survival of capitalism was at stake. There was a widespread view that the nation needed some of the elements of a safety net for the poor, the aged, and the unemployed that were already widely in place in Western Europe. The Social Security program was the centerpiece of this initiative.

At first coverage was limited, by contemporary standards. Only gradually, over several decades, was the program expanded to its present, nearly universal, form. In fact, tracing the program's history is an excellent way to understand the evolution of social insurance, generally, in the United States. Moreover, the program remains at the heart of contemporary policy and political controversy. The outcome of the current struggle over Social Security's future is likely to set the tone for, perhaps, the next half-century of domestic political debates. The reasons for its importance are straightforward: the share of the population over 65 is growing rapidly, putting more pressure on what remains the nation's most important antipoverty program.

Today, the major source of income of about half of Social Security beneficiaries is their Social Security benefits—and for some 30 percent of beneficiaries, those benefits represent 90 percent or more of their incomes. These people are among today's Americans with "too little," in Franklin Roosevelt's terms, and for them, and for those like them in the future, Social Security will remain essential.

In this context, the goal of the current debate about Social Security should be to provide certainty, not to add risk, when it comes to the safety net for older citizens. Thus, we should begin by looking beyond the campaign-style slogans and simplifications and examine the actual history and nature of social insurance in the United States. We are fortunate that much of what we need to know is embodied in the work of one man.

In this volume, the words of Robert M. Ball, who has been a part of America's Social Security system since 1939 (and who ran the program for 21 years), elucidate the rationale behind enactment, explain the program's founding as an insurance rather than a welfare program, and describe the way it has evolved. Ball penetrates the intricacies of administering such a vast and efficient system at so low a cost—overhead is just 1 percent of revenues. Perhaps more important, he also provides a roadmap to the ways in which we can ensure its survival in a manner in keeping with the original—and still valid—goals on which it was built. Ball's central point is that in thinking about this program it is always important to keep in mind that, although it is less than a century old, its roots go back to the purposes underlying our Constitution: "to promote the general welfare."

Since the promotion of the "general welfare" was also a goal of Edward Filene, the founder of The Century Foundation, it is not surprising that we have been involved with the public debate over Social Security from its earliest days. Our first foray into this area began in 1935 with an examination of the Townsend plan, a forerunner to Social Security. In the years immediately following passage of the Social Security Act of 1935, we supported numerous studies of pension programs, but it was not until the crisis facing Social Security in the 1980s that we again addressed the issue in a major way, most notably in W. Andrew Achenbaum's *Social Security: Visions and Revisions*.

Over the past few years, as the issue of the long-term solvency of Social Security came to the forefront, we again focused on this invaluable public program. One of the people we recruited to help explain the current problem was, of course, Bob Ball. And in *Straight Talk about Social Security*, which he wrote for us, with Thomas N. Bethell, in 1998, he explained the misunderstandings about the financing of the system and how the doom and gloom air about its future had emerged from the mandated 75-year-out projection of the trustees of the system. At about the same time, we published two reports by the late Robert Eisner—*The Great Deficit Scares: The Federal Deficit,*

Trade, and Social Security and *Social Security: More, Not Less*. We also published a pamphlet in our Basics series: *Social Security Reform*. At the end of that year, we published *Countdown to Reform: The Great Social Security Debate* by Henry J. Aaron and Robert D. Reischauer, and in 1999, we released a volume edited by Richard C. Leone and Greg Anrig, *Social Security Reform: Beyond the Basics*. In addition, we have set up a website (www.socsec.org) that provides information about this important subject on an ongoing basis.

When Bob Ball first became involved with the young Social Security program, more than 50 percent of senior citizens were struggling to survive with incomes below the poverty line. Today, only 10 percent find themselves in such unfortunate circumstances. In this fundamental sense, the Social Security system has stood the test of time. Of course, over the more than 60 years since its inception, the Social Security program has changed in many ways. Virtually no one, save Bob Ball, has been part of all of the public policy debates that have surrounded those changes. He has continued to be very active in the past two decades, when Social Security has been periodically in the forefront of public debate, as the nation prepares for transition of its large baby-boom population into an elderly boomer group.

Although definitely a progressive, Bob Ball is no political partisan. He has served many administrations, both Democratic and Republican. But he is a partisan of the universal insurance program for the elderly, and that is a fundamental test he applies to all remedies. One has a sense that if there were a program that offered all of Social Security's benefits, or even more, and cost less, Bob Ball would be in the forefront of advocating the change. He has retained an objectivity that is rare. But his insistence on sticking to the facts and on sharp analysis of all reform proposals has become the foundation for his abiding commitment to Social Security as we know it.

On behalf of The Century Foundation, I express our deep respect for Bob Ball's many contributions and our pride in helping to bring to the public this volume of his work.

RICHARD C. LEONE, *President*
The Century Foundation
September 2000

CONTENTS

AUTHOR'S PREFACE

Lincoln once said that "the legitimate object of government is to do for a community of people whatever they need to have done but cannot do at all or cannot do so well for themselves in their separate and individual capacities." Social Security is the embodiment of that philosophy, and as such it has long since become our most important and successful public program.

Sixty-five years ago, when Social Security was enacted, only a tiny percentage of American workers had protection against loss of income due to retirement, and even fewer had protection against loss of income caused by disability. Social Security has transformed this scene. Today the program is of major importance to just about every American family. Almost everyone is either a beneficiary, a contributor building protection for the future, or the dependent of a contributor. Ninety-five percent of people 65 and older are eligible for Social Security benefits. Ninety-eight percent of children under 18 and mothers and fathers with children under 16 can count on monthly benefits if a working parent dies, and four out of five people of working age have protection against the loss of income due to sustained disability. More than 44.6 million Americans receive a Social Security benefit each month, and about 153 million people are currently paying into the program.

In spite of Social Security's vast importance, however, the provisions of the program and the issues involved in proposals to modify it are so complex that even people who have a professional need to understand Social Security—to say nothing of those citizens who simply want to be well informed on the issues of the day—find it difficult to understand how the program works and what is at stake in the various proposals for change.

This collection of essays and commentaries, written over six decades of close professional and personal involvement with Social Security, is intended to deepen the understanding of policymakers and general readers alike. As Social Security once again takes center stage in a national political debate, my hope is to engage readers young and old in a greater appreciation of what Social Security has accomplished and how the unique protections it provides should best be strengthened in the years ahead. I believe Social Security can be as important for generations to come as it has been and continues to be for those past and present. I hope the following papers will show clearly why this is so.

*   *   *

The reader should note that throughout this collection I have updated data—and in some cases text—wherever it seemed particularly relevant and useful to do so. Updates are indicated by and contained within bracketed Author's notes.

Robert M. Ball
Bear Island, Lake Winnipesaukee, N.H.
August 2000

ACKNOWLEDGMENTS

First of all, my thanks to the editor of this volume. Tom Bethell and I have collaborated on many pieces in recent years, and he has always made an important contribution to the product. But this time, quite simply, there would not have been a book without him. This book was made possible by his skill and knowledge and his high standard of workmanship. I am very grateful to him, and to my daughter, Jacqueline Smith, for her work on the production of this book.

Thanks, too, to the copyright holders of the various pieces in this volume for their permission to reprint. The place where a piece originally appeared is stated on the first page of each essay.

The ideas expressed in this book are the result of a lifetime of interaction with the most influential makers of Social Security policy in the United States. I can't begin to name all those to whom I am indebted for information and ideas, but let me pick out a few who contributed specifically to the material in this book. Here they are, in alphabetical order: Henry Aaron, Arthur Altmeyer, J. Douglas Brown, Eveline Burns, Wilbur Cohen, John Corson, Alvin David, Karl and Beth de Schweinitz, Peter Diamond, Arthur Hess, Frances J. McDonald, Alicia Munnell, Robert J. Myers, Virginia Reno, Mary Ross, and Larry Thompson.

These friends and colleagues have contributed greatly to my thinking, but I alone am responsible for the opinions expressed, and of course for any errors of fact.

I am grateful, too, to my son, Jonathan, and my wife, Doris, for their careful reading of various pieces in the early stages of production, and to all those who in the past have read and commented on these essays.

I have borrowed my title—*Insuring the Essentials*—from a 1932 book by Barbara Nachtrieb Armstrong (published by Macmillan). A professor of law at the University of California and an authority on social insurance, Armstrong was a key staff member of the Committee on Economic Security which, in 1934, did the groundwork preparatory to enactment of the Social Security Act of 1935. Insuring the essentials is, of course, what Social Security and Medicare are all about, and in borrowing Barbara Armstrong's title I hope to honor her contributions to the nation's security as well as acknowledge her contributions to my own education in social insurance.

Finally, my editor and I want to thank Richard C. Leone and his fine staff at The Century Foundation for their careful, empathetic, and highly professional work in bringing this project to a successful conclusion. We also want to thank The Century Foundation for support that, among other things, helped us get started with this project; a grant from the Altman Fund to the National Academy of Social Insurance helped us complete it. We are most grateful for this financial support.

INTRODUCTION

We are fortunate that this collection of essays has become available during this time of intensifying national debate about the future of Social Security. It illuminates that debate as nothing else could—because no one else has Robert M. Ball's experience and expertise.

Bob Ball began working at the Social Security Administration in 1939, just four years after this most important of public programs was enacted. Since then he has had more to do with shaping Social Security, Medicare, and the federal welfare program of Supplementary Security Income than anyone else. Most of his influence, however, has been exercised behind the scenes, and he is still not a particularly well-known public figure. In fact his career exemplifies the old rule in Washington affairs that you can accomplish miracles if you're willing to let other people take the credit. Because of his low-profile *modus operandi*, the authority with which these essays are imbued may not be immediately apparent to the general reader. A few words of introduction are thus in order.

Bob Ball has been not only a key figure in every piece of Social Security legislation since 1939 and the chief administrator of the program for the 21 years from 1952 to 1973, with a total of 30 years of service at the agency, but also has been the major theoretician of the program since the mid-1940s. He has written four books, scores of articles, and volumes of congressional testimony discussing public and private pensions, the cash benefit program of Old Age, Survivors and Disability Insurance (or OASDI, for which "Social Security" has long since become the convenient shorthand term), Medicare, national health insurance, welfare, and long-term care. This collection covers the spectrum of his contributions to our thinking about and understanding of Social Security and its impact on American life—past, present, and future.

The author begins with a discussion of the nine principles that have given the program its unique characteristics—and staying power.

1

For anyone who wants to understand Social Security, this is an essential primer. It is followed by a group of essays on Social Security's evolution, why and how the social insurance approach differs from welfare, how it can be further strengthened, and—particularly relevant to the current debate—what would happen if the present program were to be partially replaced by a system of individual savings accounts.

Augmenting these essays are several that focus on an underappreciated aspect of Social Security—its highly successful administration down through the years. Bob Ball, who as Social Security's top civil servant and then as commissioner spent 21 years running the program (a record that no predecessor or successor has come close to matching), clearly conveys the importance of breathing life into a law by administering it imaginatively, decisively, and always with an acute appreciation of the constituencies it serves. (In a tribute to the staying power of this philosophy, the Vice President's Task Force on Reinventing Government found, nearly 65 years after enactment of the original legislation, that the Social Security Administration ranked high among federal agencies when evaluated both for efficiency and for humane, friendly service.)

Bob Ball's direct role in shepherding legislation through Congress and then giving it life has been complemented by unsurpassed service on the advisory councils that have been so influential in Social Security's continuing evolution. In fact, his national influence dates back to his role as the staff director of the 1947–48 Advisory Council, and his role as staff director of the first advisory group appointed by the Republicans after the election of 1952. He chaired the 1965 Advisory Council and served on the councils of 1977, 1991, and 1994–96. As a member of the 1982–83 National Commission on Social Security Reform, better known as the Greenspan Commission, he was the unsung hero largely responsible for hammering out the agreement between President Reagan and House Speaker Tip O'Neill that, in 1983, led to the most recent major Social Security legislation, averting both an immediate financial crisis and what could have become a sustained and deeply partisan wrangle over Social Security's future.

That's not to say, of course, that partisan wrangles are a thing of the past. Hardly. This year, and in the years immediately ahead, the future of Social Security, Medicare, and really the bedrock principles of social insurance will be the focus of heavily financed and highly publicized advocacy and legislative initiatives. In this climate of controversy there is a continuing need for a voice of calm reason seasoned with experience. We hear that voice in these pages. Today, at 86, Bob Ball remains one of the most active and influential participants in the debate. Retired from federal service for more than 25 years, he is still widely regarded as "Mr. Social Security"—even, as the *National Journal* has described him, as "the patron saint of Social Security."

Franklin Roosevelt might have more of a claim on *that* title, but whatever Bob Ball is called, we have in this collection the distilled wisdom of the only man who has directed Social Security under three presidents (Kennedy, Johnson, and Nixon), a man who has advised countless members of Congress, representatives of the executive branch, labor organizations, and leading senior citizens' groups. Today Bob Ball is regularly consulted by policymakers, think-tank analysts, academics, and the media, and as the founder of the National Academy of Social Insurance he has been responsible for greatly enhancing professional attention to a still widely misunderstood and under-studied field of public policy.

This timely and valuable collection, in broadening public understanding of our largest and most successful social program, is an act of generous public service by a man whose whole life has been dedicated to it. Bob Ball and Social Security are synonymous. May they long endure.

—*Thomas N. Bethell*

Thomas N. Bethell is an independent, Washington, D.C., public affairs writer and editor who has worked with Bob Ball on many projects.

1

THE NINE GUIDING
PRINCIPLES OF
SOCIAL SECURITY

Where they came from and what they accomplish.

In the midst of the Great Depression, the founders of today's Social Security system took the bold step of establishing a new institution which they expected to be slow-growing but permanent. They wanted to make a decent retirement attainable for millions of Americans who would otherwise become dependent on their families or on public assistance when they grew too old to work or could no longer find employment. They wanted to protect workers' dependents by providing insurance to make the death of a breadwinner more financially manageable. They wanted to put an end to the poorhouse by distributing program income so as to provide at least a minimally adequate benefit for everyone regularly contributing. And, foreseeing the inevitability of change—including the eventual need to insure against other major risks such as disability and illness—they sought to design an institution based on sustainable principles.

Accordingly, they took the long view. They gave major emphasis to estimating program income and expenses over a much longer period than was customarily done in other countries, and this is still true today. The time frame of 75 years that is now used for Social Security estimates is much longer than that used in almost all other

From *Straight Talk about Social Security: An Analysis of the Issues in the Current Debate*, with Thomas N. Bethell (New York: Century Foundation Press, 1998), pp. 59–64.

contexts, from foreign social insurance programs to federal budgeting. The point, then and now, was not to try to pretend that anyone could really know precisely what would be happening in 75 or even 25 years; the point was that the planners of Social Security, in making exceptionally long-term commitments, wanted always to be looking far enough ahead to anticipate necessary improvements and make needed changes in ample time to preserve the integrity of the program.

That approach has served well. The legislation of 1935 and 1939 created the basic design of Social Security, and all major legislation since then can be seen as building on that design: extending coverage to more and more workers, improving the level of protection, adding protection against loss of income from long-term and total disability, providing protection for the elderly and disabled against the increasingly unmanageable cost of medical care, protecting against the erosion of income by inflation, and abolishing all statutory differences in the treatment of men and women.

These and many other accomplishments and adjustments have taken place within a framework consisting of nine major principles. Social Security is universal; an earned right; wage related; contributory and self-financed; redistributive; not means tested; wage indexed; inflation protected; and compulsory.

As with any framework, the stability of the entire structure depends on the contribution made by each part, so it is useful to review these principles and see how they work together.

1. *Universal:* Social Security coverage has been gradually extended over the years to the point where 96 out of 100 jobs in paid employment are now covered, with more than 142 million working Americans making contributions in 1997 [153 million in 2000]. And the goal of complete universality can be reached by gradually covering those remaining state and local government positions that are not now covered.

2. *Earned right:* Social Security is more than a statutory right; it is an *earned* right, with eligibility for benefits and the benefit rate based on an individual's past earnings. This principle sharply distinguishes Social Security from welfare and links the program, appropriately, to other earned rights such as wages, fringe benefits, and private pensions.

3. *Wage related:* Social Security benefits are related to earnings, thus reinforcing the concept of benefits as an earned right and recognizing that there is a relationship between one's standard of living while working and the benefit level needed to achieve income security in retirement. Under Social Security, higher-paid earners get higher benefits, but the lower-paid get more for what they pay in.

4. *Contributory and self-financed:* The fact that workers pay earmarked contributions from their wages into the system also reinforces the concept of an earned right and gives contributors a moral claim on future benefits above and beyond statutory obligations. And, unlike many foreign plans, Social Security is entirely financed by dedicated taxes, principally those deducted from workers' earnings matched by employers, with the self-employed paying comparable amounts. The entire cost of benefits plus administrative expenses (which amount to less than 1 percent of income) is met without support from general government revenues.

   [*Author's note:* This was true from 1935 until 2000, and the principle of funding Social Security largely from the earmarked contributions of workers and their employers remains desirable for the reasons stated. As of August 2000, however, it appears that in the future Social Security may be financed partially from general revenues, as are many foreign social insurance systems. The Clinton-Gore administration has made such a recommendation, as have several Republicans, including Sen. Phil Gramm (Texas) and Reps. Bill Archer (Texas) and Clay Shaw (Florida). The rationale for this approach, which was proposed in Social Security's early days, is discussed in Chapters 17 and 18.]

   The self-financing approach has several advantages. It helps protect the program against having to compete against other programs in the annual general federal budget—which is appropriate, because this is a uniquely long-term program. It imposes fiscal discipline, because the total earmarked income for Social Security must be sufficient to cover the entire cost of the program. And it guards against excessive liberalization: contributors oppose major benefit cuts because they have a right to benefits and are paying for them, but they also oppose excessive increases in benefits because they understand that every increase must be paid for by increased contributions. Thus a semi-automatic balance is achieved between wanting more protection versus not wanting to pay more for it.

5. *Redistributive:* One of Social Security's most important goals is to pay at least a minimally adequate benefit to workers who are regularly covered and contributing, regardless of how low-paid they may be. This is accomplished through a redistributional formula that pays comparatively higher benefits to lower-paid earners. The formula makes good sense. If the system paid back to low-wage workers only the benefit that they could be expected to pay for from their own wages, millions of retirees would end up impoverished and on welfare even though they had been paying into Social Security throughout their working lives. This would make the years of contributing to Social Security worse than pointless, since the earnings paid into Social Security would have reduced the income available for other needs throughout their working years without providing in retirement any income greater than what would be available from welfare. The redistributional formula solves this dilemma.

6. *Not means tested:* In contrast to welfare, eligibility for Social Security is not determined by the beneficiary's current income and assets, nor is the amount of the benefit. This is a key principle. It is the absence of a means test that makes it possible for people to add to their savings and to establish private pension plans, secure in the knowledge that they will not then be penalized by having their Social Security benefits cut back as a result of having arranged for additional retirement income. The absence of a means test makes it possible for Social Security to provide a stable role in anchoring a multi-tier retirement system in which private pensions and personal savings can be built on top of Social Security's basic, defined protection.

7. *Wage indexed:* Social Security is portable, following the worker from job to job, and the protection provided before retirement increases as wages rise in general. Benefits at the time of initial receipt are brought up to date with current wage levels, reflecting improvements in productivity and thus in the general standard of living. Without this principle, Social Security would

soon provide benefits that did not reflect previously attained living standards.

8. *Inflation protected:* Once they begin, Social Security benefits are protected against inflation by periodic cost-of-living adjustments (COLAs) linked to the Consumer Price Index. Inflation protection is one of Social Security's greatest strengths, and one that distinguishes it from other (except federal) retirement plans. No private pension plan provides guaranteed protection against inflation, and inflation protection under state and local plans, where it exists at all, is capped. Without COLAs, the real value of Social Security benefits would steadily erode over time, as is the case with unadjusted private pension benefits. Although a provision for automatic adjustment was not part of the original legislation, the importance of protecting benefits against inflation was recognized, and over the years the system was financed to allow for periodic adjustments to bring benefits up to date. But this updating was done only after a lag. Provision for automatic adjustment was added in 1972.

9. *Compulsory:* Social Security compels all of us to contribute to our own future security. A voluntary system simply wouldn't work. Some of us would save scrupulously, some would save sporadically, and some would postpone the day of reckoning forever, leaving the community as a whole to pay through a much less desirable safety-net system. With a compulsory program, the problem of adverse selection—individuals deciding when and to what extent they want to participate, depending on whether their individual circumstances seem favorable—is avoided (as is the problem of obtaining adequate funding for a large safety-net program serving a constituency with limited political influence).

*　　*　　*

In the middle of the Depression it took courage to enact a system based on these principles. The Depression was a time of enormous and immediate needs, but Social Security was designed to be a slow-growing tree, one that could not provide much shelter in the near term. The point, however, was that, once grown, it would be strong enough to weather bad times as well as good.

A contributory retirement system takes a long time to develop, since by definition those who are already retired are not eligible for benefits. Fifteen years after the program was set up, only 16 percent of the elderly were receiving benefits, and it was not until the 1950s that politicians began to see much advantage in championing Social Security improvements. And it was only in the 1960s, three decades after enactment, that Social Security began having a major impact, paying benefits that were high enough and universal enough to significantly reduce poverty among the elderly, the disabled, and the survivors of beneficiaries. After the amendments of 1972 further increased benefits substantially and provided for automatic inflation protection, Social Security fully assumed the role planned for it as the all-important base of a multi-tier retirement system in which private pensions and individual savings are added to Social Security's defined protection.

The importance of that role would be difficult to exaggerate. Today Social Security is the only organized retirement plan—the *only* assured source of retirement income—for fully half of the total workforce. And it is the base upon which all who are able to do so can build the supplementary protection of pensions and individual savings.

Social Security continues to be the most popular and successful social program in America's history because its guiding principles enable it to work exactly as intended: as America's family protection plan.

2

THE EVOLUTION OF SOCIAL SECURITY

A broad overview of how the U.S. program has developed, from the events leading up to passage in 1935 through the most recent set of major amendments in 1983.

Social Security did not spring full blown from the minds of New Deal advisers in the 1930s. Part of the original understanding of the role, purpose, and nature of Social Security in the United States was based on what had developed in Europe.[1] Those who designed the American system studied foreign experience intensely, and although the details were American inventions, the concepts were not.[2] America borrowed the idea of a government-sponsored, independently financed, contributory and compulsory program protecting against the loss of earned income arising when people retire from work in old age, when people become totally disabled, or when a wage earner dies. By now, most countries around the world have such systems.

THE ORIGIN AND NATURE OF SOCIAL INSURANCE

The origins of social insurance are very old. The principles upon which modern government systems are based were applied in non-government plans centuries before Germany set up the first state

From "Social Security: The Original Understanding and Its Implications for Later Developments," in Theodore R. Marmor and Jerry L. Mashaw, eds., *Social Security: Beyond the Rhetoric of Crisis* (Princeton: Princeton University Press, 1988), pp. 17–38. Copyright © 1988 by Princeton University Press. Reprinted by permission of Princeton University Press.

program in 1889. Social insurance grows out of a long tradition of people banding together to help themselves. Formal benefit plans, for example, were established by the guilds of the Middle Ages. These plans required predetermined contributions from each member and paid specified benefits in the event of disability or death.[3] Another forerunner of social insurance is the "customary fund" found in the mining districts of Austria and other central European countries; some funds date back to the sixteenth century.[4] Later, fraternal orders and friendly societies were organized by the hundreds for the central purpose of providing insurance protection for their members.[5] Trade unions throughout the world developed protection plans, and commercial insurance covering some of the same risks of income loss became widely available.[6]

The origins and tradition of social insurance are clear. It is a nearly universal response of wage economies to the fact that most people are dependent on earnings and grows out of the efforts of workers to protect themselves and their families from loss of those earnings. This self-help approach is greatly preferred by workers throughout the world to the alternative of relief and assistance. One does not have to seek far for the reason. In insurance, applicants demonstrate something positive—that they have worked sufficiently to be eligible and thus have an earned right to the payment—then they receive payment based on their past earnings from funds to which they have contributed. There is no test of individual need, and the beneficiaries can add income from savings or private pensions to their social insurance benefits. In relief and assistance, applicants prove something negative—that they do not have enough to get along on. They are then given a grant unrelated to their previous level of living and designed only to bring them up to some community-determined minimum. If they have other income it is subtracted from their grant; all recipients are reduced to the same low level of living.

Neither the form of government nor the economic system seems to make much difference in the approach taken. Social insurance systems following nearly identical principles are found in market-oriented economies, in highly planned economies, and in economies where the state is the main owner and operator of industry. The common element is the need to make up for wage loss.

SOCIAL SECURITY'S ACCOMPLISHMENTS

When the American Social Security program reached its fiftieth year in 1985, we celebrated one of the major achievements of the century. When the program was enacted, only about six million persons, 15 percent of those employed, held jobs covered by any sort of retirement system; only a tiny handful—perhaps 300,000 to 400,000—actually were receiving a pension.[7] The poorhouse toward the end of life, with all its horrors, was a very real part of America.[8]

Social Security changed all that. It has gradually brought about a peaceful revolution in the way older people, totally disabled people, widows, and orphans live. It has been largely responsible for the fact that the proportion of those 65 and over who are desperately poor is now about the same as for the rest of the adult population, instead of more than twice as high, as it was as recently as 1959. Without Social Security, more than half the elderly would have incomes below the federal government's rock bottom definition of poverty; instead, 12.4 percent are in that category today. Even though eliminating much of the outright poverty among the elderly, Social Security has not moved them very far up the income scale. At the end of 1984, average retirement benefits were only $460.60; and yet 62 percent of the over-65 beneficiaries received more than half and one-fourth received more than 90 percent of their income from Social Security.[9]

But Social Security is much more than an antipoverty program. In 1986, 125 million earners contributed to the program. It has become a base on which practically all families build protection against the loss of earned income. Every private pension is planned on the assumption that the pensioner will also receive Social Security, and individuals who save on their own rely on Social Security as a base for their efforts. Today over 37 million people, retired or disabled workers and their dependents, widows, and motherless and fatherless children—one in seven Americans—get Social Security payments every month.

THE ORIGINAL UNDERSTANDING

In broad outline, then, the original understanding of Social Security was defined by the nature of the institution borrowed from abroad: insurance against wage loss, compulsory, contributory, independently financed, without a test of need, and with eligibility and benefits based on past earnings. But the more specific understanding in America was embodied in three reports and the legislation that followed: the report of the Committee on Economic Security[10] and the 1935 Social Security Act;[11] the report of the 1937–38 Advisory Council[12] and the 1939 amendments; and the reports of the 1947–49 Advisory Council[13] and the 1950 amendments.

Advisory councils on Social Security, with their representation of leaders in industry and labor, actuaries, economists, and other Social Security experts, and members of the public have frequently renewed the original understanding on Social Security as the program has developed. In addition to those already mentioned, a 1953 advisory group was very important in gaining further extension of program coverage and in winning support for Social Security principles from the first Republican administration to have responsibility for the program's management.[14] The 1959 Advisory Council reviewed the program and strongly endorsed the financing method.[15] The 1965 Advisory Council contributed importantly to the 1965 amendments.[16] The 1971 Advisory Council was important in the development of the 1972 amendments, which made benefits inflation-proof.[17] And the 1975 Advisory Council was the first to recommend stabilizing replacement rates through wage indexing, the major change brought about by the 1977 amendments.[18] The 1979 Advisory Council was the first to recommend income taxation of Social Security benefits and to explore thoroughly the treatment of women under Social Security.[19] The National Commission on Social Security Reform, appointed by President Reagan early in 1982, was the key to the 1983 amendments.[20] Several other citizens' councils and advisory groups had less but still important influence. All, whether appointed by Republican or Democratic administrations, after months of study and debate, reaffirmed the basic philosophic underpinnings of the original understanding. For example, the first recommendation of the 1983 commission reads:

> The members of the National Commission believe that the Congress, in its deliberations on financing proposals, should not alter the fundamental structure of the Social Security program or undermine its fundamental principles. The National Commission considered, but rejected, proposals to make the Social Security program a voluntary one, or to

transform it into a program under which benefits are a product exclusively of the contributions paid, or to convert it into a fully-funded program, or to change it to a program under which benefits are conditioned on the showing of financial need.[21]

THE AMERICAN SYSTEM: ITS ORIGIN AND HISTORY

How did the United States finally get around to joining the other industrial nations of the world in establishing a contributory social insurance system? The answer lies in the crisis atmosphere produced by the worst depression this country has ever known.

With nearly a third of the work force out of jobs and with millions and millions of families in desperate straits in the mid-1930s, the nation was open to new ideas as never before. In 1934 and 1935, President Roosevelt used this great national crisis as an opportunity to create permanent institutions dealing with persistent and fundamental problems of economic security. He was not at all content to deal only with the emergencies of the moment; rather, he used those emergencies to change permanently the role of the federal government in the lives of ordinary people.

This was a watershed period in the history of America,[22] and no other legislative enactment of the New Deal has had such an enduring effect on American families as the Social Security Act. The old-age benefit provisions of the act, signed into law on August 14, 1935, have grown into our old-age, survivors, and disability insurance system, which most Americans think of as Social Security, and our nationwide system of health insurance for the elderly and the long-term totally disabled, Medicare. The 1935 act, although very substantially amended in 1939, was important in defining the kind of old-age, survivors, and disability insurance program we have today because it settled some of the most basic policy issues. It spelled out many parts of the original understanding on Social Security. The 1935 act established a system that was nationwide, federally administered, compulsory and contributory, and, after considerable dispute, without provision for electing out by those with private pension coverage. Unlike many European plans then in effect, the system included all those working in covered occupations, not just those with low wages.

Although the maximum amount of earnings counted for tax and benefit purposes was limited, all in covered occupations were included for earnings up to the maximum. The principle of paying benefits only to those substantially retired was also established in the original program. [*Author's note:* In the year 2000, by act of Congress, the program was changed so that anyone who attains age 65 will receive benefits regardless of whether he or she continues to work (unless the individual specifically opts to delay taking benefits at 65 in order to receive increased benefits later). This changes the concept of the program, shifting it from insurance to partly make up for the loss of earnings on retirement to an annuity payable at a specified age.] But no one was excluded from benefits because of non-work income or because of assets; benefits were to be paid as a matter of right, related to past earnings and contributions, but weighted in favor of the lower-paid earner. The age of first eligibility for retirement benefits was set at 65. All these understandings survived the extensive revampings of 1939 and 1950. They endure to this day, although the newest set of amendments stipulates that, beginning in 2000, the age of first eligibility for full benefits will rise gradually until it reaches 67 in 2022.

But these provisions did not survive unchallenged. Controversy swirled around the old-age benefit provisions of the new Social Security Act. It was a major issue in the 1936 presidential campaign. The Republican candidate, Alfred Landon, characterized the program as "unjust, unworkable, stupidly drafted and wastefully financed." The contributory feature, he said, was "a cruel hoax."[23] Critics claimed that every worker would have to wear a dog tag with his Social Security number on it. John Hamilton, the national chairman of the Republican party, said the only indication the administration still thought of these unfortunates as human was that the tags were made of stainless steel so they would not discolor the skin of the wearers.[24] The constitutionality of the act was challenged, and it was not until May 24, 1937, that this issue was resolved by two Supreme Court decisions, *Steward Machine Co.* v. *Davis* and *Helvering* v. *Davis*.[25]

There were still other controversies. What seemed most important at the time was a continuing battle between those who favored a substantial build up of reserves that would earn interest and thus reduce the level of later contributions and those who favored raising only the amount of money needed to pay current benefits—the "pay-as-you-go" approach. Opponents of a large fund, estimated to reach $47 billion under the 1935 act, believed the build up had serious consequences for sound fiscal policy. Investing the funds in government securities, as provided by the law, would require a large, permanent national debt they considered undesirable. Yet if the Social Security funds were invested elsewhere, new federal involvement in private economic activity would have raised the specter of socialism. They argued, too, that the reserves would encourage extravagant federal spending because Social Security would have created a ready source of federal borrowing. On the other side, many supporters of a large earnings reserve looked on it as a way to avoid an eventual general revenue contribution. A pay-as-you-go approach had the inherent problem that benefits in the early years would greatly exceed the value of contributions paid, with more of the cost for early retirees being pushed forward to later generations than in a system with large reserves. Pay-as-you-go opponents feared later contribution rates would be so high that general revenues would be called on to pay for the start-up costs that had not been funded. In fact, such an eventual government contribution was advocated by pay-as-you-go supporters. President Roosevelt personally backed a large earnings reserve to prevent later costs falling on general revenues.

But financing controversies did not reach the basic nature of social insurance. No matter how these issues were decided, benefit rights would still be based on past earnings, and substantial earmarked contributions would be made by those who were to benefit from the system.

Largely because of the impasse over financing, the chairman of the Senate Committee on Finance agreed to appoint a special subcommittee to cooperate with the Social Security Board in studying the advisability of amending the old-age benefit program. There was also to be a citizens' advisory council appointed jointly by the subcommittee and the Social Security Board.[26] Arthur Altmeyer, chairman of the Social Security Board, saw the formation of this council as an opportunity to move ahead with much more than financing changes. The council was also asked to consider whether it would be advisable to begin monthly payments earlier, to increase the amount of the monthly benefits payable in the early years, to provide benefits for the disabled and survivors, and to extend coverage to additional groups. Throughout the council's work there was cordial cooperation among Brown, the chairman of the advisory council, Altmeyer, and Senator Vandenberg, an influential Republican member of the Senate Finance Subcommittee. This cooperation and the prestige of the council members, many of whom were nationally known, resulted in quick passage of the council's recommendations.

1937–38 ADVISORY COUNCIL RECOMMENDATIONS

The 1937–38 Advisory Council was probably the most important of all the advisory councils in determining the original understanding and the continuing shape of the Social Security program. The entire history of Old-Age, Survivors, and Disability Insurance (OASDI) from 1939 to the amendments of 1972 can correctly be described as rounding out the structure recommended by this council. The only major innovation this early council did not consider and take a stand on was the introduction of the various automatic provisions keeping benefits up to date with wages and prices, as provided in the 1972 and 1977 amendments. And even here it can well be argued that the additional protection provided is within the spirit of the 1935 and 1939 legislation. After all, the objective from the beginning was to provide continuing protection in real terms, not a benefit that would shrink as wages and prices rose.

In 1939, then, based on the council recommendations, the program was redesigned to set the pattern for all that was to follow. Social Security became a program of family protection, providing not only old-age benefits for workers but also benefits for wives, widows, and children. The benefits were weighted to favor lower-paid workers even more heavily than in 1935, and in several ways the system was made more effective sooner. The first date for the payment of monthly benefits was moved from 1942 to 1940. Higher benefits were paid in the early years by relating benefits to average monthly earnings in covered employment, rather than to total earnings over a lifetime.

The council recommended balancing the increased cost of higher early benefits, including the addition of a wife's benefit, by reducing the amount payable to single annuitants in the long run and eliminating a money-back guarantee payable under the 1935 act. Instead of the former lump-sum payments rebating contributions, it recommended a small death benefit.

All these changes made the benefits paid in the early years less directly related to past earnings and contributions. Workers with dependents were favored for the first time under the 1939 amendments, and lower-paid earners and those nearing retirement age were favored more under the 1939 act than under the original program. Thus, there were important modifications of equity principles in order to make benefits more adequate.

Although it favored total disability benefits in principle, the council did not recommend covering this risk at this stage in the development of the program because it foresaw much greater administrative difficulty in determining the ability to work than in proving age or death. Council members recommended extending coverage as far as they deemed feasible at the time and established universal coverage as a goal. They recommended against building large earnings reserves and favored instead a modified pay-as-you-go system, with a contingency reserve to meet unanticipated short-term needs. They favored an eventual general revenue contribution, which in a mature system would have reached one-third of outgo; this recommendation is the only major proposal of this council consistently rejected by successive Congresses and cannot reasonably be considered part of the original understanding of Social Security.

One comes away from reading the 1937–38 Advisory Council report astonished at the foresight shown by the developers of this most important of all American social programs. The Social Security program has endured in essentially the same form because it dealt well with an old and persistent problem—how to plan for the replacement of wages lost when a worker retires in old age, becomes totally disabled, or dies.

Later legislation has even adhered to the long-range goal for benefit levels. It just is not true, as is sometimes said, that the benefits have been greatly liberalized and that the program has departed from the modest goals of the system's founders.[27] Robert J. Myers, former chief actuary of the Social Security Administration, calculates that, under the formula adopted in 1939, a worker retiring today at 65 after earning the average wage would receive—in the absence of changes in wage and price levels—40 percent of his or her preretirement earnings, referred to as the replacement rate. The average couple's replacement rate today under the 1939 formula would be 60 percent.[28] These replacement rates for average wages—the goals of the 1939 amendments—are almost exactly the same as those established for now and the future by the automatic provisions of the 1977 amendments: 41 percent and 62 percent, for a single worker and married couple, respectively.

Also, contrary to what is sometimes said, the financing of the system was planned with the expectation that the ratio of workers to beneficiaries would drop substantially as the elderly population continued to grow. The 1937–38 council estimated that by 1980, 14 to 15 percent of the total population would be made up of persons aged 65 and over, compared to 6.3 percent at the time they were making their recommendations.[29] Current estimates are that the figure will not reach 14 percent until well after the year 2000.[30] Those who designed the 1939 amendments can hardly be accused of overlooking the burden that demographic change would cause. The notion that the system was planned for a ratio of 16 workers to 1 beneficiary (the ratio in 1950) and that the 1982 financing problems were caused by the ratio dropping to 3 to 1 (a favorite explanation of Reagan administration spokesmen in 1981 and 1982) is just plain wrong.[31] Both the 1935 act and the 1939 amendments took account of the future to a remarkable degree, and the financing provisions over the years have been designed to meet the expected shift in the ratio of beneficiaries to workers.

DEVELOPMENTS FROM 1939 TO 1950

Between 1939 and 1950 the Social Security system developed very slowly. The retirement features of most social insurance systems, like private pensions, take a long time to become effective because those already retired when the system begins ordinarily are not eligible for benefits. Social Security was no exception. Under the system implemented after the 1939 amendments, workers had to have been in covered employment the equivalent of half the time after 1936 in order to be eligible for Social Security benefits at age 65. Obviously no one already retired when the system started met the test, and the proportion of the aged eligible for benefits grew slowly. At the beginning of 1950, 15 years after the passage of the original Social Security legislation, only 16 percent of those aged 65 and over were getting Social Security benefits. In 1987, 90 percent of those aged 65 and over receive benefits, and 95 out of 100 children and their mothers are protected by the life insurance (survivors insurance) feature. Four out of five people in the age group from 21 through 64 now have protection against loss of income caused by severe disability.

The failure to keep Social Security benefits up to date with wage and price changes during the 1940s and the fact that few people were eligible for benefits almost proved its undoing. Social Security was simply not very important. If a senator wanted to be on record as helping older people, he introduced a bill to pay more old-age assistance, because the federal and state means-tested program was paying many more people over age 65 than Social Security was. Support was growing for radical alternatives to Social Security, such as the payment of flat benefits to all the elderly financed from general revenues or a vastly increased means-tested system. Once again an advisory council came to the rescue, convening in 1947 and issuing its report in 1949.[32]

This council, in addition to advocating changes to greatly hasten achievement of full program effectiveness, made statements of principle that were particularly important to the American system. Although important in all economies dependent upon a wage system, social insurance is perhaps of the very greatest importance in a dynamic economy like that of the United States, where industries rise and fall with some rapidity and new enterprises continually replace the old. In the final analysis, the economic security of the individual depends on the success of industry and agriculture in producing an increasing flow of goods and services. However, the 1949 council stated:

> . . . the very success of the economy in making progress, while creating opportunities, also increases risks. Hence, the more progressive the economy, the greater is the need for protection against economic hazards. The protection should be made available on terms which reinforce the interests of the individual in helping himself. A properly designed Social Security system will reinforce the drive of the individual toward greater production and greater efficiency and will make for an environment conducive to the maximum of economic progress.

The council continued:

> Differential benefits based on a wage record are a reward for productive effort and are consistent with general economic incentives, while the knowledge that benefits will be paid— irrespective of whether the individual is in need—supports and stimulates his drive to add his personal savings to the basic security he has acquired through the insurance system.

Under such a social insurance system, the individual earns a right to a benefit that is related to his contribution to production. This earned right is his best guarantee that he will receive the benefits promised and that they will not be conditioned on his accepting either scrutiny of his personal affairs or restrictions from which others are free.[33]

At a time when the future of Social Security was in doubt because of its inadequacy (benefits averaged only $25 a month and few people were getting them), the 1949 council restated the principles underlying the original understanding of Social Security and urged the extension of the system.

Opportunity for the individual to secure protection for himself and his family against the economic hazards of old age and death is essential to the sustained welfare, freedom, and dignity of the American citizen. For some, such protection can be gained through individual savings and other private arrangements. For others, such arrangements are inadequate or too uncertain. Since the interest of the whole Nation is involved, the people using the government as the agency for their cooperation should make sure that all members of the community have at least a basic measure of protection against the major hazards of old age and death.[34]

1950 AMENDMENTS

The 1950 amendments based on this council's report went a considerable way toward the original goal of universal coverage. The amendments also changed the beginning date for measuring the amount of work needed to qualify and for the computation of average earnings on which benefits were based. This was done primarily to avoid penalizing those in newly covered occupations, but it also made qualifying for benefits easier for all workers and increased benefit levels in the early years.[35]

Under the change in the benefit formula, the level of benefits promised ultimately under the old law was paid sooner but not increased. Specifically, the 1939 provision increasing benefits 1 percent for each year worked under the program was dropped, and the percentage of average wages immediately payable—the replacement rate—was increased. This followed the 1939 precedent of paying higher benefits sooner, but balancing the higher benefits by cutting back on later costs. The various changes increased the level of benefits immediately by 77 percent. Equally important, the 1950 amendments resulted in many more people getting benefits sooner, and the federal and state old-age assistance program was quickly relegated to second place.

The 1950 amendments also removed many provisions that treated women differently from men and in other ways updated the system, while continuing the basic 1939 design.[36] The 1947–49 Advisory Council recommended a limited program of total disability insurance, but this branch of social insurance was not added to the old-age and survivors program until 1956.[37] Instead, in 1950, Congress passed a federal and state disability assistance plan, based on a test of need.

The changes made by the 1950 amendments may well have preserved the system. By the time the Eisenhower administration started to evaluate the program in 1953, Social Security was a functioning institution paying significant benefits to millions of people—a real change, not in principle but in effectiveness, from the program of the 1940s. Skeptical at first, that administration over time endorsed the basic ideas underlying Social Security and worked for program improvements.[38] The task of rounding out the basic structure established in 1939 continued under the Eisenhower administration and beyond. Coverage was further extended, for example, so that by the end of 1965 the only major groups remaining outside the program were federal civilian employees and those nonprofit and state and local employees who had not taken advantage of the voluntary provisions applying to them. (All nonprofit employees and newly hired federal employees were covered compulsorily by the 1983 amendments. By 1984 about 70 percent of state and local employees had been covered by voluntary agreements, leaving only about 4 million outside the system.)

Benefit levels were increased by amendments in 1952, 1954, 1958, 1965, 1967, 1969, and 1971 that, after a considerable lag, more or less kept pace with rising wages. Thus, the replacement rate was maintained by ad hoc legislative changes. The age of first eligibility for benefits was reduced to 62, first for women (1956) and later for men (1961), but the benefits were reduced actuarially for those who claimed benefits before age 65.

In 1954, a provision was added to prevent a reduction in old-age and survivors' protection for workers who had failed to work under the program because of total disability. In 1956, cash benefits for disability were added. The United States was much slower than other countries in providing disability protection. In most countries, long-term total disability insurance, frequently called invalidity insurance, has been considered a natural accompaniment of old-age and survivors insurance. Thus, wages are partially replaced when some permanent or long-lasting event—retirement in old age, death, or long-term total disability—reduces earnings or ends the possibility of earning. Other branches of social insurance deal with short-term risks such as unemployment, short-term illness, and the cost of acute medical care. In the United States, however, it was more than twenty years after the passage of the original Social Security Act before insurance against the loss of wages due to long-term, total disability was added to protection against the risks of retirement in old age and death.

Passage of disability insurance was very controversial in the United States. It was opposed by the organized medical profession (which saw it as a first step toward socialized medicine), by the insurance industry (which had lost money on the disability policies it sold in the 1920s), and by conservatives generally.[39] Although the Eisenhower administration opposed the program, the president signed the bill when it narrowly passed over administration protests. Because of this controversy and the legitimate concern about the difficulty of disability administration, the initial program was very conservatively designed and paid benefits only at age 50 or older. It was liberalized a few years later, however, after the Social Security Administration (SSA) demonstrated that it could do the job well.[40]

But the addition of this risk, too, was within the scope of the original understanding of the nature of social insurance as borrowed from Europe and as endorsed by the 1937–38 council. It was not a philosophical departure but a further fulfillment of the basic design.

The history of Social Security legislation in the early 1960s was dominated by the fight to establish Medicare. Although it was an extremely controversial piece of legislation, strongly opposed by the doctors, insurance companies, and business generally, Medicare seemed nevertheless the only way to protect the living standard of retirees. It was all well and good to provide Social Security benefits to meet the regular recurring expenses of daily living, but there was no way for Social Security recipients to budget for the extraordinary and unpredictable expenses of a costly illness, as they could for rent or food. With the elderly using more than twice as many hospital days as younger people and with average incomes only half as large, private insurance premiums geared to the cost of care for the elderly were just too high for most retired people to pay. Thus, hospital insurance was seen as necessary to achieve the goals of the cash benefit program. The government stepped in and, using the approach already made familiar by OASDI, required contributions over the working lifetime of those who were to have the protection. The plan included voluntary coverage of part of physician costs; premiums paid by the elderly provided half the financing, with general revenues providing the other half. The only important development in the OASDI system between 1958 and 1965 was the 1960 extension of disability insurance to workers of all ages along with other liberalizations in that program. Because attention during this period was concentrated largely on Medicare, not even benefit increases to keep up with the cost of living were enacted.

All in all, the period from 1950 to 1972 represents a continuation of the work of the 1937–38 Advisory Council—expanding the insurance system to include additional groups of workers, ad hoc provisions to help keep pace with rising wages and prices, and broadened coverage to provide disability insurance and limited health insurance. The system gradually became more and more effective, and by 1970, although benefit levels were still extremely modest, it was beginning to do well the job it had been designed to do.

1972 AND 1977 AMENDMENTS

Amendments in 1972 provided for further important improvements in the basic system. Benefit levels were increased by 20 percent; even more important, the Nixon administration's proposal for automatic increases in benefits tied to the cost of living was adopted, along with several other automatic provisions. As a result, the program now does automatically what used to be done by ad hoc adjustment, an uncertain method subject to long delays. Keeping pace with wages and prices was a necessary part of the original understanding, and contribution rates had previously been set at levels to allow for such adjustments as wages rose, but now the benefit changes are made automatically.[41]

Further amendments in 1977 added other automatic provisions. Because of the 1977 amendments, future benefits will be computed so as to bear the same relationship to wages current at the time of computation as is true for benefits being awarded today. In other words, the replacement rate of initial benefits will be kept the same indefinitely; for example, workers retiring in 2020 who have earned average wages will get benefits equal to roughly 41 percent of wages then payable, as do workers retiring today who have earned average wages. All these automatic provisions have greatly increased the value of Social Security to those covered by the program, gearing the system to a rising level of living in the initial computation and making it inflation-proof thereafter.

SOCIAL SECURITY SINCE 1977

Valuable as these automatic provisions are, however, they make the system more vulnerable to poor economic performance. The income of Social Security depends primarily on the size of payrolls—and thus wage levels and the rate of unemployment. But outgo, because of the automatic cost-of-living adjustment, is affected greatly by the rate of inflation. Therefore, when inflation rose rapidly in the late 1970s and early 1980s and wages did not keep pace, Social Security reserves were drawn down to dangerously low levels. As a result, throughout 1981 and 1982 there was much talk of bankruptcy and the need to cut back on benefits or to borrow from general revenues. The Reagan administration and Congress could not agree on what should be done.[42]

The 1982–83 National Commission on Social Security Reform broke this political stalemate, negotiating an agreement supported by the president and the Speaker of the House and enacted into law in early 1983.[43] These 1983 amendments—making modest changes in benefits and taxes and providing safeguards against the recurrence of what caused the previous financing crisis—have restored financial stability to Social Security for both the short and the long run. [*Author's note:* In 2000, and for several years previously, the trustees have reported that the system is out of long-range balance. In 2000 they estimated the imbalance to be 1.89 percent of payroll per year on average over the next 75 years.] The trust funds will not only be rebuilt, but huge annual surpluses are expected for decades. The present design has, in effect, moved back to the earlier goal of building a sizable earnings reserve. For example, interest on the funds is estimated to be $259 billion during the year 2010.[44] [*Author's note:* In the 2000 Trustees' Report, the fund builds up from $1 trillion in 2000 to $2 trillion in 2005, and rises from 2.6 times the estimated annual outgo in 2000 to 2.9 times the annual outgo in 2025 before (under present law) starting to decline. In the absence of any corrective measures, the trust funds for OASDI are projected to be exhausted in 2037, although 71 percent of benefit costs would still be met by revenues from the continuance of current taxes.]

THE UNDERSTANDING TODAY AND TOMORROW

Social Security is as useful today as it was expected to be when first designed. The essence of OASDI is that while people work, they and their employers make contributions earmarked for Social Security; and when earnings are lost because of retirement in old age, long-term total disability, or death, benefits are paid. This was the original understanding, and it is the understanding today. This important principle of relating benefits and taxes to the amount of wages, where the higher-paid get higher benefits and also make higher contributions, supports the general incentive system of wage differentials. At the same time, if Social Security is to be effective in largely eliminating the need for means-tested supplementation for lower-paid workers, benefits must continue to be a higher proportion of past wages for those with low earnings than for those with high earnings. To pay the same percentage of wage replacement at all earning levels, with the percentage high enough to keep the minimum wage earner and his dependents from having to turn to assistance or relief, would mean that higher-paid workers would get much more than they do today. We have elected, rather, for a much less expensive system that can still do an effective job as part of a four-tier approach to adequate income in retirement: (1) a universal, compulsory social insurance system; (2) supplementary private pensions (in practice confined largely to average and above-average earners); (3) individual private savings; and (4) underlying the whole, as the last resort, a means-tested national system of Supplemental Security Income (SSI).

Except for the 1972 substitution of the federal SSI program for the federal and state assistance programs to the needy elderly, blind, and disabled, all this was included in the original understanding and envisioned by the 1937–38 council. It has taken a long time to develop, but today the system is working well.

This does not mean the system is perfect. Undoubtedly changes will be made in the future as they have been made in the past. Certainly the goal of universal coverage should be completed by bringing in the four million state and local employees outside the system. Once the reserves have been built up to adequate contingency levels, a decision will need to be made whether to build an earnings reserve as provided by present law or return to pay-as-you-go financing. A good case can be made for either approach.[45] And perhaps during the next 15 years further consideration will be given to whether it is wise to raise the age of first eligibility for full benefits, as planned under present law.

Many people believe it would be desirable to have Social Security administered by a bipartisan board directly under the president, as was the case in the beginning. Such a change, passed by the House of Representatives in July 1986, might help protect the system from short-term budget and political pressures. Since annual Social Security surpluses are used to help meet deficit reduction targets in the general budget (for all other purposes Social Security transactions are now "off-budget" as they were prior to fiscal year 1969), there is a temptation to increase the annual Social Security surpluses by either freezing cost-of-living adjustments or cutting back on benefits in other ways. A bipartisan board charged with protecting the separately financed Social Security system might be successful in limiting Social Security changes to those deemed desirable for reasons internal to the Social Security system. Above all, administration by a bipartisan board directly under the president would emphasize the unique trustee character of Social Security and provide an institutional setting stressing continuity and freedom from partisan political influence. [*Author's note:* Since this was written, the Social Security Administration has been established as an independent agency reporting directly to the president, and in the years 1999 and 2000 both political parties agreed to keep Social Security finances entirely separate from the rest of the budget, dedicating Social Security surpluses to reductions in that part of the public debt held in private hands.]

And, over time, we may want to change the system to provide higher benefits for those who are the worst off—beneficiaries now unmarried. Most elderly couples, given Social Security, can now get by (only 9 percent are below the poverty level). Poverty among the elderly is concentrated largely among single retired workers and single survivors. Unmarried male beneficiaries over age 65 have a 19 percent poverty rate; unmarried female beneficiaries, a 24 percent rate. And, of course, the proportion of the elderly made up of unmarried women, principally widows, is very large and increases dramatically at older ages. Of all family units over age 65, 57 percent are unmarried women. By age 85, out of a total of 1.8 million units, 70 percent or 1.2 million are unmarried women, with a poverty rate of 25 percent, even when total family income is considered for the 30 percent who live with friends or relatives. [See the *Author's note* at the end of this article.] In the long run, it would be desirable to raise the replacement rate for both single workers and widows—the primary insurance amount (PIA)—and working couples (on equity grounds, that is, they pay more) while holding the replacement rate for couples with only one worker where it is today.[46] The treatment of homemakers who are divorced after many years of marriage also needs improvement. These changes are well within the original understanding.

Over the years of Social Security development there has been tension at the borderlines between Social Security and the other three tiers of our retirement system; this, too, will continue. Reasonable people will continue to differ on how much retirement income should come from private pensions and savings and how much from Social Security. The private insurance industry, for example, although supporting Social Security, has usually opposed increasing the benefit level and the maximum benefit and contribution base, while labor has supported such expansion of Social Security's role. And reasonable people will also continue to differ on how much of the job should be left to the means-tested system of SSI, which assisted only 7 percent of the elderly in 1985. [*Author's note:* In 1999, about 5.5 percent of the elderly were receiving SSI, of whom about 35 percent were first eligible because of a disability.]

There are more than two sides to the argument over this borderline. Some would put greatly increased emphasis on equity and for the long run relate Social Security benefits strictly to the past contributions or earnings of individual workers, leaving a much higher proportion of the elderly population with inadequate Social Security benefits and dependent on SSI. And some who support the present weighting in the benefit formula and dependents' benefits and the objective of socially adequate benefits nevertheless believe that any further modifications to give low-wage beneficiaries higher benefits is wasteful because higher benefits would go to some who are not low-income people.[47] Others believe that certain modifications in this direction are desirable on grounds of both equity (couples with only one paid worker, it is argued, are treated too favorably compared to other groups) and social need, but they also agree that further weighting in the benefit formula or a high minimum benefit would be undesirable because such changes would further weaken the benefit/contribution relationship.[48] Still others, however, care little about equity considerations and would modify the tax structure (in one way or another having higher-paid people pay more and lower-paid people pay less) and reduce reliance on SSI by increasing Social Security benefits for the low paid—an approach which many believe would undermine the broad public support Social Security now enjoys.[49]

Arguments about how much each tier should do compared to the other tiers have been going on throughout the whole life of the Social Security system, and the present division of responsibilities has the appearance of an uneasy truce. But few want to emphasize only a single tier and do away with the others. Each part of the four-tier system has a role to perform, but clearly Social Security is the most important and basic tier, as expected from the beginning.

[*Author's note:* The trends noted in the early pages of this article continued after it was written. For the year 1998, 10.5 percent of those 65 and over were below the federal government's definition of poverty, the same percentage as for those of working age (18–64).[50] When children are included, the percentage for all persons in poverty becomes 12.7. Taken alone, 18.3 percent of children under 18 were in families with incomes below the poverty line.

These numbers obscure the fact that among those remaining in poverty, there is a heavy concentration of blacks and Hispanics—for the elderly, 26.4 percent and 21 percent, respectively, and for children 36.4 percent and 33.6 percent, respectively.

Social Security does a great deal for elderly widows and other women who are not currently married. Without Social Security, 63.6 percent of elderly widows and 57.5 percent of other elderly women without husbands would be below the poverty level. Social Security reduces the figures to 21.8 percent for widows and 26.2 percent for the other group. Yet these are still the two most needy groups among the elderly, even after all government programs are taken into account.

Although the poverty rate for elderly women who are married drops to 3.8 percent when all government programs are counted, the figure for widows is still 15.7 percent, and for other elderly women without husbands 18.6 percent.[51]

At the beginning of the year 2000, 44.6 million persons were receiving monthly benefits, and the average retirement benefit was $804 a month. It was estimated that 153 million workers would contribute to Social Security during 2000.[52] In spite of the relatively low average benefits paid by Social Security, Social Security payments make up 55 percent of the income of older persons and 90 percent of the income of over one-fourth of them.[53]

Social Security is a very important source of income to middle-income as well as low-income elderly people. It makes up 80 percent of the income of the two-fifths of the elderly with the lowest incomes, but it also provides 62 percent of the income of those in the next highest income one-fifth of the elderly, and 41 percent of those in the fourth highest income one-fifth. Only among the fifth of the elderly with the highest incomes (many of whom are not yet retired) does Social Security become relatively unimportant (17 percent) but even among this group, Social Security provides about one-fourth of the retirement income that can be counted on when these people are no longer at work.[54]]

3

SOCIAL INSURANCE AND THE RIGHT TO ASSISTANCE

Governments have generally relied on three methods of main-taining incomes for those no longer working and to pay for the cost of medical care: public assistance (also called relief or welfare), social insurance, and age-determined pensions (some-times called demogrants). In the United States there has always been a body of opinion in favor of abolishing social insurance or at least reducing its role vis-à-vis assistance. (In recent years the Concord Coalition has been the leading proponent of this position.) This article examines the difference between the two approaches to income maintenance and makes the case for the inherent values of contributory, wage-related social insurance.

Most people get paid only while working, whether they work for another or are self-employed. Yet people must have an income not only while they work but also during periods of forced inactivity. Furthermore, the incomes of the great majority of people while work-ing are not big enough to absorb large, unpredictable expenses. To help meet these problems of maintaining income and of paying the costs of extraordinary expenses, every industrial country in the world has developed institutions of Social Security.

The term "Social Security" is usually limited to government pro-grams which pay benefits to those whose income has been interrupted by such contingencies as old age, unemployment, disability, or the death of the chief breadwinner in the family, and to government programs which help people to meet such expenses as those of medical care and

From *The Social Service Review*, 21, no. 3, September 1947, pp. 331–44. Copyright © 1947 by the University of Chicago Press, reprinted by permission.

burial. Social Security is the inclusive term and covers social insurance and public assistance, both of which exist in most countries, and also universal pensions and allowances, where these devices are used.

As the two major parts of a system of Social Security, public assistance and social insurance have a common base in program and in administration. Similarities in the two approaches have become increasingly noticeable where, as in the United States, they are administered in the same agency. Not only are they both government programs directed at the problem of income maintenance, but in administration both are primarily concerned with the determination of individual eligibility for benefits in a situation where the conditions of eligibility have their origin in law. These basic similarities give rise to a considerable community of interest between social insurance and public assistance and make the differences between them differences within a unity.

The differences are nonetheless important. In fact, because of their common base it is necessary to stress that they are different, lest there be confusion concerning the roles which each should play in the Social Security program of the future. This paper assumes that both public assistance and social insurance will continue to be necessary and that each must be planned and administered with the other in mind as part of a total program. It is directly concerned, however, only with those elements which continue to distinguish social insurance from any program based upon a means or income test, even one which is administered as a right.

A few years ago differences between social insurance and public assistance were frequently summed up by saying that social insurance was a right, while public assistance was based on need. The right to social insurance was thought to rest on the beneficiary having paid for his insurance, while the granting of money to people solely because they were unable to support themselves was considered by many to be incompatible with the concept of a right to the payment.

Subject to considerable attack, this basis for distinguishing between social insurance and assistance is seldom advanced today. There has been at least limited recognition of a right to public relief in America from Colonial times; and, although by no means fully established in practice, it is clear that such a right exists under the Social Security Act. The real issue is not whether there is a right to assistance but the implications of that right and the extent to which it can be enforced. Moreover, critic after critic has pointed out that our social insurance benefits are not directly related to the contributions made by individual workers or on their behalf and that there are many beneficiaries for whom the contributions are insufficient to cover the cost of the risks against which they are insured. Old-age and survivors insurance favors the worker who was already old when the system went into effect, the worker with dependents, and the lower-paid worker. Members of these groups may get more than they and their employers pay for, even if contributions are figured at 3 percent each, the maximum rate to which taxes would have risen under the original provisions of the Social Security Act. [*Author's note:* This is still true at the present maximum rate of 6.25 percent.]

In unemployment insurance most states do not have an employee contribution. Furthermore, the benefit structures are so arranged that the employer's contribution on behalf of a particular employee is not necessarily related directly to the amount of the worker's potential benefit. Minimum and maximum provisions and, in some states, uniform duration of benefits mean that in unemployment insurance, as well as in old-age and survivors insurance, the worker's individual benefit has not always been paid for by direct contributions made by himself or expressly on his behalf. The right to social insurance cannot be made to rest on the private-insurance concept of individual payment covering the full value of the insurance, nor can public assistance be considered a gratuity. This once popular basis for distinguishing assistance from insurance cannot be maintained.

Recognition of the fact that the cost of social insurance for the individual is not always covered by contributions earmarked for him has led some writers to the conclusion that the program is really very much like relief and that any distinctions between the two approaches are hardly worth keeping. For example, Lewis Meriam in *Relief and Social Security* (1946) advocates the substitution of a "means test" program for social insurance, partly at least, on the theory that paying benefits to people who have not demonstrated individual need is unjustified unless they have paid the cost of those benefits through contributions. Social insurance to him is an expensive way of camouflaging relief; insofar as the insurance benefits are not paid for individually, they are relief in disguise. A believer in conditioning assistance on behavior, he would restrict the concept of right as much as possible.

At the opposite pole of social philosophy there are those who in their emphasis on an unconditional right to assistance imply that social insurance has nothing to offer which cannot be equally or perhaps even better accomplished by a public assistance program firmly established in law and administered in the spirit of right. In his excellent discussion of the implications of a right to assistance, A. Delafield Smith at the 1946 National Conference of Social Work, for example, said:

> Actually, then, public assistance is even more deserving of being described as social insurance than a more selective security system, for assistance programs frankly pay in relation to need and are financed by taxation. That, to me, is true social insurance. It is Social Security. . . .

And later, in speaking of existing limitations on the full realization of the right to assistance:

> This is the kind of thing that has given the word "welfare" an acrid flavor. It has set "charity" over against the "law." It distinguishes "right" from "need." It has made an old age "pension" acceptable, but old age "assistance" in the same amount and on the same terms unacceptable. It demands social "insurance" though the only insurable "hazard" is the bare fact of an empty cupboard. These are but words, words, words.

Both Mr. Meriam and Mr. Smith seem to me to be underrating very significant and fundamental differences between social insurance and public assistance which will and should endure, even though there are more superficial differences which will tend to be modified as the right to assistance is more fully realized. Although the differences between the two approaches are not those that were once put forward, they are nonetheless real.

THE RIGHT TO ASSISTANCE

The right to assistance is a transforming concept. It is one of those dynamic ideas occasionally met with in the history of thought that has the power to change the way men feel and act and, consequently, to revolutionize important institutions. Administration in the spirit of right and legislative safeguards such as the fair hearing and the protection of confidential information have led to such a revolution in the institution of relief and assistance in America—a revolution only half completed, it is true, but one which has already accomplished much.

The idea that assistance payments are a legal and enforceable right for all who meet the conditions of eligibility has necessarily led to an emphasis on equality of treatment among applicants, for a legal right means that those who are alike with respect to certain defined conditions must be treated alike. The concept of equal treatment in turn has led to an emphasis on objective standards for determining eligibility and the amount of the benefit—for how else can equality and right be sustained? Thus today in public assistance there is a growing awareness of the fundamental importance of rules and regulations, defining as precisely as possible exactly what an applicant is entitled to and under what circumstances. The discretion which the relief administrator traditionally possessed to determine who should get money and how much is incompatible with the concept of right.

The antithesis between right and a punitive administration purposefully designed to discourage people from applying for relief is immediately apparent. Less quickly recognized is the antithesis between right and a benevolent paternalism which seeks to improve the behavior or character of the recipient. If the recipient has a right to a payment which rests on his meeting carefully defined eligibility requirements, the administrator cannot use the threat of withholding payments to get people to do what he wants. The interpretation of the money payment provision in the Social Security Act to mean that the grant must be unrestricted—that it shall be spent as the recipient, not the agency, wants—is the Magna Carta of the assistance recipient.

All measures, statutory as well as those of individual discretion, which aim at enforcing a higher standard of behavior for the person receiving assistance than for the rest of the community are incompatible with the idea that assistance is paid as a right. Extra requirements, such as that a child must be in a "suitable" home in applying a special standard to the receipt of public assistance, mean, in effect, that the person must "deserve" his assistance payment by acting a certain way. One does not have to "deserve" a right by following a particular code of moral or social behavior. If it is truly a right, the money is the recipient's own without qualification, and the only controls to which he should be subject are those which govern the whole community. To quote Mr. Smith again:

Law never seeks to buy behavior. It seeks to give rein to moral law. It seeks to allow the individual to benefit or suffer from his choices and sacrifices as freely as possible. This is quite inconsistent with the idea that behavior should enlarge or diminish legal rights. Law insists that the free exercise of rights is essential to democratic equality.

The concept of a right to assistance means not only that the individual shall have security but equally important that he does not have to sacrifice his freedom to attain security. It is toward this goal which the right to assistance is leading us, but we are still a long way from achieving our objective.

LEGAL RIGHTS AND EARNED RIGHTS

The concept of a right to assistance has changed and is changing so much of our attitude toward that program that we are in danger of forgetting what it has not changed and what it is not capable of changing. By definition, a public assistance program pays only those who are in "need," that is, those who do not have enough income from all sources to maintain a standard of living which is considered by the community to be the absolute minimum. Furthermore, a public assistance program pays people *because* they are in need. This is the reason they receive the payment and is the most important condition of eligibility. It is what makes an assistance program assistance.

The amount of the payment, as well as who gets it, is determined by need, whether an individualized budget is used or whether an assumption is made about the need of a particular class of persons, such as the aged. Other income is deducted from the individualized budget or, in a flat-grant program, from the "presumptive budget." Thus, the total income of the individual is not allowed to exceed the minimum community standard.

Certain consequences which cannot be turned aside by good administration and a concept of right flow inevitably from this means test. Because individuals are singled out for payment on the basis of need, people will look on this payment as something different from the other money payments which they receive. Most payments to individuals are not simply a matter of legal right but are thought of as being in payment for service to the economic system. They are "earned" rights.

For the great majority of people money payments are almost entirely in the form of wages and salaries, but the other common types of money payments are also thought of as being made in return for an economic contribution. Whatever differences economists may have concerning the nature of interest, rent, and profits, the community looks on these payments as being service-connected. There is an awareness that rewards are often incommensurate with service, that there is a "windfall" element, for example, in rent and profits (thus the popular concept of a "reasonable" profit), or that wages do not always correctly compensate for the individual's contribution (witness the concept of exploitation); but, nevertheless, under our social and economic mores, the justification for labor being paid at all or for owners of capital and land getting a return is that a service has been rendered.

The recognition that economic rewards are not always commensurate with the contribution makes us willing to tamper in many ways with the particular distribution of wealth which would result from the "free play of economic forces." Our economic ethic demands that some contribution be made for what we get, but most of us do not believe that the payments which result from the automatic functioning of the system are necessarily a "correct" evaluation of the service and that additional payments for that service resulting from the intervention of the state are in any sense "unearned." The farmer feels he has earned his income even when the price of farm products is artificially maintained, and the worker who gets the minimum wage under the Wage and Hour Law is not concerned because his income is higher than the evaluation which would be put on his services by a free market.

The connection between the right to a money payment and what is assumed to be an economic service is nearly universal. With few exceptions money payments that are not thought of as earned are not considered rights but gratuities and are within the discretion of the giver.[1] This is characteristic of socialist as well as capitalist economics. People are paid wages and interest under socialism, even though not profits, and the incentive system throughout the industrial world—in those states in which either a large part or all of the productive forces are owned by government as well as where individual and corporate ownership is dominant—depends basically on this connection between the making of an economic contribution and the receipt of a payment as a matter of right.

Public assistance establishes a right to a money payment which is fundamentally different; it is not paid because of service but because of individual need. It is not strange, therefore, that attitudes toward it and toward earned rights are very different and that there is a tendency to confuse public assistance with a gratuity. Public assistance is winning acceptance as a legal right and a moral right, but it is not and cannot be thought of as an earned right. The basis for eligibility, the fundamental characteristic of the program, is not work or the payment of money contributions derived from work but is the negative fact of being without enough to live on.

The idea that assistance has been earned by work or the payment of taxes throughout the life of the recipient is a rather transparent rationalization designed to make assistance more attractive. It is an indication of the strong desire to think of the payment as earned, but it is hardly tenable. If assistance is earned, why give it only to those who are in need? Surely there is no reason to think that those who are ineligible for public assistance did less to earn a payment or paid lower taxes than those who receive it. Many who work best never get public assistance; some who work poorly, or not at all, do get it. To those it does pay, it pays not in proportion to their work but in proportion to their need. People cannot be expected to look on such a program as a reward for an economic contribution, as something to be proud of, no matter how completely they come to accept the idea of having a right to it.

ASSISTANCE IS FOR THE POOR

The means test, even when modified substantially by exempt income and exempt resources, also inevitably carries with it the separation of the community into two groups—one in which the members have enough money to support themselves and the other in which they do not. It is probable that the great bulk of workers will continue to prefer to be in the former rather than the latter group, and this in spite of any degree of sophistication which they may have concerning individual responsibility for economic success or economic failure. One may understand and sympathize with reasons for being dependent and may be willing to grant that factors other than individual worth are responsible for the ability to be self-supporting, and yet be very glad that one does not have to take assistance. A worker may believe completely in the idea that assistance is a right for those who are unable to support themselves but be very thankful that he does not have to exercise that right. A program which divides the community into two groups on the basis of income and possessions carries with it feelings of self-doubt and loss of social prestige for the one group and snobbery and prejudice for the other. It is common in public assistance, for example, for individual applicants or their friends to want to differentiate between the particular case in which they are interested and on which they look as deserving and what they conceive to be the typical case. They may be at great pains to indicate that a particular applicant was once economically successful and that subsequent failure was not his fault. This striving for a special status within the group of public assistance recipients is an indication of how strongly people feel about being identified with those who are financially unsuccessful and frequently considered by the community to be less adequate than the general run of citizens. One reason public assistance is so hard to administer in a way which preserves the self-respect of the recipient is that only the poor are entitled to the payments, and the poor are little honored.

In New Zealand, in Sweden, in Great Britain, in the states of California and Washington, wherever the concept of the right to assistance has been most fully realized and wherever the liberalization of the means test has been pushed the furthest, there is still intense dislike of a program which pays benefits only to persons with little or no income. It is exactly in these places where the movement to abolish the means test is strongest. People stubbornly prefer to receive payments to which they can transfer all the feelings surrounding earnings and which are not a badge of economic inadequacy.

Some find this hard to understand, since there is no comparable reluctance to accept such services provided by government as education, fire and police protection, libraries, and public parks, which are also supported from general taxation, are not individually earned, and are used only by those who "need" them. Perhaps people will come to feel the same about public assistance benefits as they do about these government services, but there is an important difference which has to be evaluated before coming to such a conclusion. "Need" in the case of education, fire protection, etc., is not determined by reference to whether one can pay for the service but by whether it is useful. This is "need" in a very different sense. Where the question of whether one can pay is the basis of eligibility for the service, as in medical care in America, a stigma may be attached to the receipt of the service just as it is to the receipt of a cash benefit. It is the individual test of need which introduces invidious comparisons and separates one group in the population from the other. It is the fact that all use the universally provided services of government that prevents a stigma from being attached to their receipt. The educational approach which would be comparable to public assistance would be to provide public schools only for the children of persons with little or no income.

THE COMMUNITY MINIMUM

One other characteristic of public assistance programs is also inherent in their very nature. Public assistance pays only enough to bring each individual up to a community-determined minimum. The recipient is not allowed to combine other income of substantial amounts with the assistance payment and in this way secure a higher level of living. The community minimum is his maximum as long as he remains under the program. The drive in assistance is egalitarian to the greatest possible degree, although it provides equality at a low level and only among the poor.

Since the reason for the payment is need—however this need may be defined in a given place at a given time—it does not have a comfortable standard of living as part of its purpose. Its goal must be the prevention of want or the maintenance of health and decency or some other minimum standard figured at the lowest level applicable to all. In a society where varying living standards are the rule and not only comfort but security is conceived of in different terms at various income levels, it is not possible for public assistance with its ceiling on income to promote a standard of real comfort and security. This is necessarily left to the province of individual effort and earned payments.

These three points—that the assistance payment is categorically different from other money paid as a right because it is not a reward for services; that the means test divides the community into two groups, those who have and those who have not; and that its object is limited to bringing people up to a community minimum—are inherent in the nature of the program. No amount of emphasis upon the right to assistance will change these fundamental differences. They cannot be changed without getting rid of the means test.

Social Insurance as an Earned Right

Each one of these points is in direct contrast to the social insurance approach. Social insurance payments are made to individuals on the basis of a work record and are part of the reward for services rendered. Typically, the worker makes a direct contribution to the fund, but, even if he does not "pay for his insurance" through an earmarked contribution which covers the cost of the risk, he earns the right to it through work. The insurance is part of the perquisites of the job. As in a private pension plan or group insurance, the question of who pays the cost is of the highest importance, but it is not the crucial one in determining whether there is an earned right to the payment. There is little hesitation in transferring to a payment for which one has worked all the feelings surrounding an earned right regardless of whether there has been a deduction from wages. Such a payment is a reward—something to be proud of—just as savings or high wages are. Private pensions, group insurance, and social insurance all belong, along with wages and salaries, to the group of work-connected payments, and it is this work connection, the fact that it is earned, which gives social insurance its basic character.

Public assistance in selecting people for payment because they are in need rests on an entirely different kind of right—the right to a minimum standard of living based on membership in a civilized community. As stated by Karl de Schweinitz in a forthcoming [as of 1947] book, *People and Process in Social Security*:

> The principle of self-help [in social insurance], however, is dominant. The individual is entitled to insurance by virtue of what he has done. Insurance is a positive experience. It is a measure of a person's success in the labor market. This is much more evident in old age insurance than in unemployment compensation, but the contrast in this respect between all forms of insurance and public assistance is marked.
>
> In public assistance the inherent factors are negative rather than positive. Entitlement is based not upon what

the individual has done in payment or in work but upon his lack of any such resource. It is founded upon his need, upon what he has not. The individual applying for insurance points to the record of his wages. The applicant for assistance states that he is unable to maintain himself. The right to insurance is based on contributions which the prospective beneficiary has made in money or in work. The right to assistance is founded on the individual's kinship in a common humanity recognized by a community which has undertaken to see to it—and registered the fact in statute—that none of its members shall suffer if they are in need.[2]

Although the fact that social insurance is an earned benefit does not depend on the employee contribution, this contribution does have great value in social insurance, private pension schemes, group insurance, and the like because it dramatizes the worker's direct interest in the fund. It makes it clearer to him and other people, as well, that he should have a real say in the planning and protection of the system from either undue liberalization or restriction. The contribution gives stability to the system by emphasizing both the earned right to the insurance and the proprietary interest of the worker in his benefit. To accomplish this it is of course not necessary that the entire cost of the benefit be paid for by earmarked contributions or that the benefit amounts be in direct proportion to the worker's own contribution. The basic character of the insurance as a work-connected payment remains, regardless of whether some groups are given a greater return for their money than others. In this respect, social insurance is similar to minimum-wage laws which intervene in the "free play of economic forces" and insist that some people be paid higher wages than they would otherwise be able to get. The minimum wage and the "weighted" insurance benefit are earned payments, even though the amount is not what would have resulted from "free competition."

As an earned right, social insurance, unlike public assistance, is an integral part of the economic incentive system. Under social insurance, security is earned through work and is additional remuneration for working, while public assistance provides benefits without reference to work. Equally important, in social insurance the incentive to earn and save throughout one's working life is protected because any additional income, large or small, may be used to provide a higher standard of living. On the other hand, a private income from savings, since it must be deducted from the benefit, makes no difference in the total income of the public assistance recipient. In practice, it is true, even an income which has to be supplemented by public assistance may have real value in making the recipient feel less dependent, but it is the failure of public assistance to give the same satisfaction per dollar as an earned payment which makes this so. In strictly economic terms, a person who has little hope of accumulating enough to make him entirely ineligible for assistance has no reason to strive for a private income.

Even in New Zealand, which allows fairly substantial exempt amounts before reducing benefits, there is concern about the effect of the income test on incentives. It is recognized that the system works counter to general economic incentives for those who have any possibility of securing incomes above the exemption, for above this amount the benefits are larger the less one has been able to earn and save. The very liberalizations which make the receipt of a "means test" benefit in New Zealand less subject to stigma than anywhere else in the world intensify the danger that such benefits may weaken the desire to secure a private income above the amount which allows one to get a full benefit.[3]

Partly because of the stigma attached to the receipt of public assistance in the United States, it is to be doubted that very many people deliberately avoid efforts at earning and saving in order to be eligible for a benefit or in order to get a higher benefit. However, the fear that a generous program administered in the spirit of right might be an inducement to some to work and save less is one of the reasons the community is reluctant to accept the full implications of a right to assistance and a standard of health and decency for assistance payments. Although incentives are a complex of many powerful motives in addition to the economic, no system of production can afford to ignore the relation of money payments to economic contribution. There are many faults in our present system of monetary incentives, and behavior contrary to the best interests of the community is frequently induced, but this fact argues for a closer connection between contribution and award, not for ignoring incentives in the provision of security. Some benefits must be paid on a "means test" basis, but it is important from the standpoint of economic incentives that primary reliance be placed on earned payments made without regard to need.

SOCIAL INSURANCE IS FOR ALL WHO WORK

Second, social insurance does not divide the community into two groups, putting those with enough money to support themselves in one group and those without enough money in another. It is true that certain foreign systems still have something similar to this in that they cover only lower-paid workers so that a certain class distinction does exist, but this is on the way out, and it never carried with it the same feelings as did a distinction based on a direct means test. In this country, of course, no coverage limitations based on income have ever existed. Thus, as in the case of a private pension plan, individuals of varying wage levels and varying standards of living receive payments from the same program. The low-paid wage-earner, the poor man without possessions, receives payments through the same mechanism as the highly paid salary worker or executive. There is none of the feeling in such a social insurance program, as there tends to be in assistance, that this program is for the "poor" or the "unfortunate," with all that such an attitude implies. It is not one part of the community caring for another, but the community meeting a universal need. Everyone has a stake in his earned pension and insurance benefits.

SOCIAL INSURANCE SUPPORTS A VARIABLE STANDARD OF LIVING

Finally, social insurance has as its purpose not only the maintenance of a minimum standard of living as set by the community but the underpinning of a higher-than-minimum standard of living for a large proportion of the workers under the program. This is inherent in the fact that it pays without regard to other resources, whether or not the benefits alone would allow a higher-than-minimum standard.

There is no question, for example, but that even the very low benefits of the present old-age and survivors insurance program enable many people to live at a standard considerably above what the community would consider a reasonable minimum for a "means test" program and that others who receive the payment would be able to live above such a minimum even without the benefit. This is not an accident of clumsy design but a major purpose of social insurance. As in the case of a private pension, one objective is to help people to have enough income not merely to be free from want, or to bring them up to a community minimum, but to help them to secure the economic bases for happiness and contentment. It is a program not only for the poor but for whoever is in danger of suffering a major reduction in living standards. It is a program of preventing destitution, as well as curing it.[4]

Actually, there is nothing about social insurance to prevent payments which in themselves are more than enough to maintain minimum standards. Social insurance could never pay as much as the more liberal private pension systems, but it is by no means bound to pay only an amount which will give the content of a community-approved minimum applicable to all. The question is one of what the nation can afford and of how much of the national income we want to put into such benefits—not one of principle. When many current proposals would provide family benefits under old-age and survivors insurance as high as $120 a month and when some state unemployment insurance systems already pay over $100 a month to single persons, we are no longer dealing in community-determined minimums; many people in the community will have lower incomes than these and yet not be entitled to benefits under any program. When we combine this fact with the rough generalization that those who are entitled to the highest benefits are those who may be assumed to have the most income from other sources, since they had more to save from, it is clear that social insurance is not just another way of doing the same job that public assistance sets out to do.

A major purpose of social insurance is to keep people from having to apply for assistance, but it also performs for others who would not have been eligible for assistance under any circumstances the very valuable service of helping them to live above the community minimum. This objective would be unfair, discriminatory, and completely inappropriate in a program based upon need, but it is both right and proper in a program based upon work and earnings. Under a system of relating benefits to past wages, high benefits may be paid to highly paid wage-earners and the incentive system actually strengthened thereby, just as it is strengthened by differential payments in wages, or in a private pension or disability system. There is little danger that the wage-earner will prefer the benefits to work, in those parts of the program where this is a factor, as long as his benefits are considerably below what he can earn while working. It is necessary to limit benefits for all to an amount below what the least skilled can earn only in a flat-benefit program.

DIFFERENCES IN TRADITION

These three important differences between social assistance and social insurance are inherent in the very nature of the two programs. They derive from the right to one being based on need, and the right to the other being based on work. Equally important at the present time and for a long time to come are differences in the two programs which are not inherent but which result from differences in origin and traditional attitudes toward the two programs. It is with respect to these differences that the concept of a right to assistance is making revolutionary changes.

One of the most striking contrasts between assistance and insurance in the United States at the present time is that what is freely conceded in the case of insurance requires a bitter, never completely won struggle in public assistance. For example, the right of the recipient to spend his benefit without restriction has seldom been questioned in the case of insurance but is a continual struggle in public assistance. In the same way, discretionary payments designed to enforce a code of conduct on the recipient different from that required of the rest of the community are not a problem in insurance. Yet, public assistance is carrying on a constant struggle against a tradition which used the payment as an excuse to reform or control the individual. There are probably many people who would still agree with Lewis Meriam when, speaking of those public assistance recipients whom he considers unable to manage their own affairs, he says:

> In such cases, the recipients of the benefits should be subject to the supervision of competent, professionally trained, public employees, and payments should be contingent upon suitable use and application of the public funds provided. . . . It seems reasonable to conclude that payment of public funds for persons whose need results from their personal limitations should be sufficiently contingent to make it necessary for the recipients to comply with minimum standards.[5]

He is not speaking here, of course, of those who have been judged mentally incompetent under legal procedure but of people who have a way of ordering their lives which he considers undesirable and whose behavior he considers evidence of "personal limitation." This doctrine means, in effect, that to obtain minimum security an individual would have to give up freedom of action and submit to the dictates of others on how he should conduct his life in those essentials where other citizens are allowed to make their own decisions.

Leaving aside the question of whether such supervision is practical, whether in this way you can really get people to act the way you want, an equally important point is that making security contingent on the surrender of personal integrity and freedom of action is exactly what we want to avoid in a democracy. This issue goes to the heart of the central political problem of our time—how can people obtain economic security in a way which preserves individual freedom and human dignity? How can we avoid the false dilemma, beloved of totalitarians, of having to choose between a means of livelihood, on the one hand, and freedom on the other? There is little danger of the control of one person by another if the right to security is an earned right. It continues to be a danger in assistance as long as any important section of public opinion holds the traditional attitude, championed by Mr. Meriam, that a public assistance payment is not the recipient's own but a contingent gift from public funds.

Another important difference between the two programs, at present, is that the community frequently limits the amount of funds available for public assistance in such a way as to make a mockery of the concept of a right to a minimum standard of living. No feeling of contractual obligation to supply that minimum exists in fact, whereas a feeling of obligation to supply the amount written in the law does exist in social insurance. This is irrespective of whether the legal right to the two types of payments is equally strong.

Public assistance has arrived at the concept of right by way of a long, hard road. Its history is a combination of repression and punishment, on the one hand, and of humanitarian paternalism, on the other. While its worst features have been based on the idea that the individual was at fault and needed chastisement to make him better or that relief had to be made as unpleasant as possible or people would all refuse to work, equally destructive of the concept of right has been the paternalism which held that what the individual needed was reformation and help. Punitive or humanitarian, public assistance suffers from a history and tradition in which one group or class does something either to or for another.

Social insurance bypassed this tradition both of punishment and paternalism. Its origins are not in the poor law or in the voluntary activities of the wealthy and educated to improve the lot of the poor.

Its origins are in the sturdy efforts of self-reliant workmen to do things for themselves—in the sickness and death funds of the medieval guilds, the friendly societies, the fraternal orders, and the trade-unions. It borrows much from private pension plans and from private insurance and from a tradition of protective labor laws, frequently forced on an unwilling state by the power of workers' organizations. Here is no giving of one class to another but the development of institutions by those who are to benefit from them. Social insurance is firmly fixed in a tradition of self-help and earned right. Therefore, while assistance, in implementing the idea of right, must struggle to establish new attitudes, social insurance finds these attitudes ready-made.

To make use of these ready-made attitudes and to avoid the struggle which attends the reformation of an old tradition is highly important in social planning, now at least as important as preserving what is inherently different about the insurance approach. Part of the value of the contribution by the worker in social insurance and part of the value of connecting the benefits closely with the wage record lie in using the techniques which are readily identified with the tradition of self-help, with its accompanying freedom of action and freedom from the necessity of feeling grateful. They make doubly clear to all that this program has no connection with the tradition of the poor law.

CONCLUSION

There are, then, in spite of important similarities, very significant and real differences between public assistance and social insurance. From the standpoint of freedom, democratic values, and economic incentives, social insurance is greatly to be preferred wherever there is a choice. It is important that, through an extension of coverage and an increase in social insurance benefits, it be made clear that public assistance is not a rival to the insurance method but a supplement to it, performing the residual task that will always exist for a last-resort program that takes responsibility for meeting total need. The goal of a progressive Social Security program should be to reduce the need for assistance to the smallest possible extent and at the same time to enforce it as a legal and moral right, with an administration free from the controls and the "humiliations and irritations of 'poor law' procedures."[6]

In attaining this goal, there is much to gain from the association of social insurance with assistance in the Social Security system. The fact that both devices are necessary, although different parts of a common program, reinforces the concept of assistance as a right. Insurance tends to be administered in the spirit of right, naturally and without question, and, through association, public assistance moves closer to an administration which is as firmly based in law and regulation and is as devoted to equity and definiteness as is insurance. The concept of public assistance as part of a broader Social Security program addressed to the total problem of income maintenance is important in the struggle to eliminate those undesirable features of assistance which are the result of tradition. There is no danger of assistance becoming too attractive and taking the place of social insurance, providing social insurance is made to fill its proper role. Quite the contrary, there is a long fight ahead to make assistance merely endurable in a democratic state. Assistance is never something to look forward to, since like a life-raft it performs the function of rescue and is the accompaniment of disaster—at its best, it is a necessary evil. Social insurance, on the other hand, can be a positive good, and in the preventing of disaster and in helping a family to maintain an accustomed standard of living is to be likened more to the devices and regulations which protect the safety and comfort of passengers and reduce the need for life-rafts. As long as men value self-reliance, the alternative of earning one's security through work will be preferred to payments made because of need.

4

SOCIAL SECURITY IN THE DECADES AHEAD: THE CASE FOR THE TRADITIONAL PROGRAM

A review of current issues and proposals. (To make the reader's task easier, throughout the text of this chapter—and this chapter alone—I have simply replaced earlier data with the latest data available in 2000 rather than adding bracketed updates as in several of the other pieces. To have supplied such updates in this chapter, given its scope, would have meant burdening the reader with a lifetime supply of brackets.)

Retirement policy in the United States rests on four pillars: Social Security; supplementary employer-sponsored pensions; individual savings; and the federal Supplemental Security Income (SSI) program, intended to bring the most impoverished of the elderly, blind, and disabled up to a minimum standard of living.

Each pillar complements the others, and each, by long tradition, has either been directly provided for through tax revenues or encouraged by favorable tax treatment. Medicare, the federal health insurance program for the elderly and disabled, can be seen as a fifth pillar of the system. By far the most important parts of this multi-pillar approach to retirement income are Social Security—contributory, wage-related, and now covering just about everyone—and Medicare.

Social Security is now just about universal: 95 percent of those aged 65 and over are either receiving benefits or eligible to do so but deferring receipt until they stop working. In contrast, private pensions add a supplementary source of income for only about 25 percent of those over 65 who are retired from private-sector employment. Career government pensions for federal civilian and military and for state and local employees cover about 11 percent of all retirees.

The individual savings rate in the United States is low, and, except for home ownership, accumulated savings at the time of retirement are not usually sufficient to make a significant contribution to continuing retirement income. Of those 65 and older with any income from savings, 30 percent receive less than $500 a year: only 16 percent receive $15,000 or more.[1]

When a complementary system of retirement income programs was first envisioned in the early days of Social Security, it was frequently described as a "three-legged stool" (omitting from the discussion, and the leg count, the then federal-state system of public assistance—now the wholly federal SSI—that provided a residual safety net). The three-legged stool was always more of a dream than a reality. When it was first formulated in the years of the Great Depression, there were very few pension plans covering workers in private industry, and the savings available to most retirees were even more meager, relative to their needs, than today. The hope was that pension plans and savings would develop into strong complements to the Social Security system. But the stool has always been wobbly.

Private pension coverage has remained at about 50 percent of full-time private-sector workers since the late 1970s, but there has been a significant shift in the *kind* of coverage. By the mid-90s about 33 percent had traditional coverage, while 17 percent had only 401(k) coverage.[2]

This shift makes payment in retirement, and the *amount* of payment, less certain, because 401(k) plans—named for the section of the Internal Revenue Code that permits pre-tax contributions to a voluntary salary-reduction plan—are far from adequate retirement plans. They are better described as employer-encouraged savings plans. Higher-paid workers frequently find 401(k)s attractive because they can get at the money before retirement for special needs such as buying a house or meeting medical expenses (albeit with a 10 percent penalty for early withdrawal and with the benefits taxable); they also have a say in how the funds are invested, and can stop contributing as they wish. Low- and moderate-income workers, on the other hand, are rarely able to participate in 401(k) plans. Half of all full-time, year-round workers make $26,700 or less annually and, for the most part, must focus on paying for shelter and food. Thus, while about 60 percent of workers making $75,000 or more and employed in firms offering 401(k)s are participating, only about 25 percent of those making $20,000 to $25,000 do so. This is in contrast to the more or less automatic coverage of traditional employer-paid pension systems. Moreover, participants often start making contributions late in their careers, frequently too late for meaningful accumulations; more than half of 401(k) participants between ages 51 and 60 have accrued balances of less than $10,000, which is not much for an annuity.

Employers have a strong incentive to promote 401(k)s. Instead of paying about 7 percent of payroll for a defined-benefit plan, they can offer a 401(k) for 1 or 2 percent of payroll (based on putting up 50 cents on each $1 put up by those employees who want to participate). It is not surprising that when the two kinds of plans are run side-by-side, the defined-benefit plan may be allowed to deteriorate and more attention is given to the "do-it-yourself" 401(k) plan. In short, 401(k)s can be valuable savings vehicles—for those who can afford to save—but they are not very good retirement plans.

Under 401(k) plans, lump-sum payments are common when a worker changes jobs or retires or when a company changes hands, but these lump sums may or may not be used to provide an income stream over the period of retirement. In 1994, workers over 40 receiving such lump-sum payments reported that somewhat less than half of the payments received were put into retirement savings, investments, or other savings, with the rest going to current spending. It may be that 50 percent coverage and 25 percent benefit receipt are the high-water marks of private pension effectiveness, although, depending on how they are counted in the future, 401(k) plans could increase or decrease these numbers. In any event, it is clear by now that most low-wage and many moderate-income workers will not receive substantial protection from private plans.

Even for those who do have such additional private pension protection, there is another problem: inflation. At the beginning of retirement the average replacement rates (the extent to which retirement income replaces pre-retirement earnings) are nearly as high for private pensions as for Social Security. But, unlike Social Security, the private pension replacement rates, measured in terms of purchasing power, decline rapidly because of the lack of inflation protection. Only about 30 percent of private pension recipients report that they have ever received a cost-of-living increase, and among those who have, the increases have averaged only 2.1 percent a year. In 1994, private-sector workers who began receiving annuities in 1990–94 had real replacement rates averaging 22 percent, but for those who began in 1985–89 the rate had slipped to 19 percent; for 1980–84, to 15 percent; for 1975–79, to 11 percent; and for those beginning prior to 1975, to 9 percent. By comparison, Social Security replacement rates for those receiving both Social Security and private pensions remained approximately the same (25 percent) throughout the period.

To strengthen the three-tier system, Social Security benefit levels need to be maintained (if not improved); Social Security coverage needs to be extended to all state and local government employees;[3] private plans need to be extended and improved; and those who can need to save more.

THE PEACEFUL REVOLUTION

Social Security keeps some 15 million people above the poverty line, and millions more from near-poverty. As recently as 1967, the poverty rate among the elderly was two and a half times as high as among the rest of the population; Social Security has been the key factor in bringing the rate down to 10.5 percent (on a par with rates among other adults). Without Social Security, about 45 percent of the elderly would have incomes below the federal government's rock-bottom definition of poverty.

But Social Security is much more than an antipoverty program. Because Social Security benefits are not means-tested, those who are relatively well-off are able to add other income to Social Security, providing a level of living in retirement that is not too far below what they were used to while working. That is why most people approve of Social Security and are willing to pay Social Security taxes—not only to protect their parents and grandparents today, but also to build a foundation for themselves and their families tomorrow.

In a relatively short time, our multi-pillar system of retirement-and-health protection, anchored by Social Security and Medicare, has brought about nothing less than a revolution in the way that older people, in particular, are treated in this country. But the *method* has been anything but revolutionary. Social Security emphasizes and reinforces the conservative values of work, saving, and self-help.

The future of Social Security depends on its continuing popularity. There is no constitutional guarantee of benefit payments, as there is for interest on government bonds. Nor are the benefits backed to any significant extent by accumulated funds, as is required of private insurance. Under present law, then, the future of Social Security depends almost entirely on the continued willingness of workers and voters to pay for it.

In all probability this is a much stronger guarantee than it may appear to be. Workers in the future, like workers today, will very likely continue to see Social Security as essential protection for their parents, themselves, and their children—protection that, for most people, cannot be duplicated by private savings or private pensions. Moreover, since the personal stake in Social Security increases as people grow older, any coolness toward the program among the young and unmarried tends to dissipate over time. Polls have consistently shown that most people are willing to pay more for Social Security and to support other changes, if necessary, to keep the system viable. Clearly, public support for the program reflects broad support for its basic principles.

CONFLICTS OVER BENEFIT LEVELS

Throughout the entire history of Social Security in the United States, essentially the same controversy over its proper boundaries has been at the bottom of most arguments about specific changes. On the one hand, what is the proper borderline with relief and assistance? On the other hand, where should the lines be drawn between Social Security, private pensions, and savings?

At the borderline of relief and assistance, the issue is one of the appropriateness of the social insurance approach in particular situations. Insurance against wage loss can go a long way toward meeting many, but not all, needs. How far should one reasonably go in a contributory, wage-related system, for example, in trying to meet the needs of those with only a weak attachment to the labor market? At what point does it become patently unfair to regular contributors as a whole (thereby jeopardizing their support) to skew the system to pay relatively high benefits not only to the lowest-paid but also to irregular contributors?

If redistribution is pushed too far, the wage-related character of the system is lost—and with it much of the basis for Social Security's popularity. Consequently, although there has been some consensus among Social Security supporters that steady full-time workers and their dependents should get high enough benefits that means-tested supplementation is unnecessary, few would argue for such a standard for those with only intermittent attachment to the system. This view, even in the long run, leaves a small but significant supplementary role for SSI. (There are, of course, those who disagree, believing that the primary goal of Social Security should be to end poverty for all participants.)

At the borderline of private pensions and private savings, the major issue becomes: How far should a compulsory government system go and how much should be left to private effort? Social Security can arguably furnish protection more effectively than private plans (because of its low administrative costs, protection against inflation, portability, etc.), and can do so in ways that simultaneously promote important social goals. But the system does require the dedication of a portion of workers' earnings to one fixed set of purposes: replacing earnings generally lost at retirement or because of the disability or death of a wage earner. How much is enough? How much should be left to workers to set their own priorities?

Benefits under Social Security are quite modest. As of June 30, 2000, the average annual benefit was $9,600 for retired workers living alone and $16,300 for workers with spouses. But the range is large, as would be expected in a wage-related program. A key point, however, is that in a compulsory program requiring people to save for their retirement, as opposed to a voluntary retirement plan, one has to decide how much is justified, as compared to allowing individuals to save on their own for retirement or other purposes, or to spend currently. There is a public interest in helping people attain a retirement income reasonably related to previous earnings, but there is clearly a limit to the proper use of compulsion. In providing for replacement of about one-fourth of recent earnings for the higher-paid, we may have gone about as far as we should go for them, allowing for supplementary arrangements for private pensions and private savings on a voluntary basis to provide the rest.

Over the years this issue has divided Social Security supporters. Workers themselves, at least as represented by organized labor, have in the past pushed for expansion of Social Security's role, to provide more adequate benefits at all earnings levels, while employers usually have resisted benefit increases. In recent years, largely because of the cost of health insurance, workers have generally stopped advocating expansion of the cash benefit program. As for the insurance industry and others engaged in the business of private pension and benefit planning, they have given strong support to the general concept of Social Security and to universal coverage, but, understandably, have also pressed to keep benefits relatively low so that they could sell private retirement coverage on top.

These two arguments over borderlines—one at the bottom concerning social insurance's role in preventing poverty and the specific assistance programs designed to address poverty once it has occurred, and the other at the top between social insurance and supplementary private protection—will never be completely resolved. However, they don't need to be. Some will press for a bigger role for Social Security, and others will try to put on the brakes. Some will think that the program has gone too far in helping low-income people, and others will feel that still more can be done without endangering public support for the program.

Aside from broad philosophical arguments over how much should be done by each of the four pillars of our retirement income system, however, there are equity problems in the Social Security benefit structure that need to be addressed. In particular, benefit levels for married couples are high relative to other benefit categories. Paying benefits 50 percent higher for a married couple than for a single retiree, as is currently done, probably overstates the cost of operating two-person, versus one-person, households; a 30 or 40 percent differential might be more appropriate.

Such a reduction in the spouse benefit would also help with the current perception that married women get little for their own contribution because, in effect, their benefit rate is whichever benefit is higher—as a spouse or as a worker. With this change, the majority of married women in the future would receive benefits as workers.

The benefit rate for divorced women is the same as for a spouse living with a marriage partner, although it goes to a person living alone and is frequently inadequate in that situation. The benefit for the divorced spouse is important for women who have spent most of their lives maintaining a household rather than working in paid employment, yet the present benefit takes no account of the homemaker's contribution to family income. There is a strong case for introducing a system of "earnings sharing" into Social Security, but there seem to be insurmountable transitional and technical difficulties in moving the entire Social Security system to an earnings-sharing basis. On the other hand, the concept of earnings sharing at divorce (that is, combining earnings during the time of marriage and crediting one-half to the Social Security account of each) should be carefully explored.

It might also be desirable to mitigate the penalties that wage earners now suffer when they leave the labor market to care for young children. Special treatment of the child-care years could be considered, protecting the level of a worker's benefit just as today's benefit levels are protected during periods of a worker's total disability. Benefits for young families are also in some cases inadequate, including benefits for disabled children and for a sole surviving child.

Except for the reduction in spouse benefits, these changes would cost more money. Given the perception that tax increases, even for Social Security, are likely to be unwelcome, it may well be that for now we should concentrate on restoring the long-term balance between income and expenses for the present program. It is true that benefit levels are insufficient for many of the very old, especially older women, who account for such a high proportion of the very old. This is the biggest unsolved problem in Social Security's benefit structure. [*Author's note:* For many years I have proposed a change in law that would make for substantial progress in this area: an increase in the Primary Insurance Amount (PIA)—the calculation of retirement benefits upon which all other benefits are based—of 7 percent and a reduction in the spouse's benefit from 50 percent of the PIA to 40 percent. This change would hold couples' benefits level but raise benefits for single persons, including widows and widowers, children, and workers who never married. It would add about 0.75 percent of payroll to the 75-year cost of the system.] Otherwise, the current benefit structure seems sensible for a basic system. One can argue for somewhat less here or somewhat more there, but by and large the program is doing well what it was designed to do.

FINANCING ISSUES

But is the current program too expensive—and inevitably headed for trouble? Obviously some seem to think so. But in fact only modest changes are needed to bring the program into financial balance.

The trustees estimated in 2000 that income (the sum of the revenue sources plus interest on accumulated funds) will exceed expenses each year until 2025. The trust funds will then start to decline as investments are cashed in to meet the payments coming due. The trustees estimate that although 71 percent of costs would continue to be met from current contribution rates, beginning in 2037 (in the absence of any changes in the meantime) it would not be possible to pay full benefits on time.

Expressed as a percent of payroll, the deficit over the traditional 75-year projection period is projected to be 1.89 percent. In other words, if contribution rates had been increased in 2000 by one percentage point each for employers and employees, the system would remain in balance over the long-range period.

There is little political support today for actually increasing the rate by that much.[4] But there are many other ways to bring the program into long-run balance without departing from its basic principles or undermining the economic well-being of future workers and program beneficiaries. Some would rely more heavily on benefit reductions (such as retirement age increases and formula changes) and others on payroll tax increases. Still others would rely heavily on trust fund investment options and other changes not classified as either benefit cuts or contribution increases. The point, however, is not that any one change is essential but rather that *the long-range expenses and revenues of the system can be brought into balance without drastic cuts in benefits or major increases in Social Security tax rates, and without compromising the basic purposes and principles of the present program.*

To illustrate possible policy directions, consider two approaches that would bring Social Security into actuarial balance: one based on partial advance funding and the other on pay-as-you-go financing.

Both approaches are consistent with, and could build upon, extending coverage to the one-fourth of full-time state and local employees not now covered under voluntary compacts between the states and Social Security. This is the last sizable group of workers (about 3.7 million) not covered under Social Security, and it is only fair that they, like everyone else, should be part of our national Social Security program.[5] They would generally gain from being under Social Security's inflation-proof provisions and from coverage that would be combined with work outside of their current state or local employment. And spouses would benefit from Social Security's automatic protection, which is not provided for under those state plans where workers can decide to take higher benefits rather than have survivors protection.

For Social Security, this extension of coverage saves money over both the short and long term, largely because contributions will be received for many years before benefit payments have to be made. This extension of coverage saves the Social Security system 0.22 percent of payroll over the long term.[6]

Another change that can he advocated as a matter of fairness is to tax Social Security benefits as other contributory defined-benefit pension plans are taxed. (This change is also consistent with either partial funding or pay-as-you-go financing.) The application of this policy to Social Security would be to make Social Security benefits taxable to the extent that they exceed the employee's contributions. Dedicating the proceeds of the tax on benefits to Old-Age, Survivors, and Disability Insurance, as was done when Social Security benefits were first taxed, would reduce the long-run imbalance by 0.55 percent of payroll.[7]

As a result of these two changes called for by the standard of fairness, the estimated long-range Social Security deficit is reduced from 1.89 percent of payroll to 1.12 percent. The significance of this remaining deficit, and of proposals for eliminating it, varies depending on the financing method that is adopted. The two broad options—partial funding and pay-as-you-go—are discussed next to illustrate how the projected financing problem might be further addressed.

Partial Advance Funding

As of January 1, 2000, Social Security had a reserve of approximately $900 billion. This seems large, but in fact was equal to only 220 percent of the next year's expected benefit payments.[8] In the event of an unexpected increase in costs, a reserve of this size would clearly be sufficient to tide the system over until Congress could make appropriate changes in financing.

Under present law, reserves will build to about $6 trillion in 2025, according to the 2000 Trustees' Report, before starting down. This is considerably more than enough for a contingency reserve. Because it is soon dissipated, however, even this amount contributes little to the financing of future benefits. What we have now is no longer pay-as-you-go, but it is also not a reasonable plan for partial advance funding. The fund builds up for about 25 years and then is used up over the following decade.

This funding pattern does not make a great deal of sense. A buildup followed by a drawdown could be defended as a way of financing the increased number of retirees accompanying the aging of the baby-boom generation *if* the costs of Social Security were expected to drop after the baby-boom retirees are replaced by the smaller generation that will follow them into retirement. But that is not the scenario. The cost of Social Security does indeed build to a new plateau as the result of the baby-boom generation's retirement, but the cost then stays at this high level (and even rises somewhat) because continuing increases in longevity will result in having to pay benefits longer, offsetting the drop in the number of retirees.

If we plan to build much more than a contingency reserve, it would make sense to maintain it so that earnings on the fund would make a significant contribution to the long-range balance. This is the method that private pensions follow over the shorter period (usually 30 to 35 years rather than 75) that they use in attempting to balance income and outgo.

However, relying on earnings from a substantial fund buildup as an important part of long-range financing raises the question of investment policy to a degree that it has not been raised before. With a contingency reserve, how the funds are invested doesn't make much difference, so there has been little challenge in the past to the long-standing policy of investing the trust funds almost exclusively in Treasury special obligations (which pay interest equal to the average interest on all the outstanding long-term debt of the United States). With a large earnings reserve, however, it *does* make a big difference how the money is invested. If, for the first time in the program's history, an earnings reserve of substantial size is actually allowed to build up, the traditional investment policy would seem to be unduly conservative. As the fund increases, it would be preferable—and still prudent—to increase the investment yield by putting a portion of the fund, such as 40 percent, in private equities. This could be done at minimum risk of political interference by requiring passive management of investments indexed to a broad market portfolio, under the guidance of an independent and expert board charged with selecting the appropriate index and portfolio managers. Such a policy, although still conservative, would considerably raise the return on Social

Security investments. A contingency reserve equal to 100 to 150 percent of the next year's outgo would, at the very least, be kept in government funds at all times, so the desired rates for equities would be reached gradually. (See Chapter 19, "A Public-Private Investment Strategy.")

"Partial advance financing" is a phrase that covers any buildup beyond a reasonable contingency reserve and then maintenance of such a fund long enough to make a significant contribution to long-term financing. One argument for such pre-funding is that we should have the baby boomers themselves pay more of the costs of their retirement, as compared to increasing the contribution rates for the smaller generation that follows.

This is entirely feasible. Quite modest benefit reductions or tax increases, if put into effect within the next few years in conjunction with additional state and local coverage and changes in the taxation of benefits, would build a large fund that, when coupled with increased earnings under the new investment policy, would completely eliminate the long-term Social Security deficit.

Additional changes have been suggested, including reducing the cost of benefits still more by changing the benefit formula or by further raising the age at which full benefits are first payable. However, it may be undesirable to change the retirement age further before we have had any experience with the change from 65 to 67 that will take place under present law (instituted over the 2000–27 period). First, the impact falls disproportionately on lower-paid and blue-collar workers, since they are generally least able to work longer. Second, we don't really know to what extent jobs will be available for those who want to postpone retirement. Third, we aren't sure that the basic rationale for the change is reasonable—that is, we aren't sure that because people are living longer and because some groups of older people may be healthier, most people can necessarily be expected to work longer. Perhaps the most that should be done now is to study what happens under the present retirement age provision as it gradually becomes effective before taking any further steps in the direction of increasing the first age at which full benefits are payable.

Many other options are available. For example, the proposal to tax Social Security benefits as other contributory defined-benefit plans are taxed includes shifting the proceeds of that part of the tax on Social Security benefits that now goes to Medicare. The proposal is to iron out this peculiar wrinkle when Medicare is refinanced, which has to take place under present estimates not later than 2026. Although allocating any part of taxes on OASDI benefits to purposes other than OASDI seems to make little sense for the long run, many oppose taking away any income source for the underfinanced Medicare program. If this reallocation is not adopted, it could be made up for in many ways.

[*Author's note:* Since this was written, both President Clinton and Vice President Gore have proposed shifting some of the expected surplus in the non–Social Security budget to Social Security, reducing the program's deficit by 1.06 percent of payroll. President Clinton's proposal (but not Vice President Gore's) would reduce the deficit by another 0.38 percent of payroll by investing up to 15 percent of the accumulating Social Security surplus in stocks. Accordingly, one good plan for just about eliminating the 1.89-percent-of-payroll deficit would include: extending coverage to state and local employees not now covered (reducing the deficit by 0.22 percent of payroll); taxing Social Security benefits to the extent they exceed what the worker paid in and directing all revenues from such taxes to the Social Security Trust Funds beginning in 2026 (reducing the deficit by 0.55 percent of payroll); and incorporating the Clinton-Gore proposal for general revenue support (reducing the deficit by 1.06 percent of payroll). Although I believe that all of these changes are desirable, several may be difficult to get enacted. Some alternatives that might have a greater chance of enactment include: increasing the maximum benefit and contribution base so as gradually to cover at least 90 percent of earnings, as was once the case (reducing the deficit by 0.62 percent of payroll), or, more modestly, to cover 87 percent of earnings (reducing the deficit by 0.32 percent of payroll); and investing up to 15 percent of the accumulating Social Security surplus in stock, as suggested by President Clinton (reducing the deficit by 0.38 percent of payroll), or, instead, investing up to 40 percent (reducing the deficit by 1.03 percent of payroll). A further possibility would be to improve the accuracy of the automatic cost-of-living adjustment (COLA) following the publication of an alternative Consumer Price Index (CPI) by the Bureau of Labor Statistics in 2002. The improvement in the CPI, directed at the so-called substitution bias in present law, would reduce the deficit by 0.23 percent of payroll.]

Whatever other changes are made, however, contribution rates for Social Security should be increased only modestly. Contribution rate increases could then be reserved largely for the Medicare Hospital

Insurance (HI) Program. Medicare, after all, is just as important as cash benefits to income security, and Medicare needs to be shored up. As currently financed, the HI program is expected to be able to continue paying full benefits on time until 2025. At that time, however, some restructuring of HI will almost certainly be needed, possibly including contribution rate increases.

Medicare Part B (insurance for doctors' bills) also needs attention. At the very least, the general revenue subsidy, now three-fourths of the system's financing, ought to be taxed and the proceeds used to hold down the size of future premium increases and general revenue payments. Three times the Medicare premium gets us to the amount of the general revenue subsidy, and adding that to gross income for income tax purposes would tax the subsidy simply and fairly. The larger point, in any case, is that however its financing problems are addressed, Medicare is a crucial part of Social Security, and financing for OASDI must take Medicare into account.

Table 4.1 shows how selecting among a variety of adjustments, most of them quite moderate, could restore long-term balance to Social Security. [Note that this table, which reflects the preceding Author's Note, incorporates data updated since this piece was originally written.]

PAY-AS-YOU-GO

Social Security has basically been financed on a pay-as-you-go basis. Historically there have been contribution schedules in the law that would have built up earnings reserves as a way of financing some future benefit costs, but these schedules have always been changed before their effective date, and such reserves have never been allowed to accumulate. Thus, payments into the funds have been just about enough over the years to cover benefits and administrative costs and to leave a contingency reserve. From 1937, when contributions to Social Security began, through 1999, Social Security had collected approximately $6.9 trillion and paid out roughly $6.0 trillion, leaving $900 billion in the contingency reserve at the beginning of 2000. Under present law, the funds are now building beyond what is required of a pay-as-you-go system, but most of the program's future costs would still be met on this basis, just as in the past. This is a safe enough way to finance Social Security, although not necessarily the most desirable way. Pay-as-you-go is unacceptable for private

TABLE 4.1. A MENU OF ACCEPTABLE CHANGES TO BRING SOCIAL SECURITY'S LONG-RANGE REVENUES AND EXPENSES INTO BALANCE (REDUCTION SHOWN AS PERCENTAGE OF PAYROLL)

CHANGE:	REDUCES DEFICIT:
Shift a portion of the expected surplus in general revenues to Social Security as in President Clinton's proposal:	−1.06
Improve Social Security's earnings by gradually investing up to 40 percent of the accumulating trust funds in stock:	−1.03
Alternatively, invest up to 15 percent in stock as in President Clinton's proposal:	−0.38
Extend coverage to full-time state and local employees not now covered under voluntary compacts between states and SSA:	−0.22
Tax Social Security benefits to the extent that they exceed what the worker paid in, and direct all taxes on OASDI benefits to OASDI trust funds beginning in 2026:	−0.55
Improve the accuracy of the COLA by relying on the new 2002 BLS index to reduce the substitution bias:	−0.23
Increase the maximum benefit and contribution base so as to gradually cover at least 90 percent of earnings as was once the case:	−0.62
Alternatively, cover 87 percent of earnings:	−0.32

Source: Stephen C. Goss, Deputy Chief Actuary, Social Security Administration, memorandum to Harry Ballantyne, Chief Actuary, Social Security Administration, August 4, 2000.

arrangements, because any particular enterprise or insurance company may go out of business and full funding is necessary to assure payment. With Social Security, on the other hand, the continued existence of the federal government can be assumed, and its taxing power can provide continued income for benefit payments.

It is not clear whether we will go back to pay-as-you-go or continue with partial advance financing as discussed. A reasonable pay-as-you-go schedule for the present OASDI program, taking effect after the present 6.2 percent rate is estimated to be insufficient, is shown in Table 4.2 (page 68).

TABLE 4.2. OASDI PAY-AS-YOU-GO CONTRIBUTION RATE SCHEDULE

YEARS	RATE
2000–29	6.20
2030–39	8.0
2040–49	8.25
2050–59	8.50
2060–69	8.75
2070–79	9.0[a]

[a] This rate would need to be further increased thereafter, but at a slower rate of increase.

Source: Stephen C. Goss, Deputy Chief Actuary, Social Security Administration, memorandum to Harry Ballantyne, Chief Actuary, Social Security Administration, August 4, 2000.

Another schedule, following pay-as-you-go principles once the present 6.2 percent rate is estimated to be inadequate, is shown in Table 4.3. This table assumes that the 1.89 deficit is first reduced by the extension of coverage to the presently excluded state and local employees and that benefits are taxed to the extent they exceed what the worker paid in and also that beginning in 2026 all taxes on OASDI benefits go into the Social Security Trust Funds.

Either pay-as-you-go or partial advance financing will work. But partial advance funding will avoid the need for a contribution rate increase over the 75 years for which estimates are usually made. It is doubtful that a pay-as-you-go schedule rising to 9 percent (as shown in Table 4.2) or 8.6 percent (as shown in Table 4.3) could be enacted now, so pay-as-you-go financing might invite rather substantial benefit cuts instead. Moreover, if the rest of the budget is brought into balance later on without counting Social Security surpluses [*Author's note:* as has happened since this was written], the Social Security buildup would clearly increase the national saving and investment rate and make it easier to support the retirees of the future because the future pool of goods and services would be larger.

Investing some of Social Security's reserves in equities would give Social Security beneficiaries a fairer return for the contribution that the trust fund buildup makes to the nation's economic well-being. When a dollar of Social Security reserves is accumulated and the federal government borrows it rather than going into the private market, a dollar of private saving is released for private investment. The gain

Table 4.3. Modified OASDI Pay-As-You-Go Contribution Rate Schedule

Years	Rate
2000–39	6.2
2040–49	7.3
2050–59	7.9
2060–69	8.4
2070–79	8.6

Source: Stephen C. Goss, Deputy Chief Actuary, Social Security Administration, memorandum to Harry Ballantyne, Chief Actuary, Social Security Administration, August 4, 2000.

to the nation from the trust fund accumulation, therefore, is the return on all private investment, not only on equities but on all physical capital. This return has been at the rate of about 6 percent. The proposal for investing 40 percent of the trust funds in stocks attempts to recover only part of this return for Social Security—projecting, under reasonable assumptions, an overall return to the trust funds of 4.2 percent.

Also of considerable importance is the fact that pay-as-you-go will increasingly look like a bad deal for younger workers, who will pay much more than those born earlier for the same level of protection or, as the normal retirement age is advanced, for significantly reduced protection. Even under partial advance funding, young workers in the future can argue that they could do better making their own investments. This argument can be met most convincingly if Social Security increases its investment return by putting part of the buildup in stocks. For the long run, this too is an important reason to shift from pay-as-you-go to partial advance funding, with some of the funds invested in equities.

In every generation, by definition, a redistributional system like Social Security, viewed as a closed system, will appear to do less well for the higher-paid than a system that does not redistribute. This may not be the case, however, if one looks at Social Security in combination with the Supplemental Security Income (SSI) program. For the higher-paid, whatever is lost under a weighted benefit formula will be offset to a considerable extent—perhaps wholly—by reduced reliance on SSI's means-tested supplement, which, of course, is supported by progressive taxes. The point is that those with the lowest incomes must either be subsidized under a social insurance approach, as is done today, or maintained directly. Either way, the cost will necessarily fall on the well-off, but a social insurance subsidy is both more orderly and efficient as well as more humane.

In addition to bringing the program into long-range balance, no matter how this is accomplished, it would also be desirable to include in the law protection against the possibility that the present long-range estimates understate the cost. As the assumptions governing the estimates change over the years (as they certainly will, reflecting new information on birthrates, mortality rates, immigration, and real-wage growth), forecasts too will change. Later projections of the cost of the present program may turn out to be less than now predicted, or they may be higher. In the latter case we should have a way of adjusting the system without triggering the kind of public disillusionment that inevitably accompanies reports that the system is underfunded. One way to guard against this is to more than meet the system's needs, under present assumptions, by scheduling another contribution rate increase of, say, one percentage point for employees and employers in the 2050–60 period. If, at some point in the future, changing assumptions show the system to be more costly than present estimates, the final rate would provide a cushion, and if a larger cushion were needed at some point, the effective date of the higher rate could be moved up. If not needed to make up a shortfall from changes in the estimates, this increased rate (7.2 percent) would be enough to finance the system far beyond the customary 75 years, whereas the pay-as-you-go rate of 9 percent in 2070 would need to continue to rise in later years.

Is Social Security Still a Good Deal?

Until recently, just about every Social Security beneficiary got much more out of the system than he or she paid into it, plus interest, because contribution rates were low during much of the working lives of those now receiving benefits. With contribution rates currently at levels close to what will be required over the long run, this advantage has been disappearing. Faced with the prospect of being treated less generously than those who came before, some young people have concluded that Social Security will not be a good deal for them. Although an individualized test of "money's worth" is not the most important criterion in evaluating a social insurance system, it is nevertheless important that young workers see themselves as being treated fairly.

By moving to partial advance funding and investing a portion of the funds in private equities, as discussed above, the issue of whether Social Security will continue to be a good deal for today's and tomorrow's young workers, even if not as good a deal as for their predecessors, can be laid to rest. Investing 40 percent of the trust funds in private equities would increase the real rate of return from 2.3 percent to 4.2 percent.[9] This has the effect of substantially improving the contributions-to-benefits ratio for younger workers and future generations.

But even without stock investment, in examining questions about Social Security's value, to individuals or to society as a whole, we must always ask: "Compared to what?" Can Social Security's *total* package of benefits be provided better or more cheaply some other way?

The answer is no.

The fact is that Social Security even without change continues to be a good deal for both today's and tomorrow's workers because the protection it offers can be made available to everyone and because Social Security can deliver that protection at lower cost than anything else. It will also continue to be a good deal because of its protection of parents and grandparents, protection that is of great importance to working people and their children. And Social Security will also continue to be a good deal in the future, as in the past, because it contributes values to society that may not be readily measurable but are still critically important.

In delivering a package of benefits Social Security has two great advantages: extremely low administrative costs and universal coverage. The advantage in administrative costs is very large, with Social Security spending only about nine-tenths of one percent of benefit payouts on administration, compared with 10 to 15 percent or more for most private insurance plans. And because of universal compulsory coverage Social Security is able to provide important protection—both disability insurance and retirement and survivors benefits—without adding extra premiums (as is necessary with private insurance) to guard against adverse selection and the risk of worse-than-expected claims experience.

Also, as previously noted, Social Security supplies a valuable protection that simply is not available privately: inflation protection, automatic and complete. And Social Security also provides life insurance and disability protection, which many people could not buy privately.

In point of fact, exact comparisons between Social Security and private insurance are impossible, because there is no close approximation of Social Security's package of protection available in the private insurance market. Social Security's inherent advantages, including its universality, its ability to follow the worker from job to job with a defined benefit, and its low administrative cost, make it a good buy from generation to generation, compared to anything else that a worker could purchase. Perhaps the pertinent comparison, however, is not with private insurance but with compulsory private savings plans, as proposed by privatization advocates. (This issue is discussed below.)

Private insurance and savings plans have had one cost advantage over Social Security: because they are pre-funded, they are able to realize substantial investment returns. But this advantage will diminish if Social Security is at least partially pre-funded in the future. In any case, however, Social Security's overall advantages outweigh the pre-funding advantage of private plans. The cost may be close when looking solely at future benefits for a contributing worker, but when we add the current value of family protection for parents and grandparents as well as for the worker's immediate family, along with the societal values from having a Social Security system, it becomes quite clear that Social Security is indeed a good deal for each generation in turn.

But comparative analysis can be pushed too far. Public and private efforts have different goals, and they work well in a complementary relationship. It isn't that Social Security should be taking the place of private effort or vice versa. The point is simply that there is no cheaper way of carrying out the functions of a basic Social Security system, and there is no better way to add supplementary protection to this basic system than with private plans. Each is the best way to do what it does; both are a good deal.

As surveys and focus group data show, many young workers, even those who think that Social Security will not be there for them, strongly support the current program. They appreciate that it is a mechanism for sharing with all other working families the burden of caring for the elderly and those with disabilities. They appreciate that because of Social Security and Medicare, no one family has to bear alone what could be the huge cost of caring for parents who are sicker than average or who outlive their savings. They understand that families pooled together nationwide are protected by paying for only the average risk.

Because Social Security and Medicare spread the risk and because of their nearly universal coverage, relatively few older retired people have to move in with their children to make a go of it. Similarly, millions of married couples are spared the pain of periodically having to arrive at mutually acceptable decisions (not to mention decisions that must also be acceptable to other relatives) about how much of the family income should go to supporting elderly parents and grandparents, rather than being used for themselves and their children.

Social Security also furnishes current family protection by providing ongoing insurance against loss of family income due to death or disability. Among the 45 million Americans receiving monthly benefits as of June 30, 2000, about 3 million were children under 18, mostly children of deceased workers, and nearly 6 million adults were being paid because of disability.

Social Security provided $14.5 trillion in life insurance protection in 1997, an amount about equal to the combined value of all private life insurance policies of all types in force in the United States ($14.8 trillion in 1997). The protection for young families is very substantial. For example, a 27-year-old couple with one or both persons earning average wages, with two children, one aged two and one less than a year old, have survivors protection worth $374,000. Disability protection for the same family amounts to $223,000.[10]

And Social Security has other values that are frequently overlooked. For example, Social Security is, as previously noted, keeping 15 million people out of poverty and millions more from near-poverty. Without Social Security, taxpayers would have to pump far more money into welfare. Moreover, Social Security acts as something of an automatic stabilizer whenever the economy runs into difficulty. Ongoing regular monthly benefit payments help maintain the purchasing power of very large groups of consumers who, in the absence of Social Security, would be the first to stop buying. Instead, they continue to participate in, and contribute to, the economy.

Social Security is a blend of reward for individual effort and, at the same time, perhaps our strongest expression of community solidarity. Through Social Security we recognize that "we're all in this together," with everyone sharing responsibility, not only for contributing toward their own and their families' protection, but also for the protection of everyone else, present and future. Basing benefits on past work and wages reinforces efforts to work and save, and emphasizes an earned right to benefits, with special emphasis on protecting the lower-paid and those with dependents. It is hard to imagine more broadly valuable characteristics. Unfortunately, however, the value to individuals of living in a society that has such a plan cannot be readily quantified, and what can't be measured is often overlooked. Yet all these values are part of the answer to the question of whether Social Security will continue to be a good deal. Viewed in terms of total value, and in comparison with what could be purchased privately, the answer to that question is clearly *Yes*—now and for future generations.

WHY ALL THE PESSIMISM?

Given Social Security's financial viability, it is distressing to find so little public confidence in the program's future. When the reasons are explored, what becomes clear is that most people are mainly reacting to what they are told by the media, as opposed to making an assessment based on knowledge of policy issues and choices.

The media correctly report that the program, as is, cannot continue to pay full benefits forever, but far less attention is paid to the equally important fact that relatively minor course corrections can keep the ship clear of the rocks that we can see on the far horizon. Instead, news reports and commentators tend to exaggerate both the size and imminence of the deficit and the difficulty of restoring balance. And when the talk is of the trust funds running out of money, young people assume there will be nothing left for them. It is not well understood that under the present pay-as-you-go financing, support for the system in later years comes mostly from contributions in those later years and not from assets stored in the trust funds.

Commentators are apt to point to the decline in the number of contributors per retiree as evidence that workers increasingly face an impossible burden of support. And this is often highlighted by some political activists and organizations (such as the Concord Coalition) as part of their political strategy. But the media and such activists do not note that this change in the retiree/worker ratio has not happened suddenly, does not come as a surprise, and has been fully factored into proposals to bring the Social Security program into balance over the long run.

Nor, as a rule, do media commentators consider Social Security in context. In estimating the ability of a workforce to support dependents, retirees are not the only dependents to be taken into account. We need to look at the *total dependency burden*, that is, the ratio of *all* nonworkers, old *and* young, to the active workers who produce the goods and services on which all must depend. And, as Table 4.4 indicates, the number of dependents per 1,000 workers will not again be as high as it was in 1965, when the baby boomers were children. As economist Frank Ackerman has observed, "If we could afford to live through the childhood of the baby-boom generation, we can afford to live through their retirement."[11]

TABLE 4.4. TOTAL DEPENDENCY BURDEN, 1965–2075

YEAR	DEPENDENTS (BOTH THOSE 65 AND OVER AND THOSE UNDER 20) PER 1,000 WORKERS
1965	947
1990	701
2010	660
2040	802
2075	846

Source: 2000 Trustees' Report, Social Security Administration, Table II.H 1.

Looking at the total dependency burden does not, of course, solve the problem of how to meet the needs of a growing number of elderly and at the same time meet the need for more support for children (even though there are fewer of them), particularly at a time when public programs for poor children are so inadequately funded. Yet the basic economic point is unmistakable: the picture of the worker of the future staggering under an increasing load of dependents is out of focus.

Clearly another reason why people are uneasy about Social Security is that, while they may have some understanding of the basic principles and benefits, they don't have a very tangible sense of their own stake in the system. They have only a vague understanding of the kinds and amounts of protection they currently have.

Over the years the Social Security Administration has tried in many ways to increase public understanding of the value of Social

Security protection to the individual, but it has never been particularly successful. There is, however, cause for hope. Soon the Social Security Administration will be regularly sending account statements to every covered worker. [*Author's note:* This is now being done.] This should be a great step forward in improving workers' knowledge of the protection they have under Social Security—and the more they know, the more certain it is that the great majority will favor continued support of the system.

Proposals for Fundamental Change

Despite the fact that the present Social Security system can remain strong and solvent for the long run without major benefit cuts or contribution rate increases, confusion about the program's future has created a fertile climate for proposals for fundamental change. These usually focus on means testing or privatization.

Means Testing

The means-testing or income-testing approach has been spearheaded in recent years by the Concord Coalition, an advocacy organization led by investment banker Peter Peterson and former senator Warren Rudman. The Coalition contends that Social Security should not be paying benefits to people who can get along without them, and proposes to start reducing benefits for all families whose total incomes, including Social Security benefits and the cash value of Medicare protection, exceed $40,000 a year.

For the purposes of this discussion, the details of the Concord Coalition plan are not especially important, because the proposal would, of course, be modified in the legislative process if it ever got to that. What *is* important is the key principle: relating the amount of one's benefits to one's income at the time of eligibility.

No retirement system, public or private, presently takes this approach. And the Concord Coalition would apply it exclusively to Social Security. Moreover, although private pension plans enjoy special tax treatment, the Coalition plan does not treat this public subsidy as a benefit. The target of the Coalition's high, even confiscatory, "tax" on benefits is limited entirely to a defined group of explicit federal benefits, particularly Social Security and Medicare.

Of all the changes proposed for Social Security, this is the worst. First, the incentives are all wrong. Its message to young people, for example, is: "If you are a saver, and because of your prudence are able to attain a healthy retirement income on your own, you will be penalized—your Social Security benefits will be cut." A change of this sort would make individual provision for retirement counterproductive for many workers, since saving more would merely reduce the Social Security payment for which they would otherwise be eligible.

Equally important, such a system would make *everyone's* benefits vulnerable, not just the benefits of those above the arbitrary threshold initially selected. Once the Social Security system departs from objective eligibility criteria based on prior work and prior contributions, there is no good stopping point. When political leaders want more money for other purposes, why not change the exemption to, say, $20,000 instead of $40,000—or simply peg it to the poverty level?

With the Concord Coalition's plan in place, nothing would remain of the two core principles that now protect Social Security against arbitrary reduction: (1) its universality, which assures that almost everyone has an important stake in the system, and (2) its relationship of benefits to past earnings and contributions so that payments are an earned right, not just a statutory right.

Changes along the lines proposed by the Concord Coalition would give higher-paid workers a very powerful incentive to get out of Social Security. Those who anticipate high incomes in retirement would know that their incomes would disqualify them from drawing more than token Social Security benefits, and it is hard to imagine them willingly continuing to contribute to such a system. If they succeeded in getting out, however, the increased burden on middle-income workers—the burden of supporting a redistributional system—would rapidly become intolerable.

At the very least, the program would have to drop the weighted benefit formula. But it is this redistributional formula that makes Social Security so beneficial for the lower-paid. Without it, benefits would be too low to provide a minimum level of security, and they would have to turn to welfare for help. Welfare payments would then raise the incomes of such households to the allowed maximum, and low-income workers would get nothing extra for their Social Security contributions. At that point, those at both ends of the economic scale would have every reason to be dissatisfied with Social Security.

Means testing could thus trigger the disintegration of the whole Social Security plan and make welfare our only national system. This proposal may not become a serious threat—*if* it is well understood. It is hard to imagine people willingly supporting a system to which they contribute over a working lifetime in anticipation of receiving retirement benefits, only to have those benefits withheld because they saved too much. Means testing of benefits supported by general revenues is one thing, but the public would find such a test unfair in a program supported by the dedicated taxes of the intended beneficiaries and their employers. A means test or income test would change the basic character of Social Security: benefits would no longer be an earned right, nor would the program prevent poverty ahead of time and serve as the base on which everyone can build additional income.

PRIVATIZATION

There is also considerable interest in privatizing part or all of Social Security. This has been stimulated by enthusiasm in some quarters for privatization as a panacea for the perceived ills of "big government programs," and, in part, by reports of the success of Chile's compulsory savings plan, which is gradually replacing that country's highly unsatisfactory social security system. Admiration for Chile's plan has been reinforced by a World Bank report advocating a similar approach for other countries.[12]

The idea is to compel private savings for old age that would be invested by the individual saver and held in an individual account. In the partial privatization schemes being discussed in the United States, funds for such savings would come either wholly or partly from reducing Social Security contributions or benefits. Claimed advantages include, most importantly, a greater return on savings and thus higher benefits without higher contribution rates. And supporters argue that a savings account bearing the worker's name would be more popular than a social insurance plan governed by rules about contributions and benefits that are all quite mysterious to the average individual.

The strengths and weaknesses of the idea vary, depending on whether the forced savings plan is intended to *supplement* Social Security or to *substitute* for the program in whole or in part. In the first instance—that is, if the basic Social Security plan is retained and remains reasonably adequate for both low-wage workers and those with above-average earnings—the issue becomes mainly whether compulsion is justified to force people to save for retirement benefits above the Social Security level. It has always been considered desirable to *encourage* supplementary protection through tax incentives for private pensions and individual savings, but the additional step of making supplemental plans compulsory is controversial.

It is not at all certain that low-wage earners gain by being compelled to save more, let alone by having to set aside more of their paychecks toward deferred pension income promised for old age. Perhaps, instead, they should continue to be free to spend more to meet current needs. Higher-paid workers, too, may well have current needs that take higher priority than adding to basic income protection in retirement. Assuming that everyone has Social Security to meet that basic need, why not let individuals set their own priorities, while continuing to offer them, via the tax code, incentives to encourage additional saving? Until recently, such freedom to choose has made sense to most policymakers.

But how about *substituting* a private savings plan for part of Social Security? Some advocates of privatization (such as the Cato Institute) would go further, completely replacing Social Security with a compulsory savings plan. And some (for example, Chairman Gramlich of the 1994–96 Advisory Council) would add a savings plan to a reduced Social Security system, maintaining the present contribution rate but reducing benefits to the amount that can be met by that rate. Most, however, propose taking part of the contribution rate that now goes to Social Security and investing it in personal savings accounts. That is the approach of legislation proposed by Senator Kerrey (D-Nebraska), among others.

Still another approach, advocated by a group within the 1994–96 Advisory Council, would go beyond Kerrey's individual-accounts (IA) plan by, in the long run, replacing current Social Security benefits with a low, flat benefit, and then adding a compulsory private savings account (PSA) plan supported by five percentage points of the current Social Security contribution rate. Although the emphasis in the following discussion will be on these various approaches to partial privatization, much of the discussion applies equally, or even more so, to proposals for complete privatization.

It is important not to confuse the goal of achieving long-range financial balance for Social Security with the goal of establishing individual accounts. The partial privatization proposals have to achieve both goals. But the plans are sometimes presented as if their object was to achieve fund balance for Social Security while also contributing to balancing the general budget. In fact, however, partial privatization does not help to achieve a balance in Social Security or the general budget. On the contrary, it makes achieving these goals more difficult.

Most privatization proponents advocate first shrinking the Social Security program to address the currently projected shortfall, and then they must shrink it again to permit transferring part of the contribution rate to individual accounts. The first step requires cutting benefits about 15 percent immediately, including benefits being paid to current retirees, if balance is to be achieved by benefit reductions only.[13]

The proposal advanced by Senator Kerrey in 1995 (which has become the basis for a number of subsequent proposals) provides a good example of what it takes to accomplish both goals and of the pitfalls of partial privatization. His proposal brings the Social Security program back into balance and also shrinks it further so that it can be supported by the remaining contribution rate after the amount going to the individual accounts has been subtracted. The shrinkage would be severe. The benefits payable after the year 2030 would, on average, be 25 to 35 percent lower than those provided by present law, and in some cases would be cut much more. For example, a 66-year-old retiring in 2033 who has earned average wages would have initial benefits cut 26 percent, but because of changes that are also proposed for the COLA, benefits would actually be reduced 35 percent by age 76, and 40 percent by age 86.

By that time, of course, the individual savings accounts would be generating income, but it is difficult to predict the extent to which they would be able to make up for the cuts in Social Security. *Averages* can be predicted, of course, and, over time, average retirement income under this approach would in all likelihood compare favorably with the income available under the present system, with its investments restricted to low-yield government obligations. But the *actual* income for particular people is impossible to determine. All that is known is that the amounts would vary greatly from individual to individual.

Leaving aside for the moment the question of whether a shift from Social Security's pooled arrangements to individual accounts is desirable, let us look at what has to be done to get from here to there. Problems of transition are not merely details to be worked out later. They are crucial—and daunting.

The biggest transition difficulty is what to do about current retirees and older workers. Although proponents of privatization have said on occasion that present retirees and older workers would not be affected by their proposals, this can hardly be the case. Social Security cannot be stripped of two or more percentage points of the contribution rate, for example, just because benefits for younger workers would eventually be reduced. Because Social Security is essentially on a pay-as-you-go basis, a contribution rate reduction of this magnitude in the absence of a major infusion of income to the system would also require substantial benefit cuts for current retirees and older workers, none of whom would benefit from the individual accounts. These cuts have to fall on this group because there simply wouldn't be enough money available after the contribution rate cuts to pay them anywhere near full benefits.

Proponents of the PSA approach would address this problem by raising the payroll tax by 1.52 percent of payroll. But this approach also requires heavy borrowing from the federal government. The proposed rate increase is sufficient to cover the *average* cost over the next 70-plus years, but would not be adequate to cover costs in the first 40 years. To pay full benefits to present retirees and those retiring soon would require borrowing about $1 trillion (in 1996 dollars), thus adding considerably to the national debt for a long time, with payback beginning after 40 years and completed 30 years later. This problem could be avoided, but only by requiring a much higher contribution rate increase at first—more than 3 percent of payroll. But that, of course, would be even more unpalatable.

It is true, at least theoretically, that if younger workers prefer, they can pay for present retirees and older workers in another way. In Chile, the problems of transition to a savings plan are being handled through large, permanent infusions of general tax revenues to pay for a substantial minimum benefit and for credit for past work under the old social security system. Fortunately for the success of its plan, Chile had been running large general budget surpluses. In the United States, on the other hand, this approach would require enactment of a major tax increase or, in the absence of such an increase, either a sharp reduction of support for other programs beyond what is now required to balance the budget or a substantial increase in the deficit.

[*Author's note:* Since this was written, circumstances have changed dramatically, and it is now expected that there will be a substantial surplus in the non–Social Security budget for many years. President Clinton and Vice President Gore, as previously noted, propose to transfer a major part of the non–Social Security surplus to

Social Security, reducing the Social Security deficit by 1.06 percent of payroll. Governor Bush, as of this writing, had not expressed an opinion on general revenue financing of Social Security, but his tax reduction proposals would use up just about all the surplus, pretty much eliminating this possibility. (See Chapter 5, "Making Policy: A Job for All of Us.")]

As we try to work out these schemes in practice, we find that, in the absence of new revenues, it is simply not possible to shift, say, two percentage points from Social Security to private accounts (as Senator Kerrey, for example, recognizes) while protecting the current benefit rights of older people. In practice, partial privatization plans would probably also have to drastically cut COLAs for present retirees and older workers or cut initial benefits, perhaps by moving up the effective dates for raising the age when workers become eligible for full benefits or even raising the retirement age again.

If major benefit cuts for current retirees and older workers are to be avoided without major infusions of new money, the reduction in contribution rates needs to be at least partly postponed and the money for the individual retirement accounts obtained by increasing, rather than cutting, the contribution rate, as is done in the PSA plan. The problem is that with Social Security on a pay-as-you-go basis, the first generation of those covered by these savings plans has to continue to support present retirees and older workers at the same time that they are building their own savings plan. Although infusions of general revenue can avoid Social Security tax increases as such, the only way to truly reduce the burden of doing both things at once is to impose truly drastic and immediate cuts for current retirees and older workers. In contrast, plans to bring the program into balance without establishing individual accounts do not need to reduce benefits to current retirees, although a modest reduction, say through an increase in the tax on benefits, may be desirable for other reasons. The path chosen by Kerrey et al. is to cut the COLA drastically. Given the political constraints and the antipathy to tax increases that have characterized the politics of the past two decades, this is the probable route of others who would enact privatization plans. Thus, assessment of the various provisions of the Kerrey plan and its spin-offs provides insight into problems likely to be associated, to one degree or another, with other privatization alternatives.[14]

Although Social Security's cost-of-living adjustments have been crucial to the program's success, Kerrey and other privatization proponents propose to cut COLAs for present as well as future retirees in two ways: (1) the adjustment is to be reduced by 0.5 percent pending an expert study of how the Consumer Price Index should be redefined, and (2) the size of the COLA for all beneficiaries is limited to that payable to beneficiaries with Primary Insurance Amounts[15] at the 30th percentile from the bottom. (The PIA at the 30th percentile for 1995 is about $540 per month.) The two-thirds of retirees whose PIAs are higher than this amount would receive the same flat COLA. But a capped COLA would no longer come anywhere near maintaining purchasing power—the whole point of having a COLA in the first place.[16]

The financing of the residual Social Security plan is complicated further for younger workers because of the need to maintain protection under Social Security's disability and life insurance program, or, alternatively, to set aside even larger amounts to purchase supplemental private life and disability insurance. This, too, is unavoidable, because a slowly accumulating savings plan cannot protect against these risks at younger ages. Until the worker nears retirement, current insurance protection is necessary.

If a savings program is to substitute for an important part of Social Security, before benefits are cut the savings program should have been operating long enough and at a sufficiently high rate to produce an income stream equal, at least on average, to the part of the Social Security benefit that the worker gives up. This approach is obviously essential in a voluntary scheme and, if not followed in a compulsory scheme, would create deep dissatisfaction.

Most privatization advocates, therefore, propose to have the savings plan open only to those below a given age, with older workers and the already retired continuing under a reduced Social Security system. Several plans propose using age 55 as the cutoff point. But 10 years to retirement age is not long enough to build up much of a savings plan. Accordingly, any Social Security cuts should take place gradually, in close calibration with reasonable expectations about savings accumulation. But this cannot be done if benefits have to be shrunk quickly to accommodate the loss of a part of Social Security financing. In any event, this type of calibration—a gradual reduction in Social Security benefits linked to a gradual increase in savings accounts—would be extremely difficult to explain and extremely difficult for the public to understand, with good reason.

Although major benefit cuts for present retirees and older workers are inevitable in any near-term implementation of a privatization scheme that does not involve increased income (and cutting COLAs seems to be the most practical way to do this), there are choices of how to obtain the very substantial benefit cuts that are required for middle-aged and younger workers in the continuing Social Security system. The choices made by Kerrey et al. are indicative of what would have to be done in any privatization scheme financed by cuts in Social Security contribution rates while avoiding any substantial infusions of new money.

PSA proponents would gradually increase the age at which full benefits are payable and then, as longevity increases, keep moving the age for paying full benefits automatically higher to preserve the same ratio between average lifetimes after the eligibility date and the number of years before it. Kerrey would also (1) decrease benefits for higher earners by reducing the last step in the Social Security benefit formula from 15 percent at the margin to 10 percent; (2) reduce wage indexing for the higher-paid by two percentage points a year for 25 years; and (3) reduce spouse benefits from one-half of the worker's benefit to one-third. He would also make three changes that are supported by many who do not favor privatization: cover newly hired state and local employees now excluded; transfer from hospital insurance to OASDI all the revenues from the taxation of OASDI benefits; and (in this early version of his plan) invest a portion of the trust funds in equities.

It is important to understand that not all problems with privatization are transitional. A major difficulty is that, to the extent that funds are shifted to individual accounts, the ability to redistribute income is lost. After all, the whole appeal of changing to a savings plan is to emphasize individual equity—a fair return to the individual saver—rather than adequacy for all. To take part of what the higher-paid save in order to increase what the lower-paid get would seem contrary to the spirit of such a plan.

To meet the objection of the loss of redistribution, some advocates of partial privatization propose raising benefits at the bottom and reducing them at the top in what remains of the Social Security program, keeping the same distribution as now when the residual Social Security plan and the new savings plan are looked at together. But that is not how beneficiaries would view the system. The higher-paid would see a dramatic reduction in what they get from Social Security, making participation in Social Security unappealing to those who earn above-average wages.

This "solution" is thus, in all likelihood, unstable. It is likely to lead to a situation in which the higher-paid press for the right to set aside more and more for their individual savings accounts and less and less for Social Security. Or they will want to get out of Social Security altogether. If that happens, there is no basis for continuing a redistributional wage-related program, such as Social Security is today. Thus, partial privatization could well be the entering wedge for getting rid of Social Security entirely and substituting a private savings system built entirely on individual equity principles, augmented by a government means-tested program like SSI.

This outcome may well be acceptable to some privatization advocates, but as a matter of public policy this approach has all the disadvantages of means testing, as discussed earlier. And the proportion of the population affected could be quite large. A savings plan financed as a percent of earnings will mean low accumulations for low earners (along with higher relative administrative costs for them), forcing many to turn to SSI for help. It was, of course, with the idea of avoiding this kind of problem—people paying all their lives for protection and then getting no more than what they would get on welfare—that Social Security's redistributional formula was developed in the first place.

There is also the problem of regulating and limiting the private investment vehicles for the 127 million people with individual accounts. Even if investments were limited to a menu of options vetted by the government, there would be unremitting pressure to invest in one vehicle rather than another. Some fraudulent schemes would doubtless appear, along with others that might only be inappropriately risky. In any event, we could expect a huge surge in marketing efforts and associated costs. These overhead costs, coupled with the cost of keeping track of the ins and outs of millions of individualized retirement accounts and their investments, would be many times greater than Social Security's current administrative costs—0.9 percent of benefit payments. By comparison, the administrative costs of Chile's system are at least 15 percent—"at least" because, according to some studies, they are considerably higher.[17]

There are also questions about whether an account in the name of an individual saver could be held strictly for retirement. The fact is that retirement savings may not always be the most compelling goal of individual savers. President Clinton proposed in 1995, for example, that individual retirement accounts (IRAs)—tax-favored savings accounts theoretically reserved for retirement use—be opened up for other purposes, and the Congress seemed disposed to give his and similar proposals sympathetic consideration. [*Author's note:* This was indeed done.] And 401(k) plans are available for other purposes— building a first-time house, for example (subject to payment of a 10 percent penalty and taxation of the funds withdrawn). There may be merit in allowing this leeway to savings vehicles such as IRAs and 401(k)s, but one of the advantages of Social Security is that it protects us all against having to support those who might use their basic retirement savings for purposes other than retirement. Without that kind of protection—that is, if individual retirement accounts are allowed to be used for nonretirement purposes—the cost of SSI to the general taxpayer goes up.

Somewhat similarly, what is to be done about those who invest their savings badly or who, through no fault of their own, must come into or leave an equities or bond market or invest in annuities at a disadvantageous time? In these cases, too, the general taxpayer would be called upon to help.

Another major difficulty arises from the inherent limitations of a pure savings plan. How is the retiree to determine at what rate to withdraw the savings? Generally speaking, those who are in poor health will want to withdraw at faster rates than those in good health, but, since no one can guess the proper rate for an individual, some will end up short, while others will end up with more in their account at death than they intended. The chances are that many people will be excessively cautious, to make sure their savings last, just as many will be very cautious about how they invest their savings (and thus will not achieve the high rates of return assumed by advocates of savings plans). Others may be inclined to use up their savings in a hurry, rationalizing that at worst they will then become eligible for the safety-net means-tested program accompanying the savings plan. And others might try to transfer their savings to relatives, as is done sometimes to establish eligibility for the means-tested Medicaid program.

The ordinary solution for the retiree's dilemma about how fast to spend savings is to buy an annuity, so as to receive a lifetime guarantee of regular payments based on average longevity. But annuities are a conservative investment, reducing the rate of return below what some may have enjoyed during the period of savings accumulation, and this needs to be taken into account in estimating the returns associated with privatization. Moreover, annuities necessarily require a high premium to guard against adverse selection. (As they near retirement, many older workers can guess whether their own life expectancy will be above or below average, with the result that annuity buyers tend to be relatively healthy, requiring insurers to assume long life and thus providing fairly low payments to the average person.)

Because of this failure of the private annuity market to price products fairly for the average person, some advocates of savings plans would force all savers to buy a government annuity just before reaching retirement age. That would avoid the adverse selection problem, but it would create dissatisfaction among savers with relatively short life expectancies who would have to forfeit much of their accumulated savings by being paid at the rate appropriate for the person of average longevity and dying long before they had received an amount equal to what they had saved.

Given the fact that even professional money managers usually do not, over time, match let alone beat broad-based indices of representative stocks, it is doubtful that creating individual investment choices, either within or as a supplement to the regular Social Security program, would be broadly valuable. Most people, including millions of the relatively well-off, have no experience in investing and may or may not take the time to acquire expertise. As a rule, those who do are relatively high up on the income scale, and for them the future well-being of Social Security is in any case a less pressing issue than for the less affluent. Today, with Social Security as a base for retirement income, those with other resources are free to invest them as they wish. Particularly if Social Security increases its return on contributions by investing some of its funds in equities, the arguments for substituting individual savings for part of Social Security seem weak.

In short, this approach would pose many problems. Chile's plan replaced a system that was beset with enormous difficulties, including poor administration, high cost, runaway inflation, bailouts from general revenues, and inequities in the treatment of different classes of workers. Privatization may indeed represent an improvement over what Chile, and some other nations, have had. But social security systems worldwide are not identical, and a privatized retirement security system for the United States would create many more problems than it would solve.

The present Social Security system with its weighted benefit formula has been designed to leave room for supplementation by private plans and individual savings, and the Social Security replacement rates for the higher-paid cry out for such supplementation. Present law contains several inducements to retirement savings through IRAs, Keogh accounts, private pensions, and 401(k)s. It is not necessary to make room for a compulsory individual savings plan by reducing the one universal plan. Saving, for those who can afford it, is already made relatively easy, and even more could be done to encourage people to save if that seems desirable. [*Author's note:* Both President Clinton and Vice President Gore have proposed such plans, but as additions to Social Security, not as carve-outs from Social Security.] What we need to assure is the continuance of an adequate basic Social Security plan, paying benefits as a matter of right, and with the ability to redistribute some of the protection from the higher-paid to the lower-paid.

GOING FORWARD WITH THE PRESENT SYSTEM

Social Security is, in short, admirably suited to doing what it is supposed to do, and we should essentially leave it alone. As a basic system, Social Security has many advantages over relying entirely on private pensions and private savings. Social Security benefits are kept up-to-date with wages until the beneficiary starts to collect them and then are inflation-proof thereafter. Social Security protection is portable, following the worker from job to job, and benefits are not threatened by the failure of a business or the decline of an industry. And the benefits, defined by law, are not dependent upon an individual's investment strategy and experience.

With Social Security as a base, those who can afford to do so are free to add other retirement income to it, with help from the tax system and without being penalized by a means test. And, with adequate Social Security protection in place, supplementary plans and private savings are free to seek returns that, while comparatively risky, tend to pay off at relatively high rates.

These are freedoms, however, that argue for retaining, as a foundation, a broadly adequate national program such as Social Security that everyone can count on regardless of what may happen to the returns on individuals' supplementary savings. Social Security benefits are not now too high for this purpose, and the levels promised in present law should be retained or, at most, only very slightly reduced.

Basic protection is particularly important in a dynamic, risk-taking economy such as ours, where long-established businesses may fail even as new ones are springing up and where whole industries may find themselves quite suddenly in decline. Our economy, more than most, rewards rapid adaptation to changing conditions. That is one reason why it functions well at the aggregate level—but the more dynamic the economy, the greater the need for individual protection against major economic hazards. We need the individual security that Social Security supplies regardless of mergers, bankruptcies, varying employment levels, and economic downturns.

Over time, of course, there will be changes in Social Security, as there have been in the past—and as there should be. But the system that has never missed a payday in 60 years of existence is soundly bottomed on principles that have withstood the test of time. A system built on such principles has every reason to endure—and I believe it will, in much the same form and based on the same principles.

5

MAKING POLICY:
A JOB FOR ALL OF US

It is tempting for those who are already retired, or nearing retirement, to believe that they will be immune to future changes in Social Security—and candidates for political office, seeking the support of the elderly or at least hoping not to stir them up, are not above contributing to this impression. This piece, written during the 2000 campaign, raises a warning flag.

If you are one of the nearly 60 million adults currently receiving Social Security benefits or expecting to start receiving them in the near future, you may think you have little at stake in this year's debates about the future of the program. After all, both the Republican and Democratic presidential candidates have pledged to protect your benefits, and you may assume that only workers who will become eligible for benefits in the distant future are likely to be affected by the various proposals being discussed. But you shouldn't make that assumption, because it's wrong. You really can't afford to sit this one out.

There's widespread agreement that Social Security faces a long-term funding shortfall. The trustees have estimated that, in the absence of any changes in present law, the program can pay full benefits until 2037, but after that the income from the dedicated taxes specified in current law would cover only about 70 percent of the cost of the benefits promised. It's that gap that needs to be closed.

There are various ways to do it. Social Security revenues could be increased, for example, by increasing the dedicated contributions paid by workers and employers. The trustees anticipate an imbalance of about 2 percent of payroll on average over the 75 years for which their forecasts are made. So an increase in the contribution rate of one percentage point for the employee matched by the employer would eliminate the shortfall.

There's little support for doing that, however. Instead, several plans have been put forth to reduce or eliminate the deficit in other ways. President Clinton, for example, proposes using some of the projected surplus in the non–Social Security budget to make a contribution to the Social Security Trust Funds. It's estimated that under this plan, which would also include investing up to 15 percent of the funds' buildup in stocks, full benefits could be paid until 2063 and the 75-year shortfall would be reduced to about one-half of one percent of payroll.

Vice President Gore has essentially endorsed the president's proposal, without the investment in stocks. But although many support this approach, others have suggested quite different plans. Several members of Congress, for example, propose diverting some payroll taxes away from Social Security into individual savings accounts as part of a plan to bring the system into long-range balance.

This would mean, of course, that there would be less rather than more money flowing into Social Security, which in turn means increasing rather than closing the long-term deficit. For example, diverting 2 percent of payroll to private accounts would just about double the projected deficit, raising it to around 4 percent. But proponents argue that the reduction in Social Security benefits necessitated by the reduction in Social Security revenues would be more than offset by the higher investment earnings of the individual accounts. The accounts would earn more because, unlike Social Security (which under current law is allowed to invest only in government bonds, with their relatively low earnings), they would be free to invest in higher-earning stocks.

Before looking more closely at this argument, it bears noting that there are basically only two ways to provide for a pension, whether public or private. One is to define the *benefit* that will be paid out, and then to expect the entity responsible for overseeing the pension plan—in this case the government—to make good on delivering the benefit as defined in law. That's how the present Social Security system works. The alternative is to define the *contribution* to be paid in, leaving open the question of how large a benefit will be paid out, with the amount determined by how successfully the paid-in funds are invested. Both approaches involve risk, but in a defined-benefit plan the risk is borne by the plan manager (the government in Social Security's case, or, putting it another way, all of us acting collectively through the government), while in a defined-contribution plan the risk is borne entirely by the individual. The proposed system of individual accounts would shift Social Security toward becoming a defined-contribution plan.

Governor George W. Bush, for one, has opted to move toward the defined-contribution approach. He has promised that his plan would not reduce the Social Security benefits of the elderly and the near-elderly and, because a savings plan cannot protect against the loss of support from a worker's early death or disability, he has also promised to protect the benefit level of the disability and survivors insurance parts of Social Security. He has also ruled out various income sources either as a way of reducing the long-range Social Security deficit or as a way of avoiding benefit cuts. He has pledged not to raise Social Security's taxes and not to allow any part of the Social Security surplus to be invested directly in stocks.

As many observers have noted, Governor Bush has also proposed such large income tax cuts that he leaves little if any surplus in the non–Social Security budget from which to make a general revenue contribution to Social Security. So the only route left for him to achieve the long-run Social Security balance he promises seems to be to cut benefits, and because of his pledge not to cut the benefits of older people his only apparent option is to make very large cuts in the future benefits of younger workers. (Some supporters of Governor Bush's plan argue that such cuts would be unnecessary. While conceding that a huge infusion of money would be needed to bring the system into balance while establishing the individual accounts, they maintain that the increase in corporate profits from the investment of the savings accounts would add enough to corporate income taxes to provide what is needed. But no one knows whether or to what extent this would actually happen.)

Could such a package actually be enacted by Congress? Could a President Bush honor the pledge of Candidate Bush to protect the benefits of the elderly and at the same time shift money from Social Security to the establishment of individual savings accounts for younger workers, while ruling out new sources of income?

To test the effect of the Bush plan, four economists with expert knowledge of how Social Security works recently undertook a study for The Century Foundation. The study, "Governor Bush's Individual Account Proposal: Implications for Retirement Benefits," was done by economists Henry Aaron of the Brookings Institution, Alan Blinder of Princeton University, Alicia Munnell of Boston College, and Peter Orszag of Sebago Associates. They found that if future benefits were to be cut equally for all workers age 55 and younger in 2002, a 41 percent cut would be required to maintain the long-term solvency of Social Security while carving out 2 percent of the payroll tax. This, however, would work a particular hardship on workers in their early 50s, who would have little time to build up individual accounts before retirement. So it would be more likely that benefit cuts would be phased in, with the goal of having the total retirement income from individual accounts plus the residual Social Security benefit comparable for workers of all ages. Under this approach, the economists found that future Social Security benefits would have to be cut by 29 percent for those 50 years old in 2002, while for 30-year-olds the cut would be 54 percent. *And they found that the combined retirement income from the reduced benefit plus earnings from individual accounts would still fall short—by about 20 percent—of the Social Security benefits promised (but not fully paid for) under current law.*

This takes us back to square one. To eliminate the long-term shortfall of 1.89 percent of payroll projected by the trustees solely by means of a benefit cut for those now age 55 and below, a 20-percent cut would be needed. The private-accounts approach ends up at the same place for Social Security and the private accounts combined, but with the added risk that it ends up there only on average. Those who did less well than average with their investments would see their retirement income cut by more—in some cases much more—than 20 percent.

When you think about the increased burdens on younger workers who would have to pay to maintain Social Security's commitments to the present elderly while building up their own private accounts, it seems extremely doubtful that Congress would be willing to protect the current elderly from any increased burden at all.

There are no panaceas. Those who support a Clinton-Gore approach, transferring funds to Social Security from the non–Social Security surplus, must also face up to the long-run deficit remaining after taking account of the vice president's proposed general revenue contribution, a deficit of somewhat more than 1 percent of payroll with the benefit liberalizations that Gore has proposed. The vice president, like Governor Bush, has ruled out direct investment of Social Security in stocks as well as Social Security tax rate increases, and he too proposes to protect current Social Security benefits. His maneuvering room is pretty limited. He could propose a larger general revenue contribution and perhaps an increase in the amount of earnings subject to Social Security taxes, but thus far he has made no such proposals.

Given the unanswered questions that loom over the Social Security debate, it seems inevitable that the benefits of older as well as younger people will be at risk when Congress seriously considers balancing Social Security for the long term. I don't doubt the sincerity of pledges to leave the elderly and near-elderly out of the argument, but I do doubt whether anyone can actually make good on such a pledge while establishing an individual savings account plan and at the same time avoiding all the sources of income that Governor Bush has promised not to tap.

The problem is that exempting the elderly from the cuts required by diverting some of Social Security's financing to individual accounts results in such big cuts for younger workers that during the legislative process such a plan would be portrayed as unfair, as indeed it would be. In the name of fairness and intergenerational equity, Congress might well decide to trim cost-of-living adjustments, accelerate the retirement-age increase in present law, or raise the retirement age further, among other options. Or benefits could be trimmed across-the-board.

After a half-century of experience with Social Security and Congress, one thing I know: When a pledge is being translated into law, anything can happen. No president can completely control the process. Presidents who want results have to give here and there. Older people should not be lulled into inaction by promises from either Vice President Gore or Governor Bush to protect them from change. No matter how well meant, these could become empty promises unless everyone with a stake in the future of Social Security stays actively involved in the debate.

6

MORE THAN A LAW:
THE JOB OF THE ADMINISTRATOR
IN DELIVERING A SERVICE

*The following notes for a lecture on government administration
are a good introduction to the pieces that immediately follow.
The way the Social Security program was administered by my
predecessors and during the 21 years when I was responsible
for it had much to do, I believe, with the public's strong support
for expanding the program and enacting Medicare. The popularity of the program was in part a reflection of the way people
were treated.*

*Looked at from the top down, a key element of success
was for the top staff to consider itself totally in charge and to
work to remove any barriers to good performance whether
encountered in law, in the Congress, in other parts of the executive branch, or for that matter in the upper reaches of the
Social Security hierarchy. The mission was to steer an organization through what at times were very rough waters—always
paying attention to the charts but taking full responsibility for
navigation and performance.*

As a basis for discussion I want to make some comments concerning
what I think is the most fundamental responsibility an administrator
has—not the only one, but the most fundamental one.

I believe that the most fundamental part of an administrator's job
is to set the character and spirit of the organization and its objectives

From the author's notes for a lecture on government administration delivered at
Princeton University, October 20, 1964 (unpublished).

and goals—both in the program and in the way the program is carried out. Others participate in this but the administrator is responsible.

I think that the administrator's fundamental task—frequently neglected—is to think through just what the program is, in simple, stark terms, and then in the same simple, stark terms to articulate the long-term goals in administering that program, the style and spirit of administration that is desirable, and the value system to be used in choosing alternatives.

The first implication here is that the same people feel some responsibility for the definition of the program and for its administration. I do not favor the approach which says one group has responsibility for the definition of the program in law and another takes that law and administers it. The administrator in my view administers best if he or she is taking responsibility for thinking about the fundamental purpose of the law and feels responsible for recommending changes and improving it. I think you also get a better law. I don't like the Treasury pattern under which most of the work on changing the law is done at the department level and then the Internal Revenue Service, for example, focuses almost entirely on carrying it out.

Going beyond the definition of the program in the law, the administrator then defines the program *in action* by policy decision—selecting among many alternatives according to *value* judgments. Being explicit about these values so that the whole organization can participate in making and applying them is a major part of the administrator's job. He or she must win the organization to the same general value system so that the self-direction of people all down the line—and self-direction is the only kind that amounts to much—is in general accord with the value system.

A law is not self-administering. It leaves hundreds and hundreds of choices up to the administrator.

Let me illustrate with Social Security, which has a law defining in great detail who is covered, who gets what benefits and how much, under what conditions of eligibility, and what factors cause benefits to be terminated or suspended. But the law says nothing about what proofs a person has to submit to show he meets the conditions.

It says nothing about whether the claims operation should be largely by mail or through face-to-face contact.

It says nothing about whether the administering organization should take responsibility to let people know of their rights with an aggressive informational program or whether it should wait for people to apply.

It says nothing about the kinds of people who will be chosen to interview the public or what their attitude and training shall be.

It says nothing about what a district office shall look like—and on and on and on.

I think the administrator has a primary obligation to define his or her broad goals beyond the clear intent in the law in a way that the whole organization can participate in carrying them out. The administrator has to generate *a contagion of belief and enthusiasm in the program and in a way of operating.*

The administrator's value system and attitudes will be contagious. Does she test policy and procedures from the standpoint of the public or the convenience of the organization? Whatever choice she makes, it will be contagious. Does she take the view that her job is to make the program and its administration the best possible, and does she see barriers to this accomplishment as something to be overcome, or does she see her role as more narrow, limited to a formal definition of authority shared with many others?

As a general principle, timidity is to be avoided.

Finally, the administrator sets the spirit and tone of an organization by recognizing and cultivating the organizational motivation of people—beyond salary and prestige.

The instinct to do a good job is strong: cultivate it.

Esprit de corps—loyalty to the squad even under tough conditions— does not just happen.

A sense of identification with the goals of the organization— needed for best performance—must be imparted and encouraged.

And none of this can be done by direction. Commitment to performance, to public service, is above all a voluntary act. It can't be bought or forced. It can only be inspired.

7

THE SOCIAL SECURITY
ADMINISTRATION'S OBJECTIVES

*As deputy director of the Bureau of Old-Age and Survivors
Insurance (OASI), I wrote the first* Statement of Bureau
Objectives *in an attempt to codify the organizational culture at
Social Security. The statement, published in 1958, was distributed to all current employees and to new ones as they joined the
organization. With very little change, it continued to be part of
training and planning for at least the following 15 years and, as
the organization changed, became a statement of Social Security
Administration objectives.*

FOREWORD

An organization which sets forth its objectives in writing does so to
help give consistency to its actions and unity to its planning, particularly its long-range planning. This *Statement of Bureau Objectives*
reflects the principles, the goals, and the more enduring plans to
which we are committed within the framework of Social Security
Administration policy. It reflects decision upon the ideals to which we
aspire, agreement upon basic purposes, and commitment to a way
of administration. It is a guide to our planning and a yardstick against
which we measure the adequacy of our performance.

Within the framework of the Objectives, we will continue to set
policies and goals for shorter-range planning in an annual Forecasts
and Guides statement. The Forecasts and Guides will stem primarily
from a relating of Objectives to the economic and administrative factors anticipated by the Bureau during a particular period, and will
represent policy decisions as to "how" and "how far" the Bureau
can move in that period toward the long-range Objectives. Work

plans will be evaluated to determine their adequacy in making possible the achievement of goals for the short-range period and to ascertain that they represent a reasonable rate and extent of progress toward the realization of the *Bureau Objectives*.

BUREAU RESPONSIBILITIES

We who administer the federal social insurance program have a responsibility:

I.   TO THE PUBLIC: *To safeguard and ensure the rights of the public under the program, to provide the full measure of service to which the public is entitled, and for economical administration.*

II. FOR THE PROGRAM: *To improve the program so that it will more completely achieve its purpose and play its optimum role in providing economic security to the nation's workers and their families.*

III. TO THE GOVERNMENT AS A WHOLE: *For the contributions we can make to government-wide policy and programs.*

IV. TO THE STAFF OF THE BUREAU: *For the establishment and maintenance of an administrative climate and working conditions that will foster an effective career service.*

BUREAU OBJECTIVES

I. RESPONSIBILITY TO THE PUBLIC

The OASI statute is a statement in detail of the rights and obligations of people. The Bureau is responsible for translating these statutory rights and obligations into precise and detailed operating policies and practices which guarantee that the rights are fulfilled and the obligations carried out. The responsibility has two aspects.

In the first place, we have the duty of performing the many concrete tasks necessary to protect and maintain the rights which are earned by those who participate in the program. In the second place, and equally important, we must through the *way* we perform these tasks create a personality and a character for the organization appropriate to a program based on the concept of earned right.

The OASI program is supported by a direct tax on covered earnings. The trust funds to which contributions are made and from which benefit payments come are in a very real sense the property of the contributors. Each benefit payment from this source must therefore be exactly what is due to the individual in order to preserve the rights of the group as well as of the individuals who compose it. Since our administrative expenditures are also charges against these funds, we have a special obligation to give the best in service for each administrative dollar.

Beyond the day-to-day tasks, we have the same sort of long-range responsibility which the management of a private corporation has to its investors. Our policies, our organization, our administrative procedures, our staffing practices must all be developed with the permanency of the program in mind. In each of our actions we must build for the future no less than for the present. Persons just beginning their working lives must have the same assurance of protection deriving from the stability of our management as beneficiaries currently receiving payment.

There are ten objectives under this heading.

Objective 1: Process initial claims with all practicable speed and pay continuing benefits on time. Most people who get an OASI check depend on it for the necessities of life. No goal of the Bureau, therefore, is more important than seeing that people get their OASI check every month at the time they expect it and that the initial payment of claims and the reinstatement of benefits is as prompt as we can make them. Promptness and accuracy—the right check, to the right person, at the right address, on time—is the very essence of our service.

Objective 2: Provide objective, uniform, and equal treatment of people under law. Who is entitled to benefits, how much and under what circumstances, is a matter of national law. Our job is to apply the law under a great variety of circumstances and conditions in such a way that all people can depend on getting equal treatment under law regardless of who they are or where they come in contact with the organization.

The uniform administration of law is based upon an organized system of national policies and procedures in the form of written instructions and manuals. Training programs, conferences, and similar devices are used to promote common understanding on the part of those who administer a national program.

Objective 3: Treat everyone who comes to an OASI district office or gets a letter or other communication from any part of the Bureau as deserving of respect and entitled to courteous, friendly, helpful service. OASI is the translation into operations of the spirit and objectives of contributory social insurance. The way the OASI program is administered determines almost as much as the statute itself what the concept of right means in practice. We are, of course, firm about requirements and must sometimes take actions contrary to what our "customers" want, but our goal under all circumstances is to carry out the program in a way that is friendly, courteous and humane.

Objective 4: Operate under claims policies and procedures that are as little burdensome on the public as possible but at the same time offer adequate assurance that the statutory provisions are being carried out. We have an obligation not only to see that people get what is due them but to protect the trust funds against improper payments, and we strive to earn the respect of the public for the integrity of our administration as well as for its helpfulness and its humanity. This means for one thing the adequate documentation of the claim. We want *proof* of disability, *proof* of age, *proof* of coverage and earnings. What presumptions we use must be tested to determine their validity. We must provide for reviews, and checks and balances.

On the other hand, we must guard against procedures and policies that go beyond what is needed to insure the integrity of the program, for respect on the part of the public for tight administration can easily turn to impatience with red tape.

Objective 5: Secure accurate records of all covered wages and self-employment income in a way which makes it as easy as possible for the public to do what is required. To protect people's rights, reporting of wages and self-employment income must be complete, accurate, and available on time. At the same time, it is important to our public relations, and to the public relations of government as a whole, that our procedures impose minimum costs and difficulties upon the employers and the self-employed persons who make the reports.

Objective 6: Maintain an organization in which the public has a high degree of confidence and with which it is willing to cooperate. The effectiveness and economy of our administration depend upon an underlying willingness on the part of the public to cooperate. We could not force, without prohibitive expense, what is now done willingly. What people think of us, the picture of the organization they carry in their mind, derives from the type of personnel we select to represent the Bureau, how we train them, what our offices look like, the attitude of friendly and dependable service we adopt in all our public contacts, the tone of correspondence and the promptness with which we answer inquiries, the soundness of our policies, and the correctness of our decisions under these policies—really the action of each of us every day. Such everyday matters shape our public relations even more than speeches, press releases, magazine articles, and radio and television programs.

Objective 7: Provide a helpful referral service to other programs. The people who come to our offices often bring with them problems and questions which are outside our own program and competence. While maintaining a clear focus on our own responsibilities, we should know about community resources, participate in their development, and operate a helpful referral service.

Objective 8: Maintain levels of service appropriate to an insurance program based on a concept of earned right and which will enable the Bureau to protect and maintain the rights of program participants. Inherent in the maintenance of program rights is the need to obtain and maintain adequate resources to do the work. We must develop sound budget estimates and base them on firm documentation to ensure authorization by Congress of administrative expense funds in the amounts needed. The number, qualifications, and training of staff, housing, equipment, and technical facilities must all be matched to the kind of jobs we do and the quality with which we must perform them. Particularly at the place where the public meets the program, our facilities should reflect the businesslike character of the program. It is an important part of this objective to have facilities in the field which in type of space, location, and number will provide convenience and comfort to the public and reflect credit on the program and the organization.

Objective 9: Let people know about their rights and responsibilities under the program. People need to be informed before they can act to obtain the program rights to which they are entitled and to discharge their obligations under the law. Moreover, the purpose of the program requires that people know ahead of time what rights they have, for security is not only a matter of getting the money when it is due but of being conscious ahead of time that the protection is there.

Objective 10: Attain the Bureau Objectives at as low an administrative cost as possible. We take very seriously the fact that every dollar spent on administration comes from the contributions people have made for their security. We strive to cut all unnecessary expense but, at the same time, we believe that the contributors to the program want and are entitled to a high level of service. Thus, we seek the latest money-saving machinery, improved methods, simplified procedures, and all ways in which an economical and efficient job can be done without lowering quality. There are always improvements to be made. By refusing to be satisfied with what we have achieved, we will retain the spirit of innovation, the willingness to experiment, the desire to consider new things, the capacity to evaluate the old and the willingness to drop it in favor of something better.

II. RESPONSIBILITY FOR THE PROGRAM

A fundamental responsibility of Bureau management is to contribute to the best possible statutory definition of the program. It is not enough that we should perform well the processing of work growing out of present law; we are also charged with the responsibility of helping to shape the future of the OASI program so that it makes the best possible contribution to the economic security of the nation's workers and their families.

Although work on program development and the necessary related research are areas of responsibility shared with various other organizations in the executive branch, with Congress, and with outside groups, heavy responsibility for shaping what is desirable and practical rests on the Bureau. Growing out of experience and research, the Bureau recommends to the Social Security Administration and the department, which in turn must recommend to the President and to Congress.

There are three Bureau objectives in the area of program responsibility.

Objective 11: Provide effective protection under the program for all who work for a living and for their dependents. Old-age, survivors, and disability insurance can be fully effective only if the program covers all who work for a living, and only in this way can the responsibility of protecting the nation against economic insecurity be shared by all. As long as this insurance program does not apply to all types of employment, some workers have no chance to contribute. Some pay contributions but never qualify for benefits because they work part of the time in covered jobs and part of the time in noncovered jobs. Others, who shift between covered and noncovered work, may gain benefits which are worth considerably more in relation to their contributions than are the benefits of workers who contribute regularly. Universal coverage cannot, of itself, assure effective protection; decisions as to the risks for which protection is to be provided, requirements of eligibility for benefits, and the basis for determining the amount of the benefit all play an important part in determining whether the protection afforded is effective.

Objective 12: Achieve a program that is easy to understand, that has as few administrative complications as possible, and that is acceptable to the public as equitable and rational. The broad principles and basic ideas of the program are simple, but complexity in detail has been building up over a long period of time as the program has been successively revised. Reducing the present complications in the law and reexamining the reasonableness of detailed provisions so that the program will be easier to understand, to accept, and to administer is a continuing task.

Objective 13: Carry on a program of research which will contribute most effectively to improvement of the program. Inherent in the administration of any program is the duty to improve its effectiveness. This obligation is reinforced in our case by the statutory duty of the department to study and make recommendations as to the most effective methods of providing economic security through social insurance. In addition, from both public and private sources there is a constant stream of proposals for change. The Bureau must equip itself to provide pertinent facts and to recommend policy positions on these proposals. The Bureau must have foresight and be prepared to deal with proposals and issues that will emerge as the program matures. It must also be equipped to deal with the policy issues that will arise with respect to relationships between OASI and other expanding public and private programs for income maintenance. To meet these responsibilities the Bureau must maintain an effective long-range program of research and analysis.

III. Responsibility to the Government as a Whole

We are part of a broad network of cultural, social, and economic relationships which affect our own program developments and directions, and which we in turn affect. We have, consequently, an obligation to establish objectives which will identify the special contributions we can make, over and above our specific program interests, to the wider objectives and policies of the Social Security Administration, the department, and the government as a whole in furtherance of the total public interest.

There are three Bureau Objectives in this area of broad responsibility.

Objective 14: Contribute to government-wide and community planning for the aging, the widowed, the disabled, and for children. We are deeply and immediately concerned with the economic needs of these groups. We are very conscious, too, that our own program and operations do not meet all economic needs, and that there are additional needs, too, beyond the economic ones. From our own program experience and our day-to-day exposure to other problems of the aged, widowed, disabled, and children we gain knowledge and insights which can contribute to the planning that other organizations are doing.

Of particular significance, because of the nature of our field organization and its operation, is the contribution which we can make to the establishment of adequate community resources for these groups.

The purposes of the OASI program are closely linked to the purposes of a number of other programs—vocational rehabilitation, public assistance, health and welfare services to children, unemployment insurance, and others. We should establish policy and operational relationships with these programs which will assist them and us in reaching mutually related objectives. In developing our own policies and procedures we should give appropriate consideration to the extent to which they can and should help to link in practice the mutual or related objectives of several programs. Our individual actions should be taken on the basis of a broad understanding of program relationships—of the help we can give and the assistance we can receive.

Objective 15: Contribute to the effectiveness and economy of operations government-wide. The government-wide perspective which we need in the field of program content is paralleled by a need for one of equal breadth in the management field. We are one unit in a single overall government administrative service and are able to contribute to and receive from this service.

In many areas what the Bureau can do is controlled by other government agencies and by basic statutes other than the Social Security Act. First of all, of course, is the fact that the Internal Revenue Service has a major role in Social Security administration. The Defense Department, the Veterans Administration, the Railroad Retirement Board, and various state agencies are also involved. The Civil Service Commission, the Bureau of the Budget, the General Accounting Office, and the General Services Administration, too, are involved importantly in Bureau administration. The Bureau's responsibility in relation to all these organizations and to the formation of government policy as a whole is to contribute from our experience to the development of the most efficient and the best in government service.

Objective 16: Contribute through our program operations and research to knowledge of the operation of the economy. As the collector and custodian of a vast body of statistical information about business, employment, payroll, retirement, disability, mortality, and benefits, the Bureau has an obligation to keep these data in such form that they will be available for the use of other organizations at the lowest possible cost.

IV. RESPONSIBILITY TO BUREAU STAFF

The Bureau must be run in a way that recognizes that the people of OASI *are* the organization. This calls for a democratic management in which information is shared, opinions and experience sought, and decisions mutually arrived at. It means doing everything possible to preserve and to strengthen the greatest asset the organization has—the devotion and interest of skilled and experienced people.

We have four objectives under this responsibility.

Objective 17: Make sure the Bureau deserves the reputation of being a good place to work. Such a reputation derives in part from good personnel policies, employee services—including attention to employee health, counseling, and recreational needs—good training programs, proper office facilities, and individual jobs which permit employees to obtain a feeling of accomplishment and importance. The latter must involve appreciation of the meaning of the program and its policies, challenging and frequently demanding work, mutual respect in personal relationships, and the opportunity to participate and contribute. Of basic importance is the need to ensure that individual jobs are properly classified as to grade and pay, and promptly reclassified to take into account changes that occur from time to time in the duties and responsibilities of Bureau positions.

Objective 18: So organize the jobs of the Bureau that the work is interesting and challenging and people derive prestige and satisfaction from their work. We are fortunate in the Bureau in that many of our jobs are dramatic and vitally interesting. We are fortunate, also, in that much has been done over the years to increase job breadth and responsibilities, to promote participation in common program and management concerns, and to improve methods of communication. These things are essential to job satisfaction and to enlarge the number and proportion of employees who participate creatively in matters which should be a shared concern of all. There is, of course, further work to be done on the organization of Bureau jobs to achieve this objective, and adjustments to be made in jobs as further program and technological changes occur.

Objective 19: Maintain high ethical and performance standards. The establishment and maintenance of high ethical and performance standards is a necessary means to attaining the total body of Bureau objectives since these objectives express very exacting and high ideals and concepts of service. The members of this organization hold themselves to be and act as servants of the public and executors of the public's program—operating as trustees of a permanent institution in American life. The fact that standards are set at high levels is both a challenge and inspiration to Bureau staff.

Objective 20: Recruit, train, develop, and promote Bureau personnel in such a way that all important positions are filled as they become vacant by persons fully prepared to assume exacting responsibility. Nothing is more essential to the attainment of program objectives than what we do today to develop leadership for tomorrow. This is of particular significance to the Bureau because we are still a young organization operated largely by the first generation of managerial staff. The Bureau must recruit with the future potential of employees in mind; staff members must be trained and encouraged to acquire and develop new and greater skills; we must use the opportunity as employees take on each new job to deliberately test their individual capacities and then expand their work opportunities in successive steps to encompass broader and higher responsibilities as the individual demonstrates ability.

We must consider how effectively our inter-divisional and inter-regional promotional policy works to encourage experience in more than one line of work; how completely we eliminate prejudice regarding race, sex, creed; the extent to which extraordinary ability is early recognized and rewarded by rapid promotion; whether there is sufficient recruitment from outside to fairly high levels to keep us from becoming ingrown; whether employees have the motivation that comes from the knowledge that they have every reasonable chance to develop and that they will be selected for higher responsibilities if they merit promotion.

The business of the United States is the most important, challenging, and exciting business in the world, and we must be able to attract to it the best minds and skill of the next generation. We who are in government owe it to the country to set an example of government business that will stand the competition of the very best in private industry.

8

FIELD OFFICE INTERVIEWS: NOTES FOR GUIDANCE

In 1942, as an analyst at the Training Office of the Bureau of Old-Age and Survivors Insurance, I was asked to write an instruction guide for field office interviews. This is the first document I wrote for general circulation in the Social Security Administration. It reflects both the agency's official view and my own view of what I have always thought a government agency should be.

Field personnel are Social Security's direct representatives to the public. Your success or failure in dealing with the public will in large measure determine the success or failure of the whole Social Security program. You will see more people in an official capacity than the Director of the Bureau or any other Central Office employee, and each person you see will have either a better or worse opinion of the Social Security program and, yes, of our whole government, because of the way you treated him. Yours, then, is a great responsibility and a great opportunity.

It is expected that your technical knowledge will always be thorough and up to date and that you will know the rules and regulations connected with Old-Age and Survivors Insurance which will aid you in doing a better job for the people who look to you for help. You must know not only Title II but enough about the broad Social Security program to be of assistance to those you meet who are not eligible for insurance or who need additional assistance. You are the representative of the Board as well as the Bureau. In addition, to do intelligent public relations work you must know the weaknesses as well as the strong points of the present Act, and you must be acquainted with the proposals for changes in the Act and extensions of the program. You must know the *why* as well as the *what*.

All these things you are expected to know, but even more important there are things you are expected to *be*. The mysteries of the average monthly wage and insured status are relatively easy to master, but such knowledge is only the beginning of your job. Your job is really different just because it doesn't deal with facts or things or even theories but with people in all their variety. You have much more difficult things to learn. You have to learn how to be a certain type of person.

Perhaps the one word which comes closer than any other to expressing what field personnel must be in order to be successful in dealing with the public is *courteous*. "Oh, but that's easy," you say. "I have good manners. They are really second nature to me. I would never be discourteous in business or in my private life either." Unfortunately, however, courtesy is not the same thing as good manners. If it were, we could learn courtesy as we learn the average monthly wage, and that would be that. Courtesy has been defined as the ability to make people feel at home. This ability is much more than mere politeness or the correct manners. Real courtesy means knowing each person you deal with so well that you know what makes him feel at home. It means, for instance, that you are crisp and businesslike in dealing with a busy executive and that you don't take up his time unduly with casual conversation and attempts to be friendly. On the other hand, it means knowing that it is discourteous to be crisp and businesslike to those who enter our offices shy and afraid.

Did you ever stop to think how discourteous it is to use a word that is above the vocabulary of the person with whom you are talking? Technical terms should not be used in interviewing the public not only because people do not understand them but also because they resent not understanding them. In putting them at a disadvantage you are being discourteous.

The first step toward developing the knowledge of people that is necessary in order to be courteous in this fundamental sense is to be critical of your own contacts with people. You must learn first to weigh the effect of your words and manner on others, and in time you will be able to foresee the effect you will have. At that point you will become really valuable to the Bureau. To begin, then, go over your interviews in your mind after they are completed and ask yourself—

Did that elderly gentleman really understand what I was saying or was he afraid to ask me again? Will that schoolgirl remember what I told her in the event she goes to work this summer? Was that widow, who was so obviously upset, in any frame of mind to know what I was talking about? To be a successful interviewer you must learn not only enough about people to make them feel at home, but you must learn also to express yourself so that all types of people understand you. Most important of all you must learn to be the type of person that a stranger feels he can trust.

This is a country of immigrants from many lands. Because of the variety of our origin, the task of understanding people who come to our offices is made even more difficult. The most important principle in learning about people is to remember that each individual is just a little bit different from any other and that some are a whole lot different. You must approach each new individual with a mind free of preconceived notions. Nothing is so destructive to a good interview as ready-made concepts about people, or classes of people, or races of people. The worst interviewers are those experts who can tell all about somebody from the way he talks or dresses or whatnot. A little modesty rather than cocksureness will help us to learn more about that most difficult of all subjects, another human being.

Interviewing, of course, is not a matter of either technical knowledge or courtesy or knowledge of people. We must learn to evaluate the answers we get—distinguishing between an opinion and a fact. A good interviewer draws people out and gets them talking. He is seldom satisfied with one-word answers, and he has learned to recognize evasions.

Of course, we all feel that this social program which we are called upon to administer is an important one. We hope it has become a permanent part of our American way of life. This is not necessarily true. This Social Security program will only stay with us just as long as we do the kind of a job that our visitors like and appreciate.

Success in this task requires the help of those who understand elderly people and widows and children. We must satisfy those with whom we work and for whom we work, and in addition we must know that we are satisfying them. Their reactions to us and our program must be correctly interpreted. In your capacity of dealing directly with our visitors you become the interpreter, and it is through your eyes, trained to appraise correctly, that we must look for the correct reactions to our visitors. And so we must learn not only to do the kind of job that our program calls for, but we must learn to know people sufficiently well so that we can help in developing a program that more thoroughly meets the needs of our beneficiaries.

9

A GOOD PLACE TO
DO GOOD WORK

As Commissioner of Social Security I gave this talk to first-line supervisors and mid-management staff in connection with introducing a training program. I wanted to use this opportunity to underscore the point that in getting work done, the commitment of employees to the goals of an organization is a voluntary act that cannot be forced solely by penalties and promotion but is above all responsive to leadership.

I am not going to be speaking to you this morning as a former training officer but as someone responsible for seeing that Social Security in this country does the job that the people want it to do, and as your colleague and collaborator in that effort.

This year we're going to have the largest additions to our responsibilities certainly since 1954 and perhaps since 1939. I think there is really no question that we will be administering within a very few months a new hospital insurance program and, along with that, will be involved in the conversion of benefits to a higher amount for the 20 million or more people who will be receiving benefits by that time.

This is a tremendous undertaking. The extent to which Social Security now is of major importance to every American family really can't be exaggerated. For most of you who, like myself, came into this program many years ago, it's hard to grasp the reality of the present degree of importance of this program. Just about everybody now thinks of Social Security as the base upon which he will build

Remarks delivered at Social Security Administration headquarters, Baltimore, Md., on November 23, 1964.

economic security for himself and his family in the event of death, disability, or old age. It's a sobering responsibility that we have.

My conviction is that the success or failure of any large enterprise is due more to the quality of its supervision than to any other single factor. It's not solely a matter of whether we have a good law on the books but how well we administer it that will make the difference—the real difference in the security of the American people. A good law badly administered would be a great disaster. This is not merely a theoretical possibility. There are many countries in which the social security program reads well on the statute book but is not really a particularly good thing. It's unpopular; it's not contributing to the real security of the people. I know of one country where benefits are taking two years to be paid. So the quality of the administration of the law, whether people in fact get what's coming to them according to the law, whether the right people are paid in the right amounts, and on time, and can count on it, is as big a contribution to the actual security of people as the writing of a good law. Whether the administration is good or bad depends upon the quality of supervision from top to bottom, and by "supervision" I mean a large part of what I do and what you do: the leadership and direction of people.

I want to say only a few things about supervision, and they will sound, I think, very elementary. But in these [training] seminars and discussions you will be dealing with many points that are not so fundamental and so basic—so I'll take on the role of saying the obvious.

To me a supervisor's main job, by definition, is to get a piece of work done and to get it done in an acceptable quantity and quality in an acceptable period of time. This is his job; this is what he is responsible for as such. But he doesn't do it himself, of course. He does it through people, and therein lies the whole area of skill and professionalism that is involved in supervision. I want to add, too, that I think a supervisor, in addition to having a responsibility to getting his job done through people, has the major responsibility—and this is, I think, completely consistent with his responsibility to get work done—for setting the tone and character, the style and quality, of the work group that he has.

I think a good supervisor recognizes that though he can accomplish much in a relatively short time through telling people, through penalties, through insistence upon their doing it just this way, over time and in the long run it's the voluntary desire on the part of the people under his supervision to contribute to the same goals that he has set that makes for the best atmosphere and, I would be willing to argue, the best production, the best quality, and the best job.

But aside from his major responsibility to accomplish a defined job of work, I think a supervisor has a responsibility as a human being. In the setting of the tone and quality of the place where people work, he has a responsibility to think about the fact that this is how people spend a very large part of their lives and that they have a right to spend it in a way that is meaningful, that protects their dignity, that is directed toward goals that they understand and can feel good about and that is a contribution to the basic quality of life. I really don't think it would be justified for any organization to think solely of getting the work done if it meant at the expense of a major part of people's lives being spent in ways that were not conducive to the true dignity of man. But fortunately, I believe, the best supervision can reconcile these two things and, as a matter of fact, one reinforces the other. The best supervision is supervision that is oriented toward the accomplishment of a given job or work but in an atmosphere which is respectful of the individual's own contribution, his rights, and his dignity as a human being. So I would like to leave with you the thought that the supervisor, in my judgment, is the key to our success, the big responsibilities that we have and are going to take on in terms of the quality of the administration of this whole program. In this program—which above everything else is committed to make it possible for retired people and disabled people and widows and orphans to live dignified and self-respecting lives—in this program above all others we have a special responsibility as supervisors to see that people who work here also can live their working lives in an atmosphere which is respectful of their dignity and which holds up for them goals that are meaningful and in which they can participate.

Within this general framework, I want to stress the very special responsibility that all supervisors at every level have for fairness in the area of hiring and evaluating and promoting—making absolutely certain that one's own background and associations are not in any way operating to prejudice him for or against any person on the basis of race or religion or sex or any other basis. And I'd like to stress, too, the great responsibility of supervisors for understanding and accepting the role of unions. For many of you it is quite a new experience to be part of an organization which has a union contract on an exclusive basis, but I want to say that whatever differences arise out of either immediate or more fundamental issues, it's my real conviction that organizations of employees have demonstrated that they can make a real contribution, not only to the protection of individual employees, not only to the improvement of the working conditions and level of pay of employees, but that they have and can increasingly make a real contribution to the operation and administration of a program—that they can see things sometimes that we as supervisors don't see, and I ask you to enter into discussions with them in an objective, fair, and open-minded and most of all nondefensive way, with a recognition that a previous decision you or a subordinate made could perhaps be wrong and that your job is to now make a decision in relation to additional knowledge that may have been brought to your attention. But it's also your responsibility not to give in just to pressure. The supervisor has the responsibility for deciding, and no union worth its salt wants a management that lies down under pressure. Good will come out of difference if each plays its role.

We all share together the leadership responsibility for perhaps the greatest humanitarian program the American people have ever adopted. We have this as a trusteeship throughout our careers. The quality of its administration is our special responsibility, and the worthwhileness of the lives of people who are under our direction is also our responsibility. I believe we can bring these two together in making this organization, as the Bureau Objectives have always said, "a good place to work"—and also a place that *does* good work.

10

RUNNING SOCIAL SECURITY:
LEADERSHIP CHALLENGES

In the spring of 1964, with President Johnson promoting the legislation that would create Medicare, the Social Security Administration was on the verge of a huge expansion into the field of national health insurance. The organization was also caught up in the nationwide drive for civil rights and equal employment opportunities. This address to some 10,000 Social Security employees at the agency's Baltimore headquarters was given on the eve of a threatened demonstration to be led by Dick Gregory, the prominent comedian and activist. My fear was that the demonstration—probably the first in the country against a major federal installation—would give the Social Security Administration a black eye despite the work being done to improve hiring and promotion practices for minority employees (including putting into practice the recommendations of an advisory group I had appointed that included representatives of the Urban League and the NAACP). Not everyone understood that the civil rights organizations as a matter of sound tactics attacked where there would be sympathy for their goals. I include this talk as an example of two types of situations in which administrative leaders may indeed need to lead: an unprecedented work challenge and an unprecedented challenge in national policy.

I haven't seen so many Social Security people together in a long time—it's a great sight! I'm sorry that several of you have to stand along the wall there, but I do think it's important that we all meet together. I

Remarks to employees at Social Security Administration headquarters, Baltimore, Md., May 26, 1964.

intend to do this from time to time from now on, not on any planned or regular basis, but just every once in awhile in order to bring you up to date on the program and its administration and to give you, as employees with a very vital stake in the Social Security Administration, a direct report on what I see ahead.

Today, I'd like to talk with you about two things: first, where the Social Security program stands and what I see immediately ahead for the program; and second, some matters relating to the administration of that program and your role in administering it.

First, the program. If hospital insurance is added to Social Security this year, as I believe it will be, we will then have in this country programs dealing with all of the major branches of social insurance; except for federal-state unemployment insurance, they will all be in the federal system of social security that you and I are responsible for.

In what an amazingly short time all this has happened! Many of you will remember that we started in 1935 with just old-age retirement benefits, and then only for workers in business and industry; then in 1939 a whole new branch of social insurance was added to the program—survivors insurance—and dependents' benefits for retired workers. Then not much legislation was passed in the next 10 years after that, but beginning in 1950 we have had a series of sweeping amendments that have expanded the program to just about every American, added another whole branch of protection—disability insurance—greatly increased the level of benefits, and together with the natural growth of the program have made the American system of Social Security the largest and most successful old-age, survivors, and disability insurance system in the world. We cover occupational groups that are seldom covered in other wage-related social security systems around the world—the urban self-employed and the farmer. We even cover the armed forces on a regular contributory basis! And now if we add hospital insurance for older people, we will be in, as well, what is for us the new field of health insurance.

Today, nearly 20 million people—1 out of every 10 Americans—get a Social Security benefit every month; 9 out of 10 persons becoming 65 this year are eligible for benefits; and 9 out of every 10 mothers and children in the country are protected in the event of the death of the major breadwinner in the family. The face value of this survivor protection alone is about $625 billion, just about equal to all of the private life insurance in the country added together. [*Author's note:* In

1997, the total for Social Security was $14.5 trillion, compared to $14.8 trillion for private life insurance.]

The good that Social Security is doing for the old people of this country, for widows, for motherless or fatherless children, and for the disabled is incalculable; and it is something that all of us who work for Social Security have a right to take great pride in. This is a job with great objectives and great accomplishments.

I've often wondered how it is that in such a short time America has been able to develop such a successful Social Security system and one which has such wide support among people of every kind of political opinion. My conclusion is that the wide acceptance of the program and its great success are due primarily to its basic principles. Here is a program that has accomplished truly revolutionary results. There's no other way to describe the social change that has taken place through Social Security in the way old people, widows, children, and the disabled of the country are treated; but it has accomplished these great changes through the application of old and accepted principles, emphasizing in its very design the virtues of work, self-help, and individual saving.

This is not a program in which the government or the well-to-do help people. On the contrary, it is primarily a program in which the people help themselves, using government as the instrument. The essence of our Social Security program is that people earn their security themselves out of the work they do. They work and they contribute. The basic fact that determines eligibility and how much a person gets in benefits is the amount of work he has done under the program as shown in the records kept by you in the Division of Accounting Operations. The fact that the right to the benefits is earned by work and contributions is what gives this program its distinctive character and what makes it possible to accept a Social Security benefit with dignity and pride.

Yet these basic principles are not the whole story. A law at first is only a piece of paper. It grows into a living reality through administration— through people who work for the program. It is my strong belief that another reason that this program has won wide favor in the public eye is the character of its administration. A major reason that the Congress keeps giving this organization more tasks to perform is that we have done well the jobs that have been given us before.

And this brings me to the second subject that I want to talk about today, the administration of the Social Security program and the role of each of you in it.

Our job—yours and mine—is part of a great trusteeship for the American people. How well we perform it has a lot to do with the security of just about every family in the country. If your job is to help keep the records of people's earnings or to help pay disability benefits or to see that mail and messages are properly delivered or that claims folders are filed properly—*whatever* it is—your job is a necessary part of providing dignified protection for all Americans and a necessary part of protecting the most vulnerable people in our population—the widows, the children, the aged, and the disabled. You are working to promote the security of the American family. You can be proud of your job and your contribution to this objective.

A very important reason for the success of the program is that Social Security workers have generally taken the view that getting the job done for the American people comes first. We have been an organization that looked not to our own convenience but outward to the service we give to those who are protected by Social Security. Our objective has been to give a friendly, helpful, sympathetic service to all—a service characterized by prompt and efficient handling of the work of the program at as low a cost as possible because we have recognized that money spent in administration comes from the dollars that workers contribute to their security and that any waste is a loss to them in benefit protection. I would ask you again to refer frequently to the *Statement of Bureau Objectives* (see Chapter 7), for here we have in writing our permanent goals and ideals of a publicly oriented government service. Today I would like to direct your attention to one of the objectives, which reads in part as follows: ". . . recruit, train, develop, and promote Bureau personnel in such a way that positions are filled as they become vacant by persons fully prepared to assume exacting responsibility." And, continuing to quote:

> We must consider how effectively our inter-divisional and inter-regional promotional policy works to encourage experience in more than one line of work; how completely we eliminate prejudice regarding race, sex, creed; the extent to which extraordinary ability is early recognized and rewarded by rapid promotion; whether there is sufficient recruitment from outside to fairly high levels to keep us from becoming ingrown; whether employees have the motivation that comes from the knowledge that they have every

reasonable chance to develop and that they will be selected for higher responsibilities if they merit promotion.

Much has been done since that statement was written in 1958 to help accomplish the objective described. I would like particularly to call your attention to the greater opportunities that have become available for minority group employees. At the end of 1958, a little over five years ago and shortly after this statement was written, there were 23 Negro employees in Baltimore above grade 6. Last January there were 230 Negroes above grade 6 representing more than 10 percent of the 2,183 Negroes employed by the Social Security Administration here at Woodlawn. The progress of Negro employees here in Baltimore has been accelerated in the last two years, and I am sure that the figures that become available in July will be even higher than those of last January that I have quoted. And as important as the progress in the upper grades is the movement below grade 6. The number of Negroes in grade 3 and below has not changed much since 1958, but at grade 4 the number has gone from 280 at the end of 1958 to 538 at the beginning of this year. Comparable figures at grade 5 are from 136 to 363, and at grade 6 from 30 to 73.

To make doubly sure that our system of promotion is free of bias or favoritism whether involving white or Negro, we have just recently in conjunction with a review by the Advisory Committee on Personnel Practices substantially revised the employee evaluation system and all promotional procedures below grade 7. The new system puts the emphasis on the objective measurement of the quality and quantity of work and on aptitude and other objective tests. Subjective evaluations are also important, but they belong at the end of the process in choosing among those who meet the objective tests, not in screening out people from initial consideration.

As you know, many other steps were taken in the area of equal employment opportunity while the advisory committee was meeting. These steps are listed in the committee's report, and I'm not going to review them all here. Most important, we have accepted all 17 recommendations of the advisory group and are putting them into practice rapidly. Many of these important recommendations are already in effect.

I truly believe that the adoption of these recommendations will significantly improve our personnel administration for all employees, white and Negro alike. There is nothing in any of them of any favoritism for any group. They are entirely in the spirit of fair and equal competition among employees without regard to race, creed, or color to insure that the person who will do best in the higher grade job is the one who gets it. In the words of the committee: "The Negro employees have the same rights as all other employees to fair consideration under conditions of equal competition. We believe that this is the position of the Social Security Administration management and that it is the correct position."

The committee is right that this is the position of the Social Security Administration. Our goal is the best man or woman in the job regardless of race, creed, or color, and in order to accomplish our goal we will guard our procedures against the possibility of bias, or favoritism, or cliques, or anything else that could distort the process. White employees and Negro employees alike will be fully protected in their right to fair consideration. This whole area of equal employment opportunity is a matter of major importance in our current administration of the Social Security program because it is a matter of major importance in American life.

One of the extremely significant changes taking place today is that the 10 percent of Americans who are Negroes are determined to do something about the fact that they have not been given an equal chance to participate in the good things of life in America.

What are the facts? Because of social and economic disadvantages, Negroes have much higher mortality rates on the average than whites—on the average they don't live as long. Their educational opportunities, on the average, have been more limited. Percentagewise, many more Negroes than whites are unemployed. When they have jobs, they are not likely to be such good jobs. If they travel, they find many restaurants and hotels won't serve them. They are not welcome in some places of amusement. By just about every test of equal participation in the good things of life, the Negro has been at a substantial disadvantage. There is nothing new about these facts. What is new is the determination of the Negro himself to do something about it and the strong support of the federal government in helping him to move into a position of equal opportunity.

In my judgment, all of us will need to pay very careful attention to these two new facts now and over a period of many years. The Negro is correctly going to continue to press for equality in American life on into the future and the federal government is going to back the right to full equality.

Now, this is not a simple matter of whether in a specific case there is evidence that a Negro was specifically discriminated against in promotion or hiring. That's relatively simple. It is more a matter of making sure that all our personnel and management policies, our daily dealings with employees, the atmosphere of our shop, are such as to assure people who know that they have not had equality of opportunity in American life *generally* that they *do* have equality of opportunity in the Social Security Administration. It is not solely a matter of objective fact about this or that case, but a situation involving human feelings. We must not only *be* fair—employees both white and Negro need to be *convinced* of our fairness.

Let's step up the effort of assuring ourselves that there is truly equality of opportunity in this organization. It is important to the success of our very mission, the administration of Social Security. But most important, as the president himself has said, we want to provide full equality of opportunity because it is the morally right thing to do.

Now, while on the subject of equal employment opportunity, let me say something to you about the proposed demonstration this coming Thursday. I feel it's particularly important for me to comment on it because of a paper that was distributed to employees last week that bore no names, but referred to the Social Security Government Workers Committee. Among other things, it said that "management is in accord with the march." This is not true. We haven't forbidden the demonstration, but that is not to say that we are in sympathy with it. We are not. Personally, I think it is very unwise and uncalled for.

The timing is certainly most unfortunate. What is the record? After eight months of study, the Advisory Committee on Personnel Practices in Baltimore, with representation from our union, Local 1923 of the American Federation of Government Employees, the Urban League, and the NAACP, submitted its report to me on May 6. It was immediately released to the press and copies were made available to any employee who wanted one. Thirty-five hundred copies were distributed. On May 7, the very next day, the executive staff of the Social Security Administration, after a thorough discussion, accepted in substance all 17 of the committee recommendations. On May 8, the next day, I met with the advisory committee and told them of our action. Again, the press and all employees were immediately informed. Every recommendation is being put into effect as rapidly as possible. Several are already in effect. As I am sure you all know, the National Association for the Advancement of Colored People, the Urban

League, the union, all oppose this demonstration. Dr. Furman Templeton of the Urban League and Clarence Mitchell, III, of the NAACP, from the advisory committee with the concurrence of Tom Smith, the President of Local 1923, who also served on the advisory committee, have written a letter to Social Security employees on this subject. Let me quote to you from their letter.

> As members of the Advisory Committee, which recently sub-
> mitted its report with recommendations for improvement
> on personnel policies and practices in Woodlawn, we pub-
> licly and clearly register our opposition to the proposed May
> 28 demonstration at this time. . . .
> Commissioner Ball has given us every assurance that
> prompt compliance will be given to all our recommenda-
> tions. In short, it can be said that all our recommendations
> were accepted and will be put into effect without delay. . . .
> We contend that the proposed May 28 demonstration
> represents a potential disservice in that it implies that un-
> justified lack of confidence in the Advisory Committee and
> consideration for the Administration which obviously needs
> a short time to install our recommendations as well as an
> unnecessarily embarrassing situation to that majority of
> Social Security Administration employees who are just as
> eager to have conditions improved as those who plan to
> sponsor the demonstration. . . .

I might say that some of the material that has been passed out has not been completely correct in some of the support that it has claimed for the demonstration; for example, I received this morning a telegram from the Reverend Marion Bascom, whose name was listed as a supporter of the demonstration: "I completely disassociate myself from any demon-stration at the Social Security Administration. I have given no one the right to use my name in connection with any demonstrations."—signed Marion C. Bascom, Sr. He is the Chairman of the Labor Committee of the Ministerial Alliance.

I would add to the other points about the particularly unfortu-nate timing of this proposed demonstration the fact that it coincides with the dedication of the Veterans' Memorial. The Veterans' Council arranged for this ceremony many months ago and cleared the date with the Social Security Administration. This is a solemn occasion on which all employees of the Social Security Administration, Negro and white, who gave their lives for their country will be honored. We would hope that the Veterans' Council could have its planned program without any distracting or competing activity of other employees.

This leads me to raise the question of who is organizing this demonstration? What right does the Social Security Government Workers Committee have to claim representation for Social Security employees? The Social Security Administration management in Baltimore has a contract of exclusive recognition with Local 1923 of the American Federation of Government Employees. Only they are legally authorized to represent employees in their concerns over working conditions, promotional plans, and the like. Now, of course, employees with individual grievances can take various roads. They can either ask the union to represent them or there are several other channels for pursuing grievances without the union. But the union is the only organized group that under the law can hold themselves forward and represent employees as a body. I might say any group that desires that right has to go through the same procedures.

Local 1923 won this exclusive right fairly in an election of all eligible employees, and as far as I'm concerned I'll respect that right. I believe in unions. I believe they can help us to do a better job in administration and at the same time help the employees. I don't on the other hand believe that negotiating with every group of self-appointed leaders responsible to no one advances either the rights of employees or the ability of the administration to deal effectively with the issues. Let me tell each of you that you have no obligation to such self-appointed leaders. And if there is any attempt to get you to stay away from work or join the demonstration against your will, report it to your supervisor or directly to Mr. Fred Nichols, Special Assistant for Fair Employment, in my office.

We are going to follow exactly the same policy on leave this Thursday as we would any other day before a long holiday weekend; that is we will be liberal in granting leave up to the point that in a given section there would be a serious interference with operations. As always, of course, taking leave without permission would be a serious breach of discipline.

Speaking of discipline, let me say a special word to supervisors. You bear difficult and important responsibilities. You bear the responsibility not only to promote good employee relations and help make

Social Security a good place to work. You bear responsibility not only to be fair and objective in your appraisals and free from bias, but above all you are responsible to the American people for getting a job done. You are responsible, therefore, for the discipline that is necessary for production. I will not tolerate any laxness in our administration and I count on you to prevent it. You will be backed up.

I believe I have some appreciation of the frustrations that have led Negroes and many white sympathizers to demonstrate and to march. The Negro has suffered great injustices and great indignities in American life. I consider it not only his fight to correct this situation but my fight too—everyone's fight. For until we truly have in America equality of opportunity and effective civil rights, our goal of a free and democratic society will not have been realized.

The Social Security Administration will continue to do everything it can to promote these goals. This ill-timed demonstration will only hinder the efforts being made to accomplish this purpose.

My friends and colleagues in the administration of Social Security, let us move forward to getting the job done. We want to make the Social Security Administration a model of good relations among employees and of good relations between employees and management. I believe we have been making progress, but I need your help, the help of everyone, to get the job finished.

There are exciting times ahead for Social Security, great challenges to be met in new programs and the improvement of old programs. Each of you has an important role to play in these challenges. You have the right to be proud of your work here if you give the best that is in you, no matter what your job. No matter what your job, it makes a necessary contribution to America's fight to abolish poverty. You can hold your head high every day because you are an important part of this fight to abolish poverty, this great cause. Let us then go forward in a spirit of service to the American people and with a sense of comradeship, of brotherhood, for all who work with us here in the Social Security Administration.

11

THE LAW OF RECIPROCAL OBLIGATION

At a time when "looking out for number one" seemed to be gaining ground as the nation's unofficial philosophy—sanctioned by President Reagan—I thought it might be useful to discuss, in a commencement address, the interdependence of individuals and the obligation of each to the whole.

Congratulations on your achievement. You have earned these degrees through work and thought and discipline. Today you have every right to be proud and happy.

And so do your parents and other family members. For although some of you may get your degrees without help from your families, for most of us it has been a family affair. A family affair, first, in the absorption of family values that led us to seek an education; second, in the backing of a family that helped us to stay a difficult course while others sought quicker rewards; and finally, of course, for many of us, in the sacrifice by our families of things they wanted and needed so that we could seek an education.

Congratulations need to be shared, too, with a larger family—the local community, the state, the nation and, yes, the world, because everyone gains today by the graduation of talented, trained, and educated people now better able to do the world's work, preserve those values of the past that are worth preserving, and to make increasingly better application of both technical knowledge and ethical and spiritual values.

And that is why the larger community joined with families and other relatives to give us the opportunity to go to college and in some

---

Commencement address, University of Maryland, June 1985.

cases work for advanced degrees. Without exception, we are all here, in part, because higher education, as well as elementary and secondary education, is a community endeavor.

Only the sons and daughters of the very rich could go to school—and what terrible schools they would be—if it weren't for the community decision to make education a tax-supported and, in private schools, a tax-subsidized enterprise. Almost no one could pay tuition that fully covered the cost of a university education, and where would many of us be if it hadn't been for scholarships and loans to meet at least part of the direct charges? And the economics is much the same whether the scholarship or loan comes directly from a federal taxpayer or from a fund created from tax-exempt contributions, with the general taxpayer having to make up for the loss of revenue represented by the tax-free gift.

This is all as it should be. But people shouldn't forget it. A physician, for example, who acts as if he has done everything on his own and believes that what he earns is entirely a return for his own effort has to be adept at self-deception. Let me tell you about a physician who understands what he owes the community.

Dr. Joseph Giordano was head of the trauma team that saved President Reagan's life after he was shot in 1981. The doctor's grandfather was an Italian immigrant who came to this country with nothing. One of his children was a milkman, and it was this man who was Dr. Giordano's father. The doctor wrote an article about how he became a surgeon and was in a position to save the president's life. He wrote about how his parents sacrificed for him, but he also wrote how he was helped through college by low-interest federal student loans. Yes, he said, he saved the president's life, and was proud of that, but the medical technology he used wouldn't have existed without years of federally funded research.

And he said, "My parents worked hard all their lives. But now they rely on Social Security, and more than once my father has benefited from Medicare."

This doctor understands our mutual responsibility for each other and our dependence on each other. He didn't just "go for it."

And so it is for all the health professions, for lawyers, engineers—all who have had the opportunity and privilege of going to school. To be fair we need to recognize our obligation to a society that made our education possible. To be fair we need to recognize our obligation to each other, to the past, and to the future.

We owe much of what we are to the past. We all stand on the shoulders of the generations that came before. They built the schools and established the ideals of an educated society. They wrote the books, developed scientific ways of thinking, passed on ethical and spiritual values, discovered our country, developed it, won its freedom, held it together, cleared its forests, built its railroads and factories, and invented new technology. A large part of what each one of us can do derives from the intellectual and material capital of the past. What we can do comes not only from our own effort, essential as that is, but also from the knowledge, skills, and technology we have inherited and from the continual growth of collective capital in new inventions, in the advantages we all derive from the general educational system, from public health measures, and a host of other common activities. And we not only stand on the shoulders of past generations, but as we earn our livings we are also dependent on the current contributions of others in a highly collective and interdependent economic, social, and political enterprise that now encompasses the entire world.

No one can go it alone.

For a businessman to be successful, he has to have customers, roads, railroads, airplanes—and he has to have employees who have been to school. The amount he adds to all this is important, but he can't go it alone. He didn't earn it all by himself. He owes part of it back to support the things that made his success possible.

Because we owe much to the past, we have an obligation to the future. We all have the obligation to try to pass on a world to the next generation which is a little better than the one we inherited so that those who come after, standing on our shoulders, can see a little further and do a little better in their turn.

Now isn't all this obvious? Why do I feel it necessary to say these things? A short time ago I would have thought it *was* obvious, and not really worth saying, but we seem to have moved into a period when our national leaders are teaching an extreme individualism that would make us forget our shared concerns. But greed is not enough if we are to address successfully the great challenges that face the world. If each of us pursues a life dedicated to getting the most we can for ourselves, it will not automatically follow that the community will be better off.

There is a law of reciprocal obligation. The community has given us the opportunity to succeed—although it is true that only we can seize that opportunity—and to the extent that we do succeed we owe something back. We owe the obligations of a responsible citizen to participate in the great decisions of our time. At the minimum we owe the obligation to pay cheerfully for our fair share of government, the major expression of our collective enterprise.

Government in the United States is what we have made it. It is not the enemy. It does what we have asked it to do. In many, many cases it does very good work indeed—and, like private industry, sometimes not.

In any event, we need to improve it, not teach people to despise it.

We undermine people's faith in the capacity of government at our peril. It is the only instrument we have to address many of the important issues of the present and future—war or peace, poverty or economic security, ignorance or understanding, health or disease. How do we make effective alliances and deal well with potential enemies and take responsible action toward the developing world without a dedicated and intelligent corps of people willing to work in agencies that handle our foreign affairs? How can we be convincing about our resolve to defend our borders if service for the government is held in low esteem? What about the protection of the environment so that our children and our children's children will have the fields, streams, mountains, and lakes that we have enjoyed? Can we do these things individually? How can we preserve the great research capacity of the National Institutes of Health, poised to add exponentially to its already great success in understanding and conquering many of the diseases affecting humankind, if working for the government is held in contempt? If government is the enemy, who is to protect our food and drugs, control communicable disease, prevent the pollution of air and water, promote equality of opportunity and a fair society regardless of race, creed, color, or sex? Who will take responsibility for improving the highways or safety on the city streets, protection against fire? Who is to maintain the roads and bridges, insure our savings? Who is to operate the public schools, the libraries, the city and state hospitals?

And we have so much more to do. We need to help solve the world-threatening problem of overpopulation and the depletion of energy sources and food supplies. What do we do about the fact that about a fourth of the children here in prosperous America are living in families with incomes below the federal government's rock-bottom definition of poverty? Are we going to continue to accept unemployment rates among black youth and other minorities that are scandalously high?

Of course we have made important progress. Just a few miles from here is the headquarters of our national Social Security system. Social Security is a great success story. As we celebrate its fiftieth anniversary this coming August 14th, it is right to remember that since 1959 the overall poverty rate among the elderly has been cut from 35 percent to 14 percent. [*Author's note*: In 1998, according to Census data, 10.5 percent of the elderly were below the poverty line.]

But it is too soon to declare victory even in this area. About 40 percent of elderly blacks still live in poverty. And about 20 percent of all women who are currently unmarried (i.e., widowed, divorced, or never married) and over 65 live in poverty—and this group accounts for nearly half of all people over 65. Medicare and Medicaid have accomplished a great deal, but still there are about 30 million people without any health insurance protection, and Medicaid covers only about 40 percent of the poor. [*Author's note*: In 1998, according to Census data, 26.4 percent of elderly blacks and 16 percent of unmarried women were below the poverty line.]

A more humane and just society will not come about simply by each of us single-mindedly pursuing our own self interest. We will need to take action as a community, and for many activities this must mean through government. I hope many of you will turn to government as a career. We need a responsive, imaginative, and creative public service. It is a proud career, and I am sure will again be so recognized by the great majority of the American people. You will not make a mistake. It necessarily deals with some of the most important functions of our society, and government needs an important share of the best and brightest minds we have. It can be an exciting, fulfilling, and adventuresome career. I can personally testify to that.

But one can make contributions to the common enterprise from any position in society, and that is what I am pleading for: For a sense of common obligation. For a selection of life goals based on an understanding of mutual concern and participation in a common enterprise. Banker, artist, industrialist, writer, union leader, health professional, engineer, teacher, government worker, computer specialist— everyone can have a part. But we will continue to be a truly great society only if we care about each other. "Go for it"—looking out for number one—does not quite capture the spirit of civilization or the spirit of the people of this great country. Perhaps it would be better to return to the spirit of community expressed by John Donne in 1624:

> No man is an island, entire of itself; every man is a piece of the continent, a part of the main; . . . any man's death diminishes me, because I am involved in mankind; and therefore never send to know for whom the bell tolls; it tolls for thee.

12

ONE WILLING TAXPAYER

A brief statement of my belief in interdependence (memorably described by E. B. White, toward the close of World War II, as "the word with the big new syllable") and the role of government as the instrument of our collective will.

Now don't get me wrong. I am not a masochist trying to make things unpleasant for myself. During the past few years, for the first time in my life, I have had a small amount of money for what they call "discretionary spending"—that is, after what has seemed essential for food, clothing, shelter, medical care, and other family needs, there has been a little money left over that we could save or decide to spend as we wished. A good feeling.

Then a strange thing happened. As I was making out my income taxes, it occurred to me that I would get a better bargain if I spent somewhat more of my money on those things that benefit us all and a little less on what I selected individually. That is, I found I had a marginal preference for public goods versus private goods. This will not lead me to make a gift to the federal government, but it *will* lead me to vote for those who will see that everyone helps pay a fair share of increased expenditures.

Let me take first that *bête noire* of my liberal friends: defense expenditures. For many of them, the decisions about federal expenditures seem to be easy—just cut the defense budget and leave social programs alone. But I am glad we are planning to increase our defense capability over the next decade relative to the Soviet Union's, and that shouldn't be hard to do. We have a gross national product almost

An op-ed published in the *Washington Post* on April 18, 1980. (At that time I was a senior scholar at the Institute of Medicine of the National Academy of Sciences.)

three times as large as theirs, and they are apparently locked into a very low-growth or no-growth situation for many years. Now, I am annoyed by the fact that we seem to be letting the Germans and the Japanese get away without paying a reasonable share of their own defense, thus increasing the total cost to us, but that doesn't change my main point: there is nothing that I can do in the marketplace with my money that will do as much to help create the conditions of a safe and stable world as what the federal government can do if it spends some of that money for me.

And I feel the same way about area after area in the federal budget. Although it is not supported by the income tax—but rather by special contributions—I like the idea that I live in a country that has a contributory social insurance system that provides dependable and inflation-proof benefits to retired elderly people, the totally disabled, surviving spouses, and motherless and fatherless children. I like the fact that we have a Medicare program that sees that older people and totally disabled people (and their sons and daughters) are not made bankrupt by serious illness. I like the "entitlement programs" that are supported by income taxes, too—veterans' benefits, the federal government's contribution to the unemployed, to poor women and their children, food stamps for the hungry, medical care for the poor, and so on. I like it that these programs are "uncontrollable"— that they are a commitment in law that people can count on.

I want to buy more, and not only in these areas of very large expenditures, defense and "entitlement programs." But how can I as an individual help to protect the food and drug supply through expenditures in the private market? How can I buy the new knowledge to reduce disease and promote health? How can I buy in a way that prevents water pollution and promotes clean air? I like the Forest Service, the Park Service and hundreds of other services I get for my federal tax dollar. I want to buy more of these public goods. In my opinion, they do much more toward creating the kind of world I want to live in than anything further I can buy in the private marketplace.

Now, all was not sweetness and light as I made out my tax return. I wish the IRS would spend more money to catch the cheaters. I feel about them as I do about the shoplifters who run up retail prices. And I am annoyed at waste, inefficiency, and dishonesty that run up the cost of either public or private goods. I guess I am even more annoyed when it is a public agency that is at fault. If some of the people in the General Services Administration, say, stole public money, I would hold them to a stricter accounting than those private entrepreneurs caught bilking the public. Public service should have the highest standards, and they are usually observed. All in all, I'm greatly pleased that less than two cents of each dollar contributed to the Social Security program is spent on administration, with 98 cents-plus going out in benefits. That's what I call getting my money's worth!

There was one matter above all that I found irritating on April 15: the notion I kept running into in casual conversations that "they," the government, were taking away "my" money for "their" purposes. It has always seemed to me that, almost exclusively in the history of the world, the U.S. government is not "they" but "us," and it has always seemed to me fatuous that whatever income one could manage to lay one's hands on was somehow to be thought of as entirely the result of one's own work. Obviously, the major part of our income derives from the collective capital that we have all inherited from the past. Our income comes not only from our own effort but also from the knowledge, skills, and technology that others have developed and, for example, the advantages we all derive from public health activities and the products of our educational system (it makes sense to print this paper only because someone else has taught children to read).

And we not only stand on the shoulders of all the generations before us when we earn our living, but are also dependent on the current contributions of others in a collective, interdependent economic enterprise. It seems to me, therefore, that the government, expressing the collective will of the people, has the responsibility to take back for broad social purposes a significant share of what we like to think of as our own earnings.

Anyway, I hope that when the next budget is submitted and the focus is again on the value of public goods versus private goods, those who make the decisions will keep in mind that there are some of us out here who like what we buy from the government—and that goes for local and state governments, too.

13

SOME REFLECTIONS ON OUR SYSTEM OF SOCIAL INSURANCE

These remarks were prepared for a Princeton University symposium in June 1967 honoring J. Douglas Brown on the occasion of his retirement from Princeton's faculty. Doug Brown was one of the founders and long-term guiding lights of Social Security.

There was a time, not so long ago, when many of us were quite concerned that Social Security was not attracting as much interest from the academic and other research communities as we believed it deserved. That time has passed. It is encouraging, as well as important to the country, that during the past few years there has been increasing discussion about the Social Security system, welfare programs, private pensions, and other benefit arrangements, and related programs and proposals.

Let me begin by making a point that may be overlooked in our search for ways to improve Social Security. The point is that the system as it exists today is tremendously successful. It has changed the face of America in one short generation. Twenty-four million people who would otherwise be among our most economically vulnerable group—the retired aged, widows and orphans, and the totally disabled—have income they can count on as a matter of right. That this has been accomplished with the enthusiastic acceptance of the vast majority of Americans speaks well for the principles on which the program is founded. In broad outline these principles have

From William G. Bowen et al., eds., *The Princeton Symposium on the American System of Social Insurance* (New York: McGraw-Hill, 1968), pp. 241–49. Copyright © 1968 The McGraw Hill Companies. Reprinted by permission of The McGraw Hill Companies.

been widely accepted and have stood the test of practical operation for a generation.

Economic security for American workers has changed radically from just 30 years ago, when few had pension rights of any kind, let alone continuing income protection for their families in case of death or disability. Yet the methods used have been anything but radical. They are built on traditional values and concepts: self-help, mutual aid, insurance, incentives to work and save. To bring about great social change with small disruption, using traditional ideas and motivations, is the ideal approach to social reform. Social Security is our most successful experience in recent times with a planned and deliberate effort to bring about a major and permanent social reform.

The most succinct of recent statements summarizing the principles and purposes of Social Security is in the introduction to the 1965 Advisory Council's report:

> The Council strongly endorses the social insurance approach as the best way to provide, in a way that applies to all, that family income will continue when earnings stop or are greatly reduced because of retirement, total disability or death. It is a method of *preventing* destitution and poverty rather than relieving those conditions after they occur. And it is a method that operates through the individual efforts of the worker and his employer, and thus is in total harmony with general economic incentives to work and save. It can be made practically universal in application, and it is designed so as to work in ongoing partnership with voluntary insurance, individual savings, and private pension plans.
>
> Under the Social Security program the right to benefits grows out of work; the individual earns protection as he earns his living, and, up to the maximum amount of earnings covered under the program, the more he earns the greater is his protection. Since, unlike relief or assistance, Social Security benefits are paid without regard to the beneficiary's savings and resources, people can and do build upon their basic Social Security protection and they are rewarded for their planning and thrift by a higher standard of living than the benefits alone can provide.
>
> The fact that the program is contributory—that employees and self-employed workers make contributions in the form of earmarked Social Security taxes to help

finance the benefits—protects the rights and dignity of the recipient and at the same time helps to guard the program against unwarranted liberalization. The covered worker can expect, because he has made Social Security contributions out of his earnings during his working lifetime, that Social Security benefits will be paid in the spirit of an earned right, without undue restrictions and in a manner which safeguards his freedom of action and his privacy. Moreover, the tie between benefits and contributions fosters responsibility in financial planning; the worker knows that improved benefits mean higher contributions. In social insurance the decision on how to finance improvements is always an integral part of the decision on whether they are to be made.

Because of these characteristics of social insurance the Council believes that where it can be properly applied it is much to be preferred to the method of public assistance, with its test of individual need, and the Council therefore strongly favors the improvement of social insurance as a way of reducing the need for assistance. The Council recognizes the need for an adequate public assistance program, but it believes that assistance should play the role of a secondary and supplemental program designed to meet special needs and circumstances which cannot be dealt with satisfactorily by other means.

No matter how well designed and administered, assistance has serious inherent disadvantages in terms of human dignity and incentives to work and save. People view receipt of assistance as meaning a loss of self-support. In contrast, they view social insurance as an extension of self-support. People who had led productive lives and have supported themselves through their own efforts do not want to see their self-reliance end with their ability to work.

Moreover, applying for assistance is at best a negative experience. Eligibility for assistance depends upon the individual's asking the community for help and proving that he is without the resources and income to support himself and his family. On the other hand, under social insurance the individual proves, not that he lacks something, but that he has worked and contributed, and has thus earned a right to a benefit.

Like the United States Constitution, these fundamental principles allow for much leeway in interpretation and application. But they *are* fundamental; they appeal strongly to workers everywhere. People like to earn what they get and they like to have other people earn what *they* get. The relationship to work explains much of the great strength of contributory social insurance.

I do not believe at all, as some have evidently come to believe, that the difference between people's attitudes toward an income-determined or needs test program and social insurance is primarily a matter of "style of administration." I believe we should do everything we can to make the needs test less onerous and to make an assistance or income-determined program as considerate of individual self-respect as possible. But it is not in the nature of people brought up to work for a living to feel as comfortable about receiving money payments because they can prove that they otherwise lack enough to live on as they do when they get the money payments in return for work and contributions.

Although in Europe social insurance started out as a program for low-income people, in the United States from the very beginning it has applied to those who work without regard to the amount of their earnings. Our Social Security system is therefore not primarily a poor man's system, but instead is of great importance to people at all income levels including the poor and middle-income people, and is important even to those with more than average income. The fact that this is increasingly true has been brought home to me very clearly by the reaction that I now get in talking to audiences of businessmen and executives, as compared with the reaction from such groups in the 1940s. In those days the questioning made clear that the audience was interested in the program solely from the standpoint of social policy; their questions related in a very impersonal way to the nature of the institution and what it might do for others. Today, a high proportion of questions for such a group show clearly that they are interested in what the system will do for them as individuals—how much will they have to pay, what will they get—and all have a question about some friend or acquaintance of theirs who had this or that sort of situation.

Social Security is an important system for the supervisor, the executive, the farm owner, the businessman, the skilled worker, the unskilled. But it is also a system for the very low-income person. It just is not true, as has sometimes been implied, that the program leaves him out or treats him badly. In fact, in relation to contributions paid, the system does the most for the lowest paid.

Social Security has been our most effective weapon in the war on poverty to date. It has made the difference between poverty and non-poverty for more people than all other programs combined. On the basis of the poverty index developed by the Social Security Administration, a person aged 65 or older living alone now needs at least $1,565 a year in the city and an aged couple in the city needs $1,970 a year to remain above the poverty level. Even after the increase in benefits resulting from the 1967 amendments, there are still about 5.4 million aged beneficiaries who are living on incomes below the standard; another 6.7 million older people, however, are kept out of poverty because they are getting Social Security benefits. Only 4 million aged beneficiaries have other income sufficient to keep them above the poverty level without Social Security benefits. For a high proportion of this group, the source of income that makes the difference is continuing earnings either of the beneficiary or a younger wife—income which will, of course, not continue throughout their lifetime, and so these people, too, in considerable part will in turn look to Social Security benefits to keep them out of poverty.

We have, then, a system of universal usefulness, relied upon by people at various income levels, but because of the nature of the risks insured against, a very high proportion of the people drawing benefits from the program would be below the poverty line in the absence of these benefits.

The Social Security program has always given special consideration to low-wage earners by providing a weighted benefit formula. The theory has been that although the benefit should be essentially wage-related, paying higher benefits to those who earn more and pay more, nevertheless the replacement of earnings should be on a higher percentage basis for low earners than for middle and high earners. It has been thought that the program would not serve the interest of the low-wage earner unless it paid him benefits that were at least enough to make it unnecessary for him to turn to assistance for help.

One important idea in social insurance has been to make the modifications in structure that are necessary if the institution is to be useful for the low-paid worker. Strictly from the standpoint of a transfer system designed to cure poverty, one could well question whether low-paid wage earners should be asked to contribute toward their own protection and whether they might not be better off in a separate program that paid them income-determined benefits from general revenue. But there are values in the tradition of self-help and earned rights of social insurance that cannot be gained in any other way. In fact, one can generalize beyond this to say that to the extent possible the poor are served best when served by the same institutions as the rest of the community rather than separately. Our interest, as individuals and as a people, in institutions that we all have a personal stake in, seems to hold up better than our interest in institutions that are designed to help other people. We want the institutions that serve all of us to be good all the time; our interest in institutions specially designed for the poor tends to be sporadic and occasional.

Some say that this is wrong—that we should have a social insurance program that gives no special advantages to low-income people, and that we should treat their special problems in a separate program supported by general revenues. Others say that the only point of the social insurance program is what it can do for the poor and that it should be entirely redesigned in their interests. I would agree that to a considerable extent we can and should combine the two goals in a single program of income insurance. I believe that to the extent feasible we should plan to use our growing social insurance machinery to prevent poverty among low-income people—including special adaptations as necessary—while keeping the system useful for and acceptable to the community as a whole. This involves compromise in benefit structure. We have here one of the two basic theoretical problems on the benefit side of the program. How far should we go with a weighted benefit formula or with a minimum benefit within the contributory social insurance system? How much of the job of providing a minimum income guarantee to all is compatible with the social insurance method?

The fundamental idea of social insurance—the partial replacement of work income which is lost or reduced as a result of defined causes—is an extremely powerful idea and can go a very long way in preventing poverty and economic insecurity. However, a program which undertook to provide a minimum income guarantee to every last person would at some point have to abandon the method of partial replacement to lost income from work. It is, of course, possible to combine two programs into one and to use two different methods in the same administrative structure. Perhaps the first point, though, is how far should we go with the concept of partial replacement of the loss of work income. At what point does a weighted benefit formula or a high minimum benefit endanger the fundamental values of a wage-related contributory system and risk the general support that such a system now has?

I don't have a precise answer to this question. I will point out, however, that we have a different problem in relation to each of three different groups.

We can easily provide for the steady worker who earns low wages over most of his lifetime through contributory social insurance without significant weakening of the basic idea. In fact, to a very large extent, we are doing this in a satisfactory way now. Under present law, following the 1967 amendments, the worker who has had average earnings equal to the current federal minimum wage will with his wife get benefits equal to about 71 percent of the minimum wage. Such benefits are in themselves more than sufficient to keep a couple above the defined poverty level. Even for steady workers who earn below these minimum levels over most of a lifetime, the social insurance approach can easily do an adequate job, although of course this requires some liberalization of present benefit levels.

It is not so easy to handle the problem, however, for people now retired or about to retire when a major part of their earnings were in jobs that were not covered under Social Security until the last 10 or 15 years. These people have low covered wages that result in minimum or near-minimum benefits because their main jobs were not covered under the program soon enough. People in the future who have earnings patterns like theirs will ordinarily get adequate benefits, but in this first generation of covered workers there are many who have very low benefits for this reason.

Then there remains the problem of the truly marginal worker, the in-and-outer, with only a slight connection with the labor force over a large part of his working life. Here the method of social insurance is not entirely applicable, if one is focusing on the extreme of the problem. The problem can be mitigated, however, and has been by special provisions in social insurance, such as dropping out years of low earnings or no earnings in figuring benefits (we already have a precedent of a five-year dropout). Perhaps some liberalization of the "disability freeze," which protects the benefit level during periods when an individual is unable to work because of disability, would also help in this area.

Undoubtedly, however, there is a point at which it is unwise to provide fully sufficient benefits through a contributory system for people who have been under the program very little. In the long run

I do not believe that this is a problem involving very many people, but to the extent that it exists it could be met either by adding a minimum benefit supported from general revenue and available to all in a given age group, or through improvements in the public assistance program. Incidentally, a good public assistance program, to which people can turn as a reasonably acceptable alternative to social insurance, can help to preserve the values and principles of the contributory program by making it unnecessary for social insurance to try to do the whole job. A negative income tax, which is one approach to a national assistance program, would have the same effect.

One temptation that we are faced with right now is that in this first generation of coverage under social insurance, there are so many of the poor among retired people in the second group—those whose jobs were only recently covered—that one is tempted to push up the minimum under contributory insurance so that it is reasonably adequate in itself. But to go too far in this direction is to risk the principle of the benefit-wage relationship to solve what, in major impact, is a relatively short-run problem. Thus we compromise correctly, I believe, when we try to arrive at a minimum for the short-term contributor that will do a lot of good now, but will not be so high as to endanger for the long run the important principle that essentially benefits grow out of work and contribution. [*Author's note*: For the reasons discussed, the regular minimum benefit of $122 was eliminated for those eligible after 1981, and a special minimum for those with at least 10 years of coverage was substituted. This minimum, which now applies to very few people, should be liberalized.]

The other basic issue on the benefit side is how much social insurance should do for middle-income and higher-paid people. To what extent is the federal system to be thought of not as guaranteeing a minimum level of living but as aimed at maintaining in retirement a reasonable relationship of income to the past earnings of workers at all levels?

There is now widespread acceptance that our arrangements for retirement should be made up of a universal federal system supplemented by private pensions. There are, however, a number of unresolved policy problems relating to specific aspects of this interrelationship of public and private plans. There is a growing concern that, after a period of rapid growth, the rate of supplemental private plans is slowing down, despite the fact that a large share of the labor force is not yet covered.

It probably is not true that we can count on most workers in the future having protection under both Social Security and private pension plans. Just about everybody will have protection under Social Security or the civil service system or railroad retirement. Today an estimated 18 percent of the elderly receive private pensions (either as annuitants or as their surviving spouses). But on the other hand, it seems unlikely that private pension supplements even by 1980 will be available to as many as a third of all older people over 65. [*Author's note:* In 1998, 25 percent of the elderly received private pensions, and 11 percent received government pensions other than Social Security.]

For most of those who will have combined private and public retirement incomes there will almost certainly be a reasonable relationship of benefits to previous earnings. There is less reason to be optimistic about the situation of the remainder of older citizens. We need to give some careful thought to ways in which we can assure that the adequacy of post-retirement benefits will be sufficient for persons who do not have a private pension supplement so that the income of such people does not fall below socially acceptable standards.

In addition to concern about the limited coverage of supplemental pensions, the President's Committee on Corporate Pension Funds and Other Private Retirement and Welfare Programs pointed out in 1965 that many of the covered persons may not ultimately enjoy the benefits they anticipate. The committee solidly endorsed the further development of private pensions, as do I, but indicated that, unless vesting of pension rights could be improved, funding provisions strengthened, better controls established over those exercising fiduciary controls, and certain other improvements implemented, we might find the ultimate results disappointing for millions of workers.

In considering the proper course of development for Social Security, it is important to consider what effect a given course of action or inaction will have on private pensions. How much of the total job do we want done by private plans and how much can they do? There is, in my opinion, a great need for more analyses comparing the social efficiency of the two approaches. Although it is clear that we will have both approaches in the future and that both are needed, it is important to ask whether we have obtained the right balance between the two or whether one set of arrangements should be encouraged to grow at the expense of the other.

Such analyses need to take account of similarities as well as differences. For example, questions are raised around the issue of supplying more than a minimum income guarantee in a compulsory Social Security system, but little recognition is given to the fact that private pension plans are by now not individual provisions for security but institutional arrangements enabling people to earn protection as they work, just as Social Security is, with little choice left to the worker as to whether he is to be covered or not.

As to the differences, given Social Security's ability to protect a worker's freedom to move from job to job, the security of payment, the ability of the system to adjust to rising price and wage levels, the ability to provide universal coverage, and other attributes pertinent to social efficiency, I am inclined to think that a proper mix between public and private systems calls for greater recognition that the public plan must in itself be adequate for at least the average worker, with private plans encouraged to supplement this broad base.

One of the most important issues in connection with the long-range financing of the Social Security program is whether, if benefits are to be raised substantially, we are willing to raise the contribution rate sufficiently, or whether some of the additional financing should come from general revenues.

There is of course some leeway for improvement in the future without a government contribution and without increasing the contribution rate. The base to which the rate is applied can be significantly increased, which would have the additional effect of making the program more effective for the somewhat-above-average worker. Moreover, I don't believe there is general realization of the extent to which the present financing would allow for increased benefits as wage levels rise. Because of the weighted benefit formula, if the maximum earnings base is increased from time to time, the contribution rates in present law will produce sufficient income to considerably more than keep benefits up to date with future increases in prices. Of course, it may well be that we will want to increase benefits substantially more than this. It is at this point that the issue of a government contribution will be seriously considered. A government contribution comes up in connection with both of the matters already discussed— that is, the role of the system in the war on poverty and the role of the system for average and above-average earners. If benefits at the lower wage levels are to be substantially higher than they are, most of the disadvantaged need more of a subsidy. And those at average and above-average earnings levels don't want too much of the subsidy to come from payroll contributions that would otherwise be available for them.

There are other as yet unresolved problems. For example, we are developing a problem of low benefits under Social Security arising out of the provisions for actuarial reduction of benefits when people retire before age 65. More than half of all people now retiring do so before age 65 and therefore get reduced benefits. The amounts are very substantially below what they would get if they waited until they could receive their benefits in full. The evidence indicates that generally they claim benefits early because they cannot any longer secure employment or are in ill health and unable to continue at their regular occupation, and they thus have little real choice.

In the long run, if this situation is allowed to continue, it might actually reverse the long-range trend of reduction in the old-age assistance rolls. On the average, the longer a person is in retirement, the more likely he is to have used up whatever resources he took with him into retirement, and the more he becomes wholly dependent on his Social Security income. Thus, those people taking low early benefits may later on have to apply in increasing numbers for assistance. This is a serious problem. It may require some modification of the actuarial reduction provisions, or perhaps some liberalization in the disability program as it applies to older workers would be helpful.

Another issue involving the disability program is whether it should take on somewhat shorter term illness, say by reducing the waiting period for disability benefits from six to three months and dropping the requirement that the disability must be expected to last for at least 12 months.

Health insurance is, of course, just getting under way. Is extension of the program to cover prescription drugs feasible and desirable? We have recommended the inclusion of the disabled Social Security beneficiary. Should other Social Security beneficiaries—surviving spouses and children—be included later on? What can be done about incentives for efficiency in the delivery of quality service by institutions? What can be done about helping to control the increasing cost of medical and hospital care?

It seems likely that the basic protections provided by the Social Security system will continue to be adjusted to economic changes in the future as they have been in the past. We have not as yet, however, resolved the important question of whether or not the adjustment process is to be entirely on an ad hoc basis as in the past, or whether the adjustments should in part be made automatic by relating benefits not to a career average but to, say, a high five or ten years, or perhaps even by introducing automatic increases in benefits after people come on the rolls.

These are all important issues, in large part, internal to the Social Security program. There are many others of perhaps lesser importance.

As over the next several years we consider the next steps to be taken to improve the economic security of the American people, I believe that social insurance will be called upon to do an even bigger job than it is doing today. I believe this is true because there is a great advantage in building on a functioning system of universal application based upon principles that have proven popular and enduring. At the same time, I believe we will have to ask ourselves what is appropriate for social insurance and what is not. The idea of insuring against the loss of work income has wide application in any attempt to improve our economic security arrangements—but the institution of social insurance should not be expected to cure the problem of income deficiency singlehanded, nor should its failure to do everything make us value less the great contribution to security that this institution can appropriately make. In my judgment, solutions to the many-sided problem of income deficiency will be found not in a single program but in a variety of programs, both public and private.

14

MAJORITY RECOMMENDATIONS
OF THE GREENSPAN COMMISSION

*The most recent major amendments to Social Security were
enacted in 1983. They were based on the recommendations of
the bipartisan National Commission on Social Security, chaired
by Alan Greenspan. I was the chief negotiator for the five members of the commission appointed by Democrats and was the
chief architect of the proposals that won majority support in the
commission and in Congress. The reasoning behind these
amendments is of current importance as further changes are
considered.*

We have arrived at a number of consensus recommendations which,
taken as a group of interrelated recommendations, I fully support.
The recommendations are endorsed by all five of the commission
members who were appointed by Democrats[1] and seven of the ten
appointed by Republicans.[2] As you know, the proposals are backed by
the president, the Speaker of the House and the Majority Leaders of
both the House and the Senate, among many others.

There is no member of the commission who is pleased with each of
the recommendations taken separately. No one would have come up
with exactly these recommendations if he or she had been free to design
the proposals alone. They represent a compromise within the commission and between the commission members and the administration,
but, taken together, they are, in my opinion, as good a compromise as
could be designed to get the widespread legislative support and the sig-
nature of the president that are necessary to solve Social Security's

From testimony before the Senate Finance Committee, February 15, 1983, in a joint
appearance with Chairman Greenspan.

financial problems. In the words of the *Washington Post*, "It is as close to absolute fairness as any Social Security revision can ever be."

Given the fact that between now and 1990, Social Security income is estimated to fall about 5 to 10 percent short of expenditures, it is necessary during this period to increase income or reduce expenditures. To get agreement within the commission and to design a group of recommendations that could win wide support, it was clearly necessary to do both—to have some reduction in expenditures and some increase in income. This the plan achieves in a fair and balanced way. All share in the sacrifice necessary to restore full financial health to Social Security—current beneficiaries, contributing workers, employers, and the general public—but none are asked to bear a large additional burden. The changes proposed are modest and reasonable.

Taken together, the consensus recommendations eliminate the shortfall between now and 1990, and according to the more pessimistic of the intermediate estimates (II-B) of the trustees, the trust funds will return to fully satisfactory levels in the 1990s. The agreed-upon recommendations also bring the long-term deficit of the program within the range of what has traditionally been considered close actuarial balance, that is, plus or minus 5 percent of expenditures over the 75 years for which the estimates are made. That is, the consensus recommendations reduce the official 1.8 percent of payroll deficit (1982 II-B estimate) to 0.58 percent of payroll, which is 4.5 percent of what the estimated expenditures over the next 75 years would be after the adoption of the commission's recommendations.

The consensus was, however, that we would go further and propose ways of reducing the 0.58 percent of payroll deficit to approximately zero. We could not agree on how best to eliminate this final 0.58 percent, but the five members who were appointed by Democrats have proposed scheduling an increase in the contribution rate of a little less than one-half of one percent of earnings in year 2010, with the employee share to be offset by a refundable tax credit.

It now appears that the 1983 Trustees' Report will show a slight increase in the remaining deficit, perhaps 0.70 percent as compared to 0.58, and the Congress will need to decide whether it is desirable as part of strengthening public confidence in the long-run financing of the program to cover this additional small deficit. Clearly, treating 75-year estimates as if they could be made with such a high degree of exactness is unrealistic, but there may be some public relations advantage in having the official estimates show no deficit at all. It does not seem to me of great importance either way.

[*Author's note:* Congress added a provision to the commission's recommendations that, beginning in the year 2000, gradually raises the age of first eligibility for full benefits from 65 to 67. This was intended to bring the program into 75-year balance. By the early 1990s, however, changes in the way the long-term estimates are made, coupled with more conservative economic assumptions, were largely responsible for the trustees' forecasting a new long-range deficit, estimated in their 2000 Report to be 1.89 percent of payroll. The attached appendix to the report of the 1994–96 Advisory Council explains how this new long-range deficit arose. It is important to note that the commonly held view—that it was caused by the declining ratio of workers to retirees—is incorrect: the ratio had been fully taken into account. The new forecast of a deficit was entirely the result of other factors, including changed assumptions about wage growth and the cost of disability benefits.]

The commission also agreed on three steps that would strengthen the financing of the system should actual economic performance fall outside the range of the rather pessimistic assumptions that the commission used. First, the commission agreed that authority for Old-Age, Survivors, and Disability Insurance (OASDI) to borrow from the Hospital Insurance (HI) fund should be continued as a fail-safe procedure through 1987. Second, the commission agreed on a "stabilizing provision" to the effect that beginning in 1988, a drop in trust fund assets to unacceptable levels would trigger a temporary change in the indexing procedure. Third, the commission agreed that the law should contain a provision that would ensure timely payment of benefits if unexpectedly adverse conditions occurred with little advance notice. The commission did not agree on specifics of this ultimate fail-safe, but the five members who were appointed by Democrats recommended that the law be amended to allow short-term borrowing from the general fund at interest in the unlikely event that the other measures recommended prove insufficient in some emergency situation.

There has been some suggestion that it might be desirable to strengthen the short-run financing of the program even further. For example, a group of private insurance actuaries appearing before the Social Security Subcommittee on Ways and Means testified that under the commission plan the estimated assets in the funds at the beginning of some years seemed low to them in relation to the next year's estimated outgo. This perception of a possible cash flow problem in some years arises because of the practice of crediting Social Security taxes to the trust funds gradually over the course of a month, while Social Security checks are, of course, charged against the funds at the beginning of the month when issued.

If in the future Social Security receives credit at the beginning of the month for taxes collected during the month—as has been proposed—there would be a considerable difference in the ratio of trust fund assets to the outgo in a subsequent period, since on average, collections are quite close to outgo. Under the conservative II-B assumption for the 1983 Trustees' Report, the commission's plan, given this new procedure, would produce trust fund ratios of 20 percent or more through 1988, rising to 33 percent in 1989 and increasing rapidly thereafter. These ratios are clearly ample. With the three changes described above—inter-fund borrowing, the introduction of a stabilization procedure, and authority to borrow from general revenue—the commission's proposals will provide for the full and timely payment of benefits under even much more unfavorable economic conditions than those assumed in the new II-B estimates.

All in all, the commission's proposals solve the short-term and most of the long-term financing problems of OASDI.

DEFINING SHORT-TERM AND LONG-TERM FINANCING GOALS

The commission decided early in its deliberations not to deal with the Medicare program. The current statutory advisory council on Social Security will be concerned exclusively with making recommendations about that program. We did not feel that we could deal adequately with both HI financing and the financing of OASDI in the time available. Moreover, the considerations involved in HI financing are quite different from those involved in the cash benefit program. The increasing costs of HI under Medicare are caused by the same factors in medical economics that are driving up the cost of private insurance, and many of us felt that in this program the proper emphasis was not merely to increase the funds or reduce benefits to conform to actuarial projections, but rather to consider the extent to which the rate of increase in the cost of providing services can be controlled. The entire report of the commission and its recommendations, therefore, relate to OASDI, except for the recommendation to extend the inter-fund borrowing provision that expired in 1982.

SHORT-TERM

Under present law, there is a shortfall in expected income for OASDI as compared to expected expenditures between now and 1990. The gap is not large relative to the size of the program—5 to 10 percent—but it is real and must be addressed. The boundaries of the shortfall would appear to be between $75 billion and $200 billion, depending upon the economic assumptions used.

The members of the commission have agreed that since trust fund balances for OASDI are now at dangerously low levels, it is prudent to set short-term goals on the basis of quite pessimistic economic assumptions. We are not necessarily agreed that there is a shortfall between income and expenditures in the range of $150 billion to $200 billion as has been publicized, but we are convinced that it could be this high under adverse economic conditions. Should the economy perform better than was assumed in setting these target figures, the resulting more rapid buildup in trust fund balances would be desirable, in any event.

MID-TERM

The shortfall between now and 1990 is followed by a period of 20 to 25 years when OASDI, even under present law, will have substantial annual surpluses of income over outgo, with the trust funds building up at a rapid rate. Although it is possible to construct economic projections where this buildup would not occur under present law, the commission's recommendations—including a shift to indexing by wages or prices, whichever is the lower, should the trust funds drop below 20 percent of the next year's outgo—would go a long way toward guaranteeing that the expected buildup in the 1990s and the early part of the next century takes place.

Basically, the reason for the favorable period from roughly 1990 to 2015 is demographic. Birthrates were low in the Great Depression years, with the consequence that the increase in the number of older people which we have been experiencing will slow down. In addition, the baby-boom generation born after World War II will be swelling the labor force so that the ratio of workers to beneficiaries is expected to stay about the same as it is today—three workers for each beneficiary—for at least the next 30 years. Under these circumstances, increases in productivity reduce the cost of Social Security measured as a percent of payroll or gross national product. At the same time, the present law already provides for an increase in the contribution rate beginning in 1990, with the result that very large annual excesses of income over outgo are expected. In the one year, 1991, the excess is expected to be over $20 billion, and during this middle period the excess will grow year by year.

LONG-TERM

The commission also agreed that the estimated long-range deficit of 1.8 percent of payroll (1982 II-B estimate) should be reduced to approximately zero. We differed among ourselves as to why we took this position. Personally, I have considerable skepticism about our ability to know, within very wide limits, what the demographic, economic, and social situation of the United States will be 50 to 75 years from now, and the projected deficit occurs almost entirely in that far-off period. However, as a matter of restoring confidence in the financing of the program, it seemed best to all of us to design a plan that would result in the trustees saying officially that the program was in actuarial balance in both the short and long run.

The consensus agreement alone comes very close to this goal, providing for a reduction of 1.22 percentage points in the 1.8 percent deficit. The five members of the commission who were appointed by Democrats proposed, in addition, that the law be amended to provide a contribution rate increase of 0.46 percent of payroll in the year 2010 (refundable to the employee) as a way of eliminating the remaining 0.58 percent of the long-term deficit. Such an increase may not actually be needed and, of course, as 2010 approaches such an increase would not be allowed to go into effect unless estimates then being made showed that it was desirable. Moreover, by that time there might be support for some other way of financing part of the Social Security program. Yet it is of some importance to put the increase in the law now and thus show the intent of Congress to meet the full cost of the program over the entire 75 years for which the estimates are made. The proposal made by other members of the commission to meet this remaining 0.58 percent deficit would be to raise the age of first eligibility for full benefits to 66 by 2015, and then after that date have the age rise automatically in accordance with increases in longevity, ultimately reaching 68 in about 2055 under the assumptions in the 1982 Trustees' Report.

We have agreed on the specifics of so much within the commission—a plan to meet the short-run problem, and a plan to meet by far the largest part of the estimated long-run deficit—that I hesitate to spend much time on this difference of opinion about two approaches to a problem which may very well not even exist. The five members of the commission who were appointed by Democrats have included a supplementary statement in the commission report that tells why we are against raising the age of eligibility for full benefits. Suffice it to say here that, aside from whether or not it is desirable to raise the age of first eligibility for full benefits, it seems to me unwise to index additional Social Security provisions. Under the indexing proposal, no one would know ahead of time at what age full benefits would be available. Private pension planning and private savings for retirement would be made more difficult. Surely some Social Security questions can be left to the determination of future Congresses.

THE CONSENSUS AGREEMENT

The major provisions affecting the financing of the program are as follows.

Rescheduling the Social Security tax rate. Under present law, the OASDI tax rate rises from the 5.4 percent of earnings now being charged to 5.7 in 1985 and to 6.2 in 1990. Under the agreed-upon plan, workers would not have to pay any more than under present law until 1988, and then there would be a higher rate for two years, an increase of 0.36 percentage points in 1988 and 1989, with a return to the present schedule in 1990. (The OASDI trust funds would get additional income from moving the rate to 1984, but the increased Social Security tax for workers would be exactly offset in that year by a refundable tax credit.) Employers, who can count the Social Security tax as a business expense, would be charged 0.3 percentage points more than present law in 1984 and, as is the case with employees, 0.36 percentage points more in 1988 and 1989.

Although this rescheduling of tax rates contributes $40 billion to the short-term goal of $150 billion to $200 billion, the increase for individuals is relatively slight—nothing until 1988 and then, for a $20,000 earner, for example, $1.38 per week for two years.

Putting the Social Security tax for the self-employed on a basis comparable to other covered workers. When the self-employed were first brought under Social Security, the rate for them was established at one and a half times the employee rate, and although it has varied somewhat from that basic rate from time to time, it is approximately at that level today and under present law would soon be exactly one and a half times the employee rate again. The self-employed, of course, get the same protection as everyone else, but for others the rate paid is the employee rate plus a matching amount by the employer. Because the self-employed pay less, everyone else under the system pays somewhat more. This isn't fair.

The proposal is to remedy this inequity by charging the self-employed two times the employee rate and to treat one-half of it as the employer's contribution is treated—allowing the self-employed to deduct one-half of their total contribution as a business expense. This proposal will increase income to the Social Security system between now and 1990 by $18 billion, but $12 billion will be offset in the general budget because of the business deduction. This change also reduces the long-term, 75-year average estimated deficit by 0.19 percent of payroll. One way of easing the transition to this new tax basis for the self-employed would be to allow them a refundable tax credit in 1984 for the increase in the employee rate, 0.3 percent of earnings. The commission's report does not address this question, but such treatment would be consistent with the recommendation to treat half of the self-employed payment as an employer contribution and half as an employee contribution.

Crediting the trust funds for past military service credits and unnegotiated checks. Employers and employees have to pay for Social Security benefit credits when they are earned, but in the case of certain military service credits that are paid for by the federal government, the amounts due are not paid to Social Security until the benefits are paid. Putting payment for military service credits on a basis more comparable to other benefit credits and recrediting to the trust funds outstanding checks which have gone uncashed for a considerable period of time would mean that the OASDI trust funds would receive a lump sum payment of $20 billion in 1983.

The military have been covered under Social Security for many years, but they pay contributions only on the cash paid to them. The government pays the cost of the benefit credits made in lieu of allowances for room and board. However, under present law, the government does not make payment currently (but only when benefits are paid) for these credits. Moreover, prior to 1957 free credits of $160 per month were granted for service in the armed forces and these credits, too, are paid only when benefits are paid, and the cost is amortized over a long period of time. The proposal is to pay up for the back amounts owed by the government in a lump sum, and then in the future to pay currently the equivalent of employer and employee contributions on the wage credits in lieu of allowances.

Mandatory coverage of all nonprofit employees and federal employees newly hired after 1983. Social Security is a system with a national purpose through which just about everyone who works contributes toward the payment of benefits to make up for income lost because of retirement in old age, total disability, or the death of a wage earner in the family. It is anomalous that federal employees do not take part in this national effort.

The commission recommends mandatory coverage of newly hired employees and establishment within the civil service retirement system of a special supplementary plan for these newly hired employees, independent and completely separate from Social Security in every way, just as private pension plans are supplementary to Social Security and separate from it. The supplementary plan should be designed so that when combined with Social Security it will supply, overall, as good protection as the present civil service system does alone. Current civilian employees of the federal government (the military are already covered under Social Security) would continue to be covered by the present civil service retirement system for their employment by the federal government, but would not be under Social Security.

For many new federal employees, this arrangement of Social Security plus a supplementary plan would undoubtedly be better than the present civil service plan alone. Social Security with its weighted benefit formula is generally more favorable to low-paid employees than the civil service system, and frequently Social Security is better for those who move in and out of federal employment. Moreover, full survivorship and disability protection is more quickly achieved under Social Security.

Covering those nonprofit employees not now covered (15 percent) and newly hired federal employees will add $20 billion in income to the Social Security system between now and 1990. Moreover it will reduce the long-range deficit in Social Security by 0.3 percent of payroll. This is true because today, while about 80 percent of federal annuitants age 62 and over are also eligible for Social Security when they reach 65, they will have paid into Social Security for relatively short periods and will receive benefits that are excessive in relation to the contributions that they have made. For this reason, everyone else in the country is paying somewhat higher Social Security contribution rates because federal employees are not covered.

One would think that present federal retirees and present federal employees would not have much standing in making a case against the coverage of federal employees who have not yet been hired, but they have been arguing that (1) new federal employees will be asked to "bail out" the Social Security system to their own disadvantage, and (2) present retirees and present employees will be hurt because the new employees will not be paying into the civil service retirement system or not paying in as much as they otherwise would. Both of these arguments are fallacious. Under the plan, new employees will be asked to do just what all other employees in the country are asked to do: pay into Social Security throughout their working careers in return for Social Security protection. Then, in addition, they will share with about half of the private labor force the additional protection of an independent, supplementary plan. Far from "bailing out" Social Security, this arrangement will end the unfair situation where others have to pay more for Social Security because federal employees get Social Security benefits at bargain rates from working in Social Security covered employment for short periods of time. Secondly, it just is not true that the present civil service retirement system will be less well financed because of the proposal. At the present time, the protection furnished by the civil service retirement system is worth about 40 percent of payroll. Employees are paying only 7 percent of their earnings toward this protection. Under present law, the benefits of present workers will be paid for mostly from general revenues, not the contributions of the newly hired.

The contribution that the newly hired employees would make toward a specially designed benefit plan within the civil service system would mingle with all other contributions to that system, which today is not a single plan and will not be in the future. Today the system covers, with special provisions, members of Congress and congressional employees, air controllers, etc., as well as the bulk of executive branch employees. The lower contributions to be paid by new employees (because, of course, the supplementary plan on top of Social Security will be cheaper than the design of the present plan for the presently employed) will be balanced by the fact that the newly designed plan will have lower long-term costs and create less liability for the civil service retirement system. The system as a whole will not be injured.

There is apparently widespread misunderstanding among federal employees about these facts, some even believing that the civil service retirement system is adequately financed by a combination of the 7 percent contributions that they pay and matching contributions from their agency. It is important that these misunderstandings be corrected.

Delaying the cost-of-living adjustment (COLA) for six months so that in the future any automatic increases will be made for the month of December rather than for June as in present law. The five members of the commission who were appointed by Democrats agreed to this change with great reluctance. We did so because it was essential to an agreement which we believe, overall, is in the best interest of present beneficiaries and contributors. It is worth some sacrifice on the part of all to assure both the short- and long-range financing of the system and remove the fear of drastic cuts that has haunted beneficiaries and contributors for the last two years. It is worth some sacrifice on the part of all to get this done promptly and without the bitter fight that might well have followed the failure of the commission to reach agreement.

The agreement does not include any other reductions in present or future benefits—no reduction in replacement rates or cuts disguised as increases in the age at which full benefits are first paid, although one-half the benefit of the 10 percent of beneficiaries with the highest incomes would be subject to income tax. It looks now as if the automatic increase in benefits due to the cost-of-living adjustment payable for this June under present law will be below 4 percent—perhaps an increase for the average retired beneficiary from the current monthly benefit of about $420 to a new rate of about $435.

Under the plan, the new rate of $435 for the average retired beneficiary would be delayed until the payment for the month of December. Moving the cost-of-living adjustment to the calendar year basis will reduce expenditures about $40 billion between now and 1990 and reduce the long-range deficit by 0.27 percentage points.

It is possible that the increases in the Consumer Price Index (CPI) from the first quarter of 1982 to the first quarter of 1983 might be slightly less than 3 percent so that under present law no cost-of-living adjustment would be made in 1983. There would be widespread mis-understanding if at the same time that the COLA is moved to a calendar year basis there is no increase at all for 18 months. Because of this possibility, I believe it would be desirable to provide for the COLA for next December without regard to the 3 percent trigger in present law.

Under the agreement, those Social Security beneficiaries who also get Supplemental Security Income (SSI) because their benefits and other income are too low to meet minimum standards of need will have their SSI benefits raised by $30 a month. In the future, $50 of Social Security benefits would not be taken into account in determining need under the SSI program instead of $20 as at present. The agreement did not cover the question of whether the cost-of-living adjustment for the SSI program should be advanced six months from present law, and the administration has now proposed this as part of its new budget proposal. I hope that the Congress will not agree to postponing the July cost-of-living adjustment for SSI recipients. By definition, these people need all the purchasing power they have and more. Two million of them—30 percent of the elderly SSI recipients and two-thirds of the disabled recipients—are not Social Security beneficiaries and will not gain from the increase in the disregard from $20 to $50. Indeed few have anything but SSI.

I recognize that it is desirable in the future to keep the timing of the COLA for both programs the same. Otherwise what the dual beneficiaries gain from an earlier SSI increase, they may lose from the OASDI increase later, as it is offset dollar for dollar against the means-tested SSI program. Keeping the timing of the COLAs together is as readily accomplished by an SSI adjustment in July and again in January as it is by skipping the July increase. This is what I would recommend.

Income taxation of one-half of Social Security benefits of higher-income beneficiaries. Social Security benefits are not now subject to income taxation simply because in the early days of the program the Treasury ruled—I believe erroneously—that Social Security benefits are a gratuity. There is no legislative history. On the basis of this ruling, Social Security payments have been treated differently than other retirement income. The rule generally for retirement income is that it is subject to income taxation once the recipient has recovered what he has paid toward the retirement benefit, exclusive of interest. Thus, employer-paid-for pensions are subject to income taxation immediately and in full, and contributory plans such as federal civil service are taxed after the benefits exceed the employee's own contribution.

The special treatment of Social Security benefits hardly seems justified for higher-income beneficiaries. Thus the commission proposes that for single filing units with $20,000 or more in non–Social Security income and for those filing as couples with $25,000 or more (10 percent of beneficiaries), one-half the Social Security benefit be included in gross income for income tax purposes. The limitation to one-half rests on the rationale that although one-half the benefit can be thought of as being derived from the employee contribution on which a tax has been paid during one's working life, the other half, derived from the employer contribution, has not been taxed. It has not been taxable income for the employee and is treated as a business deduction by the employer.

The commission recognized that this proposal needs refinement to eliminate triggering the taxation of a sizable amount of Social Security income by having other income just barely over the thresholds recommended. One possible way of meeting this problem would be to include in taxable income $1 of Social Security benefits for each $2 of non–Social Security income above the thresholds, but the committee will undoubtedly want to study other possibilities. This proposal results in additional income to the system of $30 billion between now and 1990 and reduces the long-range deficit by 0.6 percent of payroll.

Measures to protect the future financial stability of the program. The short-term financing problem in Social Security is entirely due to recent poor economic performance. The present program is very sensitive to changing economic conditions, particularly the relationship of wages and prices and the amount of unemployment. Income varies according to the level of payrolls while benefits rise with increases in the Consumer Price Index. Usually wages rise faster than prices, and the resulting higher payrolls finance the more slowly rising cost-of-living increases. This is how the pay-as-you-go financing of the system ordinarily works. In several recent years, however, prices rose faster than wages, causing larger pay-out and lower income than expected. In addition, high unemployment has further reduced payrolls.

As part of the agreed-upon package, the commission proposes the adoption of an economic "stabilizer," which would go into effect in

1988 when reserve ratios are expected to have improved under these proposals. If ever again the OASDI reserves drop below 20 percent of the next year's outgo, wages or prices, whichever is the lower, would be paid until the 20 percent fund ratio was restored. When the fund ratio reached 32 percent, additional benefits would be paid to make up for any payments that were less than the increases called for by the price adjustment. The payback would be limited to amounts that would maintain a 32 percent fund ratio.

In addition to this modification of indexing designed to reduce the sensitivity of the program to economic factors, the consensus agreement includes a recommendation to extend the authority of the OASDI trust funds to borrow from hospital insurance funds from the effective date of the amendments until the "stabilizer" goes into effect. It is not expected that either of these devices will be needed, but it is important to have insurance against the possibility of poorer economic performance than is assumed in the projections underlying the basic recommendations.

The commission has gone further and recommended that beyond the stabilizer and inter-fund borrowing, there should be an ultimate fail-safe arrangement to tide the program over some completely unexpected short-term development. We were unable to agree on the exact nature of such a provision but, as indicated earlier, the five members of the commission appointed by Democrats recommend that authority be granted to the program, under such limited circumstances, to borrow from general revenues at interest, or if it is considered preferable to issue its own bonds, a device which would show that the debt was clearly a Social Security obligation.

Other proposals that either have no financial effect or a relatively small financial effect. The commission has made several other proposals, many unanimously, which are important, even though most do not contribute significantly to the solving of the financial difficulty. These recommendations include prohibiting the withdrawal of state and local government employees, the great majority of whom are now covered under Social Security through voluntary agreements. (This proposal may have a significant financial effect.) Other recommendations include the elimination of windfall benefits for persons with pensions from noncovered employment, several proposals for providing greater equity under the program for certain groups of beneficiaries (primarily women), the gradual increase from 3 percent to 8 percent (after 1990) for each year up to age 70 in which the individual postpones taking benefits, the reallocation of the amount of the Social Security tax now going to the OASI and the DI trust funds, the elimination of opting out of part of Social Security coverage through the use of a salary reduction plan (section 401(k) of the Internal Revenue Code), new investment procedures for the trust funds which will make clear that the investments are being properly handled, and the addition of two public members to the Board of Trustees. I support all of these proposals and their rationale is adequately developed in the report itself. The short-range and long-range cost effects of the commission's proposals are summarized in Table 14.1 (see page 168).

The removal of Social Security from the unified budget and the establishment of the Social Security Administration as an independent agency under a bipartisan board. Although the majority of the commission favored taking the Social Security program out of the unified budget and treating its financing entirely separately, as was the case prior to fiscal year 1969, the division of opinion was fairly close. I agree with the majority. Only by such a separation can it be made unmistakably clear that Social Security decisions are being made for reasons internal to this separately financed program and not for the purpose of making a unified budget look better. Since Social Security funds can be used only for Social Security benefits and to pay for the cost of administration, I believe that separation is also better accounting practice.

It is easily understandable, however, that many are reluctant to make this change just when the adoption of the commission's recommendations—which have been made entirely because of the internal needs of the Social Security system—would, as a by-product, reduce the unified budget deficit.

In any event, the administration has agreed that the OASDI program will be presented in the budget from now on as a separate budget function rather than being included with other income programs. I believe this is an important step in the right direction, and even though this change could not be implemented in time for the budget just submitted, it is my understanding that during the current budget process OASDI will not be placed in competition with other programs.

There was more general agreement in the commission on setting up Social Security as an independent agency, although some members felt that more study was required before action was taken. I believe it should be done now. I believe that setting up Social Security as an

TABLE 14.1. SHORT-RANGE AND LONG-RANGE COST ANALYSIS OF OASDI PROPOSALS AS OF 1983

PROPOSAL	SHORT-TERM SAVINGS, 1983–89 (BILLIONS)	LONG-RANGE SAVINGS (PERCENT OF PAYROLL)
Cover nonprofit and new federal employees[a]	+$20	+0.30%
Prohibit withdrawal of state and local government employees	+3	—
Tax benefits of higher-income persons	+30	+0.60
Shift COLAs to calendar-year basis	+40	+0.27
Eliminate windfall benefits for persons with pensions from noncovered employment	+0.2	+0.01
Continue benefits on remarriage for disabled widow(er)s and for divorced widow(er)s	−0.1	−0.01
Index deferred widow(er)'s benefits based on wages (instead of CPI)	−0.2	−0.05
Permit divorced aged spouse to receive benefits when husband is eligible to receive benefits	−0.1	−0.01
Increase benefit rate for disabled widow(er)s aged 50–59 to 71.5% of primary benefit	−1	−0.01
Revise tax-rate schedule	+40	+0.02
Revise tax basis for self-employed	+18	+0.19
Reallocate OASDI tax rate between OASI and DI	—	—
Allow inter-fund borrowing from HI by OASDI	—	—
Credit the OASDI trust funds by a lump-sum payment for cost of gratuitous military service and past unnegotiated checks	+18	—
Base automatic benefit increases on lower of CPI or wage increases after 1987 if fund ratio is under 20%, with catch-up if fund ratio exceeds 32%	—	—
Increase delayed retirement credit from 3%/year to 8%, beginning in 1990 and reaching 8% in 2010	—	−0.10[b]
Additional long-range changes[c]	—	+0.58
TOTAL EFFECT	+168	+1.80[d]

[a] Includes effect of revised tax schedule.
[b] Assumes retirement patterns would be only slightly affected by this change. If significantly affected, the cost increase would be less; possibly even a small savings could result.
[c] As described in the text.
[d] Leaving a positive balance of 0.02 percent of payroll.

independent agency headed by a bipartisan board would improve the operation of the program and help restore faith in the program.

We need to make some institutional changes in the way Social Security is handled in order to assure people that the program will continue to operate as an independent insurance system, protected against the short-term policy swings of elected officials and political appointees. Under Social Security, workers are creating rights for their retirement which may not occur for 40 or more years down the road. They should feel secure that those rights will be respected. It is not enough to have the system operate as part of a cabinet department with a president appointing both the cabinet secretary and the commissioner of Social Security. Social Security should be handled in a way more in keeping with the obligations of the huge pension and group insurance plan that it is. I believe that the policy functions should be performed by a board of directors with staggered terms, appointed by the president and approved by the Senate, and that the board, in turn, should have the right to hire and fire the chief executive officer without regard to usual civil service rules. The power to set benefits and the financing of the program would, of course, remain with the Congress and the president as it is today.

It would add significantly to public understanding of the trustee character of Social Security as a retirement and group insurance plan if the program were administered by such a board directly under the president. Social Security has about 85,000 employees and some 1,300 district offices across the country; it is one of the very largest direct-line operations of the federal government. It does not make sense administratively to have this huge program, which intimately touches the lives of just about every American family, operated as a subordinate part of another government agency. The management of Social Security could be made more responsive to the needs of its beneficiaries and contributors if it were free from the frequent changes in the levels of service to the public which grow out of short-term decisions about employment ceilings and the varying management value systems which follow the frequent changes of HHS secretaries and their immediate staffs. But most importantly, an independent board would be visible evidence that contributory social insurance was separate from other government programs.

Just about every American has a major stake in protecting the long-term commitments of the Social Security program from fluctuations in politics and policy. The administration of Social Security by a separate bipartisan board would strengthen public confidence in the security of the long-run commitments of the program and in the freedom of the administrative operations from short-run political influence. It would give emphasis to the fact that in this program the government is acting as trustee for those who have built up rights under the system.

Conclusion

There is one recommendation of the commission that I have not yet commented on, and which, in some ways, may be the most important of all. The last few years have seen many sweeping attacks on the Social Security program and many radical proposals for change have been offered. However, the commission's number-one recommendation is as follows:

> The members of the National Commission believe that the Congress, in its deliberations on financing proposals, should not alter the fundamental structure of the Social Security program or undermine its fundamental principles. The National Commission considered, but rejected, proposals to make the Social Security program a voluntary one, or to transform it into a program under which benefits are a product exclusively of the contributions paid, or to convert it into a fully-funded program, or to change it to a program under which benefits are conditioned on the showing of financial need.

The Social Security system in essentially its present form has served the American people well. I do not believe that the American people want to change the program fundamentally or to cut back on Social Security protection. I believe current workers are willing to pay for a good system of social insurance in which they have confidence. Our task is to give them once again a firm basis for full confidence.

Workers have a common interest with the retired, disabled, and surviving families of deceased workers in sound planning for income insurance. Everyone who is fortunate enough to live until retirement will need a regular, permanent income to replace the earnings that were previously the main source of support. We are all headed in the same direction—no one stays young. Also, any worker may become totally disabled before retirement, or he may die and leave surviving dependents. Planning for income security is not primarily a matter in which those at work help those who are not. We are planning together for the kind of protection that we all need.

*   *   *

SUPPLEMENTARY STATEMENT BY COMMISSIONERS BALL, KEYS, KIRKLAND, MOYNIHAN, AND PEPPER ON LONG-TERM FINANCING AND ISSUES OF SPECIAL CONCERN TO WOMEN

All of us supported the compromise agreement which is being recommended by a vote of 12 to 3 of the full commission.[3] The agreement provides for fully meeting the commission's short-term financing goal and also for meeting about two-thirds of the commission's long-term goal—1.22 percent of payroll out of the 1.8 percent projected need.

We recommend that the remaining 0.58 percent of payroll deficit be met by providing additional revenues starting in the year 2010, in advance of the period when the bulk of the deficit is projected to occur. Sufficient additional revenues would be provided by an increase of less than one-half of 1 percent (0.46 percent) in deductions from workers' earnings beginning in 2010 and a like amount in employer payroll taxes (with an equal combined rate for the self-employed), or the revenue could be supplied by an equivalent general revenue contribution, or some combination of the two. For purposes of present legislation we would support putting in the law now an increase in the contribution rate beginning in 2010 of 0.46 percent of payroll (with the employee contribution offset by a refundable income tax credit), recognizing, of course, that in the next century the Congress may prefer to raise the money in some other way and that, in fact, such a rate increase would not be allowed to go into effect unless estimates at the time of the scheduled increase showed that it would be needed.

An increase of less than one-half of 1 percent in the contribution rates in all probability would not mean an increase in the burden of supporting OASDI because: (1) by 2010 real wages are likely to be substantially higher than they are now; and (2) although levied at a higher rate, the rate will apply to a smaller portion of total compensation than today if the expansion of nontaxable fringe benefits projected in the estimates actually occurs. (If such expansion fails to materialize the contribution rate increase would be unnecessary.)

In contrast to our plan for meeting the part of the long-range deficit not addressed by the compromise agreement, some members of the commission seek to meet the remaining deficit by raising the age at which full benefits are first payable and then continuing to raise the age automatically in relation to improvements in longevity. This proposal is a benefit cut. If the age is raised to 68, benefits would be reduced by 20 percent relative to those received at age 65; if it is raised to age 67, the cut is 13 percent; and if set at age 66, the cut is 7 percent.

The cut would be concentrated on those unable to work up to the newly set higher age and on those unable to find jobs. It would cut protection for those now young, the very group being asked to pay in more and for a longer period of time. And an automatic provision changing the age of first eligibility for full benefits would make it very difficult for people to plan for retirement. It would also greatly complicate private pension planning. In our opinion it is unwise to try to index Social Security for all possible future changes in society. Social Security has enough indexing. Congress can act to make changes affecting the long-run future as needed.

We favor the maintenance of the full range of retirement options in present law so that the program will be responsive to the great variety of occupations in the American economy and to the great variety of individual circumstances. It is one thing, for example, to consider a higher age of first eligibility for full benefits for white-collar workers, and something else again for those required to do heavy work. The system today has the required flexibility. It provides: (1) full benefits at any age for qualified workers who have long, continued total disability, (2) actuarially reduced benefits for those who apply between ages 62 and 65, (3) higher benefits for those who postpone retirement and continue to work between 65 and 70 (3 percent a year additional benefits under present law, to be raised to 8 percent during the 1990s under the commission's recommendations).

Some have argued for raising the age at which full benefits are first payable on the ground that as life expectancy increases, so will the ability to work. However, two leading government authorities on health and aging testified before the commission that data on increased longevity carry no evidence that health improved commensurately. If anything, they said, what evidence there is indicates the contrary: more people living longer, but with more chronic illness and impairments. Moreover, recent increases in longevity may be related to retirement at earlier ages.

It is, of course, highly uncertain what the economy and the labor market will look like in the next century. Two major possibilities exist. A labor shortage may result from projected shrinkage of the proportion of persons in the 20–64 age group. In that event, greater market demand for the services of older people would produce greater paid-work opportunities for them. Employers would be seeking older people and the benefit increase for work after 65 recommended by the commission would encourage older people to work. If, on the other hand, a labor shortage does not materialize, raising the age of first eligibility for full Social Security benefits would force a large number of elderly persons into early retirement with lower benefits than current law provides.

We should not cut benefits in an attempt to keep older persons at work. Instead we should recognize and remove the impediments that stand between older workers and employment. Most important of all, economic arrangements should favor full employment, and then the voluntary approach—the incentives proposed by the commission—will have a chance to work. Social Security benefits are not so large as to cancel the lure of good wages. The best medicine for Social Security is full employment and economic growth, not benefit cuts.

Meeting problems of special concern to women. Since enactment of the 1964 Civil Rights Act, federal law has sought to prevent and redress unequal treatment of women. Despite those efforts, substantial inequalities persist and much remains to be done.

In general, gender-based discrimination has been eliminated from the OASDI program through legislative change and court decisions, but in recent years there has been a growing concern regarding the extent to which the Social Security system has adapted to the changed roles of women in society and the economy. The labor force participation rate for married women has almost doubled in the last 25 years. Over 65 percent of all women aged 20 to 54 are now in the labor force. In addition, the divorce rate has increased significantly. Two decades ago, there was one divorce for every four marriages; in 1976 that rate had risen to one divorce for every two marriages.

Although the scope and urgency of economic considerations appropriately consumed most of the time of the commission, it did give attention to some of the problems that currently exist for women in Social Security coverage. Four specific recommendations were made for important changes affecting certain groups of widows, divorced women, and disabled women.

Social Security has indeed given extensive protection to women and men. It provides benefits for 91 percent of women over 65 today (compared to 10 percent of women who received benefits from a private pension system in 1980). Nevertheless, the significant changes in women's roles in society and the economy have caused many inequities and unintended results for women beneficiaries.

Today the majority (65 percent) of working-age women are in the labor force; yet their benefits may be greatly reduced if they leave the labor force for a period of time for homemaking or child-caring. Also lower family retirement and survivor benefits exist for two-wage-earner couples than for one-wage-earner couples with the same family earnings history. Although there are some advantages to having benefits based on one's own earnings that are partly offsetting, this is basically unfair.

Homemakers have no individual coverage or eligibility for Social Security and no credits of their own on which to build with later employment because of early widowhood or any other reason. Divorced women may be severely affected by the arbitrary 10-year duration-of-marriage requirement and the inadequacy of the 50 percent dependent benefit for their independent economic needs. Currently, the benefit for the divorced woman depends upon the actual retirement of the former spouse; however, the commission has recommended a change which will correct this problem. Disability protection exists only for women who remain quite continuously in the labor force and not at all for homemakers. It is often lost to working women during a period of time spent in the home.

Since the introduction in 1976 by Reps. Martha Keys and Don Fraser of legislation to implement the concept of earnings sharing, many have believed this to be the best solution to these anomalies. Earnings sharing is a recognition of marriage as an economic partnership with equal respect given to the division of labor chosen by each couple. It accords the right of each individual to a retirement income based on half of the total retirement credits earned by the couple during their marriage. This is similar in concept to the sharing of income in the joint tax return of a married couple. Working women would have a continuous record of Social Security credits when they retire instead of zero credits for years spent in the home. It would respond to, and recognize, the economic value to the couple of full-time work in the home by either spouse.

Earnings sharing has been proposed in many forms and was recommended for consideration by both the 1979 Advisory Council and the 1980 President's Commission on Pension Policy. Obviously, such a comprehensive change in structure requires careful development of a detailed proposal and thorough analysis of its impact. There are many technical and administrative questions to be worked out and special consideration must be given to continued strong protection for the family against death or disablement of its primary wage earner. These are not insurmountable problems, however. We believe that earnings sharing is the most promising approach to the solution of Social Security problems of special concern to women and we urge renewed efforts to develop a comprehensive proposal based on this concept. [*Author's note:* Since this was written, much additional work toward developing a practical earnings-sharing proposal has been performed. Now, in 2000, I am convinced we can't get there from here. If we were starting a new program, I would enthusiastically support such a plan, because I fully accept the rationale of economic equality between husband and wife, but because of the practical difficulties involved, I think only earnings sharing at divorce is worth considering further.]

*   *   *

DEVELOPMENTS SINCE 1983

[*Author's note:* This is the text of Appendix I to the Report of the 1994–96 Advisory Council.]

The last major tax and benefit changes in the Social Security Act occurred in 1983. These amendments followed the recommendations of the National Commission on Social Security Reform (the Greenspan Commission), except that about one-third of the long-range deficit was met by a proposal added on the floor of the House of Representatives to gradually extend the age of eligibility for full retirement benefits from age 65 to 67 beginning in the year 2000 and concluding in 2022.

The 1983 Trustees' Report, following these amendments, found the system to be in balance for both the short and the long run, with a long-run balance over 75 years showing a slight surplus of 0.02 percent of taxable payroll. Actual short-term experience has generally been more favorable than estimated at the time of the 1983 amendments, with income exceeding outgo by more than had been projected.

Nevertheless, looking ahead 75 years, the trustees have found reasons to be concerned. The 1995 Trustees' Report shows a continued surplus of Social Security taxes over outgo until 2013, and counting income from interest on the funds, the surplus continues to 2020. But beginning then it will be necessary to start cashing in bonds in order to meet full benefit payments on time. Unless changes are made, after 2030, annual income would meet only about 75 percent of annual costs. The trustees in 1995 reported that the average shortfall over the 75 years would be 2.17 percent of taxable payroll. [*Author's note:* In 2000 the trustees reported that the shortfall would be 1.89 percent of taxable payroll.]

What Has Happened since 1983 to Produce the Long-range Deficit?

Beneficiary/worker ratio much the same. The usual popular explanation of the present deficit has been to repeat the underlying reason why the Social Security system will be more expensive in the future than it is today. It is pointed out correctly that while today there are 3.3 active workers paying into the system for every beneficiary now drawing benefits, over time this ratio will change to two workers per beneficiary and in the long run to perhaps 1.9 or 1.8. This is the main reason why Social Security will be more expensive in the future than it is today.

However, this has almost nothing to do with why there is a 2.17 percent of taxable payroll deficit. The estimate of the future relationship between beneficiaries and workers was just about the same in 1983 when the program was last in balance. In other words, the fundamental ratio of beneficiaries to workers was fully taken into account in the 1983 financing provisions and, as a matter of fact, was known and taken into account well before that. The current deficit has a different explanation, resulting from an accumulation of relatively small annual changes in the actuarial assumptions and in the method of making the estimates.

Shifting estimating period. Of the 2.17 percent of taxable payroll deficit, 0.55 percentage points (one-quarter of the deficit) are the result of the fact that as each new 75-year estimate is made, it includes a more expensive out-year because higher benefits will later on be paid to more beneficiaries. All three of the proposals made by the advisory council try to correct this situation by having a stable trust fund ratio at the end of the 75-year forecast horizon.

Of course, correction of this problem will not guarantee that there will not be deficits, or surpluses for that matter, arising because of changes in future assumptions. Any 75-year estimate will be subject to change. But when the problem arising from the moving 75-year period is dealt with, there will be no factor now on the horizon that will cause the deficit to worsen over time.

Disability assumptions. One of the significant causes of the current deficit is the change in the assumptions as to future disability allowance and termination rates. Looked at separately, the experience in this part of the program over the last 12 years has differed significantly from what was expected. Changes in the assumptions to bring the long-range projections in line with that experience account for 0.70 percentage points of the 2.17 percent of taxable payroll deficit.

The council urges the new Social Security Administration Advisory Board to work with the Social Security Administration and the Congress to monitor developments in the Disability Insurance program. This council had neither the special experience and skills nor the time needed to make an important contribution to understanding the causes of and possible remedies for the increase in the estimated cost of the disability insurance part of the program.

Economic assumptions. Changes in the economic assumptions underlying the 75-year projections are also a significant cause of the deficit. They account for some 0.79 percentage points in the 2.17 percent of taxable payroll deficit. The change in the real wage growth assumption, which gradually came down over the 12 years since 1983 from 1.5 percent per year to 1.0 percent per year, accounted for 0.50 percent of taxable payroll. Another important factor was the decline in the portion of total compensation which is now assumed to be taxable in the years ahead. The council's Technical Panel on Assumptions and Methods has studied both matters and finds the new estimates to be reasonable.

Methods. Improved methods of estimating costs have also played an important role in producing the 2.17 percent of taxable payroll deficit, causing an addition to the deficit of 0.93 percentage points. These changes involved revisions in the age distribution of immigrants, improvements in consistency between short- and long-range estimates, and higher projections of future benefit levels based on new data on benefit awards. Also, beginning with 1991, the cost of providing for trust funds equal to one year's outgo at the end of the estimating period is taken into account in calculating the long-range balance.

Demographic assumptions. Curiously, changes in demographic assumptions over the last 12 years have had the effect of reducing, not increasing, the deficit by 0.83 percent of taxable payroll. Increased immigration assumptions and higher near-term fertility rates more than offset the higher costs attributable to a reduction in the ultimate fertility rate and mortality. Whereas the Technical Panel on Assumptions and Methods was not quite so sanguine on these demographic assumptions, in the end it did not propose changing them either.

These changes in the OASDI actuarial balance, 1983–95, are summarized in Table 14.2.

TABLE 14.2. CHANGES IN OASDI ACTUARIAL BALANCE (AS PERCENT OF TAXABLE PAYROLL)

Balance in the 1983 Report	+0.02
Balance in the 1995 Report	−2.17
Change in balance	2.19
Reason for change:	
Legislation	+0.10
Valuation period	−0.55
Economic assumptions	−0.79
Demographic assumptions	+0.83
Disability assumptions	−0.70
Methods	−0.93
All other	−0.15

Source: Office of the Actuary, Social Security Administration

[*Author's note:* The 2000 Trustees' Report attributes the changes in balance from the 1983 report as follows: Legislation +0.16; valuation period −0.94; economic assumptions −0.32; demographic assumptions +0.68; disability assumptions −0.74; methods and all other −0.73.]

15

A SYSTEM FOR
MUTUAL SUPPORT

In the 1980s critics of Social Security increasingly argued that the elderly were being coddled at the expense of younger Americans. This essay puts the "intergenerational equity" debate in perspective while also looking at some of the unfinished business of social insurance.

The media, with a push from those interested in cutting back on Social Security and Medicare, have recently begun to look at social policy through the prism of something called "intergenerational equity." The thesis goes that working-age generations have been having a tough time and that it would help them if we cut back on our "overgenerous" treatment of the elderly, particularly by cutting back on Social Security and Medicare and, of course, on the taxes that pay for these programs.

Governor Richard D. Lamm of Colorado, for example, in his novel, *Mega-Traumas: America at the Year 2000*, has a committee send the President of the United States a memorandum as follows:

> Simply put, America's elderly have become an intolerable burden on the economic system and the younger generation's future. In the name of compassion for the elderly we have handcuffed the young, mortgaged their future, and drastically limited their hopes and aspirations.
>
> The policymakers of the 1960s and 1970s . . . set up unsustainable pension systems. . . . They placed the bill for

From remarks delivered at the Third Annual Conference on Older Adults, Calvin College, Grand Rapids, Mich., October 17, 1986 (unpublished).

all these programs on succeeding generations who consequently inherited the crippled economy their excesses
caused. . . . The biblical story of the prodigal son has been
turned on its head: we now have the sad but true story of the
"prodigal father."

There may be some truth in the idea that much of America's current working-age generation—the baby-boom generation—has been
having a tough time, but there is no truth in laying the blame for this
on "over-generous" treatment of the elderly.

The baby-boom generation—those now approximately age 20 to
45—because of its sheer size has had to face many economic problems
unknown to those a bit older and unlikely to be experienced by those
a bit younger. Its problems have not been as bad, of course, as the
problems faced by those who grew up in the Great Depression, and
who are now drawing Social Security, but they have been bad enough.
One can understand and sympathize with the frustration of this age
group, which has experienced nerve-wracking and never-ending competition, starting with overcrowding in the schools and colleges, continuing in the search for jobs, in slow advancement once on the job, in
the virtual freezing of real wage growth from 1973 to 1984, in the
inability to find affordable housing, and frequently in the need for both
spouses to work to maintain a decent level of living for their families.

Perhaps the remarkable thing is not that the baby-boom generation found less economic opportunity but that it has done as well as
it has. I am not surprised at an unemployment rate hovering around
7 percent since 1975, but rather at the creation of 37 million new
civilian jobs in the last 20 years, an increase of over 50 percent.
Almost all those who were a part of the huge increase in the number
of those seeking work—caused not only by the baby boom but by a
great increase in the proportion of women in the labor force—have
found work. It is a remarkable achievement. But it has not been
accompanied by much in the way of real wage increases. This is not
surprising. If in a short time there is a great increase in the supply of
labor relative to capital, one would expect real wages to grow slowly if at all. But surprising or not, the result has been difficult for the
baby boomers, and competition for jobs and promotions will continue
to be keen.

As they grow older, however, their work should be valued more
as the pressure of new entrants on the labor force eases. It is the new

generation of the young, today's teenagers, who will find things much more to their liking. Colleges are recruiting students, not making it difficult for them to enter. Almost anyone can get in somewhere. And so with summer jobs, and later with full-time jobs and promotions. This new generation will be in demand because there are relatively few of them, and their real wages, on average, will go up. In 1984, there were almost 10 percent fewer young people and children under 18 than in 1965, even though the population as a whole was 22 percent larger. It looks as if we will never again have to create millions and millions of jobs just to stay even.

Obviously, there are many good things about being part of a smaller generation, but the question posed by Governor Lamm and others is whether because they are few in number they will be overwhelmed by having to pay the Social Security, Medicare, and long-term care costs of the big baby-boom generation as it starts retiring some 20 to 25 years from now.

Let me say, first, that I agree with the part of the intergenerational argument that says we should stop piling up a huge national debt and passing it on to future generations. We are the most under-taxed of all modern industrial societies, and government needs more money now to balance the budget, to improve and extend government services, and to reduce poverty. We should raise taxes over the next several years.

The main point, though, is that this generation of workers just now entering the labor force, in all likelihood, is going to be much better off than those who preceded them. They will not only earn more but, by and large, will have fewer dependents to support than the workers of 20 years ago. Don't be misled on this issue by talk of the great increase in the number of old people compared to those of working age. The truth is that despite the increase in the number of the elderly, it is unlikely that the ratio of *all* nonworkers to workers will ever be as high as it was in the recent past.

There will, of course, be a large increase in both the number of people over 65 and in the ratio of the over-65 group to the group aged 20–64, which includes most workers. At first blush the numbers are startling. According to Social Security area population figures,[1] the number of those over 65 on July 1, 1985, was 29.1 million, or 11.8 percent of the population. In the year 2000, the number is expected to be 36.5 million, or 13.2 percent. By 2020, the number is expected to be 54.5 million, or 17.7 percent, and by 2040, when it is expected to level off, 70.8 million or 22 percent. But if one considers those under 20 as well as those over 65, then the age groups comprised mostly of nonworkers compared to the working-age group has been *coming down*, and rapidly. In 1965, there were about 950 young people and children under 20 and people over 65 for every 1,000 in the age group 20–64. Because of the decline in the birthrate, this figure is now down to approximately 700. Even when the size of the elderly population peaks some fifty years from now, the ratio of the non-working-age population (both elderly and young) to those age 20–64 is expected to be lower than it was in 1965. There will be more older people and fewer children, not an increase in the total number of dependents per worker. [*Author's note:* As of 2000, these estimates were proving to be quite accurate. The number over age 65 was 35.5 million; by 2020 the number is now estimated to be 53.1 million, and for 2040 is estimated to be 74.6 million. The number of nonworkers compared to the working-age group in 2000 is still approximately 700. By 2035 it is expected to be 810, and by 2075 to be 850.]

The division between public and private expenditures will be different because most children are largely supported by their parents, whereas we have chosen to provide a major part of the support of elderly retired people through social insurance, but the fundamental ratio of current workers to dependents will not be unfavorable. (On a per capita basis it is probably more expensive to support the elderly than children but, on the other hand, not all those over 65 will retire, and higher education costs have been increasing rapidly.)

In any event, it will be easier to bear any higher costs in the next century because even modest productivity increases help meet the burden of supporting those who are not currently working. Beyond that, we have chosen to pre-fund a considerable part of the future cost of retirement income by establishing funding standards for private pension plans, funding most state and local plans, and, under present Social Security policy, returning to a very large buildup in Social Security earnings reserves. If ultimately the rest of the budget is balanced by raising general taxes without the use of Social Security surpluses, Social Security would come to own a large part of the national debt, freeing private funds for productive investments that would help finance future retirements.

Let's look at what Social Security does for today's young workers. Will they get their money's worth? First of all, it is frequently overlooked that Social Security is much more than a retirement plan. It gives the families of current workers protection against the loss of the worker's wages from death or total disability as well as from retirement in old age. Frequently the value of this insurance protection can be very large. In fact, the total value of life insurance in force under Social Security roughly matches that of all private life insurance in the United States.

And young workers will do well on retirement protection. It is true that those now contributing to the program or already receiving benefits will get more protection for what they and their employers pay than will be the case for those who come after. This is the inevitable result of paying full benefits before full-rate contributions have been effective for a lifetime. However, young workers as a group will get their "money's worth." Workers aged 18–22 in 1983, for example, will get somewhat more than the full value of their own and their employers' contributions compounded at an interest rate that exceeds prices by 2 percent, a reasonable return for a safe investment.

Some analysts have produced what appears to be a different result by computing a separate rate of return on contributions for certain sub-groups of workers at the end of their working lives. For example, it can be shown that young, male workers who never marry (thus having no use for the survivors or dependents benefits), do not become disabled, and always earn the maximum will have received protection worth their own contributions but not those of their employer. But this is a questionable way to assess the value of a group insurance and pension plan like Social Security where the risks are pooled for all workers over a lifetime. A correct evaluation doesn't wait until the end of life and then look back and see who suffered what risks. It is not possible to tell at the beginning of a working life who always will get maximum earnings, who will have dependents, who will be disabled, or who will die before retirement age. These are some of the risks insured against.

But the value of Social Security protection is not fully captured in *any* of these computations. Social Security provides unique protection not available elsewhere: the protection follows the worker from job to job, guarantees a fixed replacement rate of recent earnings at retirement (in other words, it keeps up to date with rising earnings), and pays inflation-proof benefits thereafter. And those of working age benefit from Social Security not only because of what they will get individually, but also because they are now pooling the support of their parents with all other workers. Because of Social Security, no one has to fully meet the cost of maintaining parents who live longer than average, those who have not saved enough on their own, those who are sicker than average, or those who have such low incomes in the absence of Social Security that they need to move in with their sons and daughters. And taxpayers have savings from taxes that partly offset their Social Security contributions, because without Social Security relief and assistance costs would be much higher.

Some critics reject the conclusion that the young will make out well under the system because they argue that present law is inadequately financed and that young workers will have to keep paying higher and higher taxes. This argument is no longer about the next 25 years. During this period even the most pessimistic assumptions used by the trustees for their highest-cost estimates show a substantial surplus. In fact, the argument has now become whether the system may in fact be collecting "too much" during this period rather than concern over whether Social Security will "go bankrupt," the big concern in 1981 and 1982. It is now expected that the excess of income over outgo will be about $200 billion in the next five years and that the trust funds will grow much more rapidly in the following 20 years.

Even looking ahead 50 years, all but the most pessimistic assumptions show substantial surpluses. Beyond that, out to 75 years from now, assumptions can differ widely and still be plausible. The official estimates showing the system to be in close actuarial balance over the whole 75 years for which the estimates are made seem reasonable enough, but certainly they may be wrong and the system may be somewhat over- or under-financed over the long run. How can one possibly be sure either way? But in any event, with anything like the large surpluses planned, any changes in the estimates for the long run, either up or down, can be accommodated gradually, year by year, and need not be a problem. Contrary to what the doom-sayers claim, our Social Security system is in good shape, working well on behalf of all segments of society and all age groups. [*Author's note:* This statement, based on the 1986 Trustees' Report, seems too optimistic in 2000—but not by very much. In 2000 the trustees forecast a 1.89-percent-of-payroll average annual deficit over the following 75 years, with a trust fund exhaustion date of 2037. President Clinton's proposal for dedicating to Social Security part of the expected surplus in the non–Social Security budget and investing up to 15 percent of it in stocks would reduce the average annual deficit to 0.48 percent of payroll and move the estimated trust fund exhaustion date to 2063.]

There are, however, two remaining issues of overwhelming importance to the well-being of elderly people:

1. how to eliminate poverty for those elderly who in this wealthy country still barely eke out an existence; and

2. how to provide adequate health care and long-term care.

In spite of great advances, poverty is still the lot of many elderly people. Poverty among the elderly is now heavily concentrated in three groups: unmarried (widowed, divorced, and never married), the very old, and minorities. Among family units with one person over 65, couples have a poverty rate of 9 percent, but unmarried men have a 19 percent rate and unmarried women a 24 percent rate. Unmarried women make up a very large proportion of the elderly and this proportion increases dramatically at older ages. For elderly blacks, the poverty rate is very high. For all black family units over 65, the rate is 40 percent. The poverty rate for the elderly of Hispanic origin is also high: 23 percent. [*Author's note:* We have continued to make progress in reducing the poverty rate for the elderly, although obviously more needs to be done—not only for the elderly but even more importantly for children, among whom the poverty rate in 1998 was 19 percent. The figures for 1998 in the above categories were: 29 percent for blacks and 22 percent for Hispanics, 4.4 percent for couples, 10.8 percent for unmarried men, and 16.3 percent for unmarried women.]

In the long run, changes in Social Security could be made that would help the most needy groups. Such changes, however, would increase the cost of Social Security and are not likely to be adopted in the near future. After the negotiated settlement of Social Security's financing problems in 1983, there is little likelihood soon of Congress opening up the program to major legislative change. In the meantime, help for the low-income elderly might have more chance of approval by raising standards in the means-tested SSI program supported from general revenues. This, as well as help for low-income children, could occur in the next several years when the United States realizes that there is a pressing need to raise general taxes, not only to balance the budget, but also to improve human service programs and reduce the incidence of poverty.

HEALTH CARE AND LONG-TERM CARE

Unlike the situation for retirement cash benefits, health care and long-term care for the elderly need much improvement—not only for the sake of the elderly but for their sons and daughters who are faced with the prospect of making up for the inadequacy of present arrangements. What should be done to improve Medicare?

Much has been made recently by friends and foes of Medicare alike of the idea that the Medicare design is flawed because it is borrowed from health insurance plans that primarily cover younger people. A shift in emphasis from acute care to chronic care, it is argued, would make the plan more suitable for older people. Some of those who make this point imply that money now spent on what Medicare covers could be shifted to pay for a new range of services without any, or much, additional cost.

I disagree. Most elderly retired people have the same health insurance needs as younger people. They are healthy and active, and usually when they get sick they need hospital and physician services to make them well again. Of course, more often than younger people they have chronic conditions and limitations on activities and when they go to a hospital the typical stay is longer, but health insurance needs for most of the retired are still met by protection against the high and unpredictable costs of hospital care and physicians' services, just as is the case for most younger people.

A relatively small proportion of the elderly do have very large expenses for a type of care that does not loom very large for younger people: long-term care for devastating incurable illness. Relatively few people need such care before 75 or 80, but of those over 85, more than 20 percent are in nursing homes and many more at that age need help with the activities of daily living at home. These are costs now largely left uncovered by either Medicare or private insurance.

Let us first address Medicare's design as a health insurance plan for the healthy and active elderly, the great bulk of the retired population. Part A, hospital insurance, by and large works reasonably well from the viewpoint of beneficiaries. It costs too much but covers about three-fourths of the hospital costs of older people, and most of the cost is covered by paid-up insurance as a result of Social Security contributions made while at work. What is missing in benefit coverage can be added quite easily. For the few who need to be in a hospital for a very long stay—the 5 percent of elderly hospital patients with stays of over 60 days—the costs can be very high. The special copayments beyond 60 days and the lifetime limits should be dropped. Also the deductible set by Congress in October 1986 for all hospital stays, while much better than would have been the case under the old law, is still too high. The amount of $520 set for 1987 and rising in the future at the rate of increase in the cost of an average day in the hospital should be cut in half and allowed to rise each year no more than the automatic increase in Social Security benefits. With these easily made corrections, the benefit design of hospital insurance under Medicare seems fine and as well adapted to the elderly as to younger people.

Hospitalization for elderly people does have its problems, but they are not problems of benefit design. There are three important issues concerning the appropriateness of hospital care that have particular relevance to the elderly. These issues are the high cost of terminal illness, the explosion in the technology of transplants, artificial organs and other body parts, and the hospital treatment of patients best treated elsewhere. These issues involve patients of all ages, but they arise most frequently among the elderly, and deserve comment.

TERMINAL ILLNESS

Most deaths today—about 70 percent—occur after 65. This is a great triumph of public health, general affluence, and medicine, but it has made the role of the hospital more ambiguous. It is no longer taken for granted that under all circumstances the physician and the hospital should do everything possible to keep a patient alive. Some 30 percent of Medicare costs go for expenses in the last year of life, 15 percent in the last 60 days. Is all this necessary or even desirable? Probably not, even though in many cases it is not possible to know ahead of time that a last illness is the last. Still, as the AMA has recently declared, "It is not the duty of a physician to prolong death."

One of the most significant recommendations of the most recent advisory council on Social Security, the one devoted exclusively to Medicare and chaired by the present Secretary of Health and Human Services, Dr. Bowen, was to make "living wills" conveniently available to all older people, so that well ahead of time they could make clear that they opposed the prolongation of their own deaths. The Social Security Administration is in a very good position to carry out this recommendation and to help overcome the tendency to postpone a declaration of this sort. SSA is in touch with just about every older person in the country. And Medicare now does cover hospice care as a substitute for hospitalization.

Thousands of decisions by patients, their families and physicians are being made informally every day in this difficult area. The decision probably never should be formalized by a health insurance plan deciding what to pay for or not to pay for. The worst thing that could happen would be to get the courts more and more involved in these decisions. What is needed is an increasingly supportive climate of opinion for individual decisions reflected in the living wills and family and physician decisions. I believe we are on our way. There is no evidence of large-scale inappropriate treatment of the terminally ill.

TRANSPLANTS AND ARTIFICIAL BODY PARTS

Because we are such a wealthy country we have not yet had to face directly and on a large scale the question of the extent to which we are willing to pay for the elderly to have expensive transplants, artificial parts, and life-prolonging procedures like kidney dialysis. In contrast, Britain has decided that with a limited amount of money and available technology they will use what they have for those with the best chance for a long and healthy life. We do, too, but on a much more limited scale. At the extremes the decisions are relatively easy, nor are they especially difficult when costs are manageable and supply plentiful, as in the case of hip replacements, but down the road, with the aging of the population and an explosion of technology, we face excruciatingly difficult ethical and economic decisions.

The main health insurance device used so far to control costs in this area is to declare certain procedures nonreimbursable because they are experimental—for example, the artificial heart. But for many procedures this is only a delaying action. We have no way of saying that a widely accepted and proven procedure should not be reimbursed because the patient is 80 years old and it will cost $100,000. In fact, we have set up elaborate administrative appeals and appeals to the courts to force equal treatment by health insurance agencies, and we have fostered malpractice suits to force physicians to do everything possible for the patient. Age alone is not and should not be a criterion for approving or denying care. In short, we do not yet know what to do about this problem, but I do not believe it can be left to health insurance administrators to decide on their own. Perhaps this is one of the few situations where we really do need a commission of wise and expert citizens, followed, perhaps, by continuing advisory bodies.

Over-reliance on Hospitals

The final area of hospital practice that affects the elderly more than others involves keeping people in the hospital unnecessarily because there is no other appropriate place for them to go. Here Medicare reimbursement is now designed to apply pressure for discharge, and although it holds the potential for harsh treatment in the short run, perhaps the long-run results will be productive. When hospitals were reimbursed on a retroactive cost basis, unless a hospital was pressed for space the incentives were to keep a patient on, especially if a discharge meant there was no good place for the patient to go during a recovery period—no one at home or no approved nursing home bed available. Now, since the hospital is reimbursed the same amount for each diagnosis regardless of length of stay, the incentives are all for early discharge if the patient no longer needs intensive hospital care, regardless of whether he or she is still unable to function on his or her own. Hopefully the long-term response to this situation will be more adequate long-term care outside the hospital. The old way led to unnecessarily high hospital costs; the new way, in the short run at least, may well be leading to inadequate care.

But although there are aspects of hospital care that affect the elderly more than others, there is nothing about this difference that calls for a special design for hospital insurance for the elderly. Modified, as suggested, the benefit design of the hospital insurance part of Medicare would be quite satisfactory. The same is not true for physician coverage under Part B of Medicare. Here many changes are called for. Part B is just not very good insurance. Before any payments are made, the elderly person has to pay a premium of $15.50 a month, $31 for a couple, and meet a $75 annual deduction. And the reimbursement is for only 80 percent of an allowable charge. The physician can and very often does charge more than the amount on which the Medicare payment is based. Thus in many instances the real co-payment is not 20 percent of the physician's charge but 30, 40, or even 50 percent. [*Author's note:* In 1999 the Part B premium was $45.50 per month for individuals and $91 for couples, and the annual deductible was $100. Under the law as it stood in 1999, non-participating physicians—that is, those who do not accept Medicare fee schedules in all instances—ordinarily receive 5 percent less than the schedule, and can charge at the most only 115 percent of the schedule, based on their customary charge.]

This part of Medicare is voluntary in that those applying for Social Security can opt out, although 99 percent of the elderly covered for hospital insurance and 92 percent of the long-term disabled do choose to take physician coverage. Inadequate as it is, it is a good buy in the sense that 75 percent of the costs are now paid from general revenues.

To try to make up for Part B's inadequacies, about two-thirds of the elderly buy private insurance, so-called Medigap policies. These in turn are inadequate and expensive. By and large they are designed to fill in the deductibles and co-payments of Medicare and cover some additional days in the hospital or skilled nursing home, using the same definitions as Medicare. They do not effectively cover the gap between what physicians charge and what Medicare will reimburse and do not deal at all with the cost of long-term care where the need is primarily for personal services such as feeding, dressing, toileting, or helping the patient move about.

It is surprising that Part B has endured with little basic change for 20 years. It was a last-minute add-on in the original 1965 amendments and was not part of the original Medicare proposal. What happened was that the House Ways and Means Committee, after several years of debate, accepted the Kennedy and Johnson administrations' proposals for hospital insurance based on the traditional social insurance approach of paying the costs while at work through deductions from workers' earnings and matching amounts from employers. But for physicians' services the committee, in pursuit of bipartisan support, added a private insurance model sponsored by the Republicans that was voluntary, had co-payments, allowed the physician to charge his normal price and was financed in part by a premium paid after retirement and in part by a subsidy from general revenues.

What should be done? First, both parts of Medicare should be combined in a single plan and made compulsory. The deductibles and co-payments of the new combined plan should be eliminated or greatly reduced and, if retained, subjected to an annual cap applying to all services, a total of, say, $1,000 or $2,000. Physicians should be reimbursed on a negotiated fee schedule and not allowed to charge more than the amount determined reasonable for reimbursement.

Under this approach, private Medigap policies would no longer be attractive and the total health insurance coverage for elderly people would be greatly simplified: one administering agent and one set of provisions instead of the three or more typical today.

Premium financing, too, should be eliminated and, at the same time, the well-off elderly ought not to continue to get a large tax-free subsidy from general revenue. In fact, there is much to be said for substituting new earmarked taxes for the present large general revenue subsidy altogether.

Most important, the new combined plan should cover additional services and additional people—prescription drugs, basic dental care, and services designed to prevent disease and promote health and rehabilitation.

The expanded plan should be extended to all the disabled receiving Social Security benefits, not just those who have been receiving them for two years, as under present law. Elderly persons should be eligible at 62, not 65, since most now retire before 65 and wives typically are three years younger than their husbands. All Social Security beneficiaries should be included; widows and children need the protection as much as older and disabled people.

Long-term Care Insurance

The most important emerging issue of the late 1980s for the elderly is long-term care insurance. Medicare has not been designed to pay for either the cost of long-term care in a nursing home or to provide many of the services that would allow elderly and disabled people to remain in their own homes or in protected community housing instead of going to a nursing home, and neither has private insurance. Many people don't know this. They think that with a combination of Medicare and Medigap policies they now have protection. They don't. Protection should be provided by the public plan.

First of all, long-term care insurance should include an assessment service open to all beneficiaries as they come on the rolls to determine medical and other needs and to help develop disease prevention and health promotion activities. It should be available at any later point when changes in health or social status may call for a choice between additional community services and institutional care.

In the event that the assessment determines that nursing home care would be appropriate, Medicare should provide it or alternatively pay the cost of appropriate community-based services under a plan not to exceed the average cost of reimbursement for nursing home care. Some of the services that might be included in such a plan are those already available such as home health care visits to Medicare beneficiaries, but the services would be provided also to those who are not homebound. In addition to the services already available to some Medicare beneficiaries such as home health care visits, social services necessary to keep an individual from having to enter a nursing home should be considered—particularly homemaker services, chore services, and help with the activities of daily living, such as bathing, eating, and helping with food preparation.

Nursing home care is, of course, an essential part of a long-term care program, and present arrangements are very unsatisfactory. Much of the cost is now paid for by the means-tested federal-state Medicaid system, and frequently Medicaid is unable or unwilling to pay for quality care. The cost of more than half of nursing home care falls on the individual and on relatives. Few people can pay for extended stays in a nursing home, and a high proportion of those who start out in nursing homes as private payers end up on Medicaid, with their funds exhausted and, in many instances, after considerable expense to friends and relatives. Medicare and private insurance play almost no part in protecting people against long-term nursing home costs. Yet as we look ahead it is clear that provision of nursing-home care will become increasingly important. The threat of exhausting resources and ending up in a Medicaid nursing home is a major concern for a high proportion of elderly people and their children.

A way of greatly reducing the cost of extending Medicare to nursing homes would be to separate out the basic room-and-board component of nursing home costs and include as part of a health insurance payment only the nursing home costs above room and board. Room and board would be paid for by the recurring retirement income of the patient, supplemented, if necessary, by Supplemental Security Income (SSI). The purpose of Social Security, private pensions, and government career retirement plans is to meet the ordinary living expenses of the recipients. After retention of a small allowance for personal expenses, it would seem reasonable to devote these payments to meeting the room-and-board part of nursing home costs. Long-term care insurance would take responsibility only for costs above the basic room-and-board allowances paid by other programs. This approach needs further development, but it may well be the most feasible way of providing nursing home care on a largely non-means-tested basis.

I believe it will turn out that a public plan is the only practical way to meet the need for long-term care insurance. However, as with Medicare, we may first have to go through a demonstration that private insurance can't do it. Many private companies are now looking at the idea of cash indemnity payments for each day in a nursing home, albeit with strict limitations on the total amount of liability. They are correctly concerned about the risks of selling plans on an individual voluntary basis. They know there will be a tendency for those with the greatest risks to buy—the very old and others who for other reasons are most likely to need such care. They fear that once the care is paid for, families now taking care of the elderly will stop doing so and will increasingly rely on nursing homes. And they know that because of these factors the cost for those who buy the policies will be high.

Group insurance, on the other hand, with contributions starting for workers while young, would be quite cheap because relatively few over a lifetime will have expensive long-term care needs and because payments accumulating over a lifetime at interest would greatly reduce premiums. Perhaps some large employers and unions will come to see this protection as a good substitute for some of the Medigap policies now being supplied retired employees, but it is doubtful that this risk will be seen as a high priority by many. If anything, employers are now interested in cutting back on the health insurance protection now being provided to retirees.

But there is a big social need—and not just for old people. Many couples today are faced with a painful choice: to take a frail parent into their own homes, with the possible disruption of a career—typically for the wife—and less time and money for the children, or to turn to an inadequate and feared Medicaid nursing home for the parent. Thus long-term care insurance through a public plan, probably as an add-on to Medicare, may well be our next big social program. I believe in the end it will be voted in, not just by the power of the elderly, but by their sons and daughters, and that it will be popular not so much with the poor as with the great bulk of Americans who consider themselves middle-class. They will want the protection on a social insurance basis, not with a means test, and they will want it to cover comprehensive services at home as well as in nursing homes. [*Author's note:* In 1989, I developed a modification of this approach to long-term care insurance as a branch of social insurance (described in *Because We're All in This Together*, with Thomas N. Bethell, Families USA Foundation, Washington, D.C., 1989). Under this approach, which I still support, the plan would provide comprehensive home care services for those with a need for assistance with two or more activities of daily living and nursing home care with 15 percent coinsurance for this group, covering the first year of care and extended indefinitely while a spouse was living independently in the community.]

We need to start intensive planning for such a program now. We need to be ready. Self-financed, as such a program should be and as Social Security is, it does not need to be in conflict with a budget-balancing and conservative mood in the electorate. This issue will be a good test of whether Americans are really against the use of government for social purposes, as has recently been stated with increasing frequency, or whether they like President Reagan more than they like his philosophy.

As we build permanent institutions providing retirement income, health care, and long-term care for the elderly, we do it for *all* generations—not just for those who are old today. No one stays young. We owe our children and our grandchildren a secure old age. We are all in this together. "Generational equity" arguments are destructive of the best interests of all age groups.

To be fair, we need to recognize our obligation to each other, to the past, and to the future. We owe much of what we are to the past. We all stand on the shoulders of the generations that came before. What we can do comes not only from our own effort, essential as that is, but also from the knowledge, skills, and technology we have inherited. And as we earn our livings we are also dependent on the current and future contributions of others in what has become a highly interdependent economic, social, and political enterprise that now encompasses the entire world.

Social insurance is built on awareness that no one can go it alone. True generational equity means acting on that awareness so that those who come after us, and who stand on our shoulders, can see a little further and do a little better in their turn.

16

ADAPTING TO CHANGE

In the early 1970s, Social Security district office managers across the country formed an organization to further their common interests. It performed some of the functions of a union while at the same time promoting the managers' professional interest in good administration. Some six years after leaving the government I was asked to address their annual meeting. Among other things, these remarks describe some 1979 Advisory Council proposals that were not adopted—for example, a proposal that the two parts of Medicare be combined and financed from earmarked portions of the personal and corporation income taxes, with the part of the payroll tax now going to Medicare reassigned to the cash benefit program, thus solving the long-range financing problem of OASDI and avoiding the problems for Medicare that arise because so much of its financing comes from undifferentiated general revenues.

This is the first time I have talked to a group of Social Security managers in the last six and a half years, and I thank you for the opportunity. The field organization of the Social Security Administration has always embodied my idea of the federal civil service at its best—ever since March 1939 when, as a recent graduate of the Washington training class for new employees, I proudly joined the staff of the Newark district office as a grade-3 field representative at $1,620 a year. I had spent many weeks in classroom training, learning what there was to know about Social Security in those days—not only the details of what I would be expected to do, but the historical background, the issues, hopes for future development, causes of poverty

Remarks to the Social Security Administration District Office Managers' Association, Atlanta, Ga., October 11, 1979.

and economic insecurity, etc. As a matter of fact, the only really useful thing I learned in the Washington course was the broad background material because, although I learned, word for word, Section 205 of the 1935 Social Security Act, on lump-sum payments, and learned in great detail the 1935 monthly benefit formula, etc., they were very soon replaced by a very different kind of Social Security program as a result of the amendments of 1939.

But it is significant how important training in the broad background of social insurance was thought to be in the very early days of the program. Social Security in 1939 was a pioneering movement for the United States, and those responsible for the program at that time—from Arthur Altmeyer, the Chairman of the Social Security Board, to John Corson, head of the old Bureau of Old-Age and Survivors Insurance, and his associates, people like Oscar Pogge, Ewell Bartlett, Joe Fay, Hugh McKenna, and the head of the Training Office, Francis McDonald—looked on Social Security not just as a job but as a great cause in the service of the American people. And all those who came to work there under their direction in those early days, and all who have grown into leadership positions in the years that followed, have looked on Social Security as a great cause, the cause of eliminating poverty and economic insecurity for the elderly of this country, the motherless and fatherless children, the widowed, and the disabled.

Tremendous advances have been made since those early days, and in spite of the huge size of the program and of the administering organization today, I know that the spirit of the Social Security Administration, of providing a friendly, helpful, sympathetic service to the public, remains in the hearts and minds of you who lead the field organization.

Of course there have been difficult times, setbacks as well as victories. Sometimes a particular crisis seemed almost unmanageable, and then in later years we found a new crisis that made the old one seem, in retrospect, not nearly as difficult as we had imagined at the time. How many of you have been with the organization long enough to remember the inundation of claims from farmers when coverage was first extended to them? Grappling with the material participation provisions? Days when an itinerant station in a farm area that ordinarily had five or six callers for each employee had a hundred or more? How many remember even earlier when in 1939 and 1940 we struggled to clear up the old "John Doe" files, created when so many items had been reported in 1937 and 1938 without Social Security numbers? And then, of course, the launching of a whole new branch of social insurance—disability insurance—which required district office people to conduct entirely different types of interviews than they had ever handled before, with a different clientele—inquiries of great complexity and with a division of responsibility between the Social Security Administration and state agencies.

Perhaps the toughest job of all was Medicare. I truly believe that no other organization could have done what we did at that time. In addition to everything else that had to be done we had to set up a brand-new program of great magnitude, involving all the hospitals in the country (and requiring their desegregation before they could participate), just about all the doctors in the country, all the state health departments, thousands of skilled nursing homes, home health agencies, laboratories, and some 19 million people past 65 who had to be given the opportunity to sign up for the voluntary part of the program and had to learn what it was they needed to do to file claims, what was covered, etc. And you will remember that before the deadline, 95 percent of all the older people in the country had signed up for the voluntary program. When we started, I didn't believe we could *find* 95 percent of the people over 65. But you remember that we had forest rangers looking for hermits in the woods, post-office trucks carrying the deadline date in billboards on their sides, and the Railroad Retirement Board and the civil service retirement system and the military and state and local systems circulating information. There was a great cooperative effort that Social Security created and led. The problem as far as older people were concerned was primarily to reach them. Once they had an explanation of the program they knew they wanted it.

It was a time of tremendous overwork, great pressures, and scare stories in the newspapers. Some people got the idea that on the first day there would be lines of old people around every hospital waiting to get in, to get a hernia repaired or a cataract removed which they had not been able to afford before. During the final two weeks before the effective date, President Johnson had us set up a "war room" with maps showing the hospitals of the country, and we had veterans' hospitals, public health hospitals, and military hospitals alerted to take patients, with army helicopters standing by. And, of course, nothing happened. Everything worked very smoothly, considering. After all, an increase in utilization of hospitals by older people by 20 percent meant only an increase of 5 percent overall, and most hospitals were readily able to absorb that.

The Social Security Administration has met and surmounted a series of crises. One of the most difficult things about Medicare was that we had to throw so many resources into that program to make it work that the regular cash benefit programs bogged down somewhat, pending loads increased, claimant dissatisfaction increased, and so on. The same thing happened when we were handed the black lung program overnight and told to administer something we had no hand in planning for. Supplemental Security Income, too, was not only an extremely difficult program to implement—amended, as it was, twice during the implementing period, and with the fundamental problem of working from frequently erroneous state and local records—but, again, the problems with SSI spilled over onto the regular program, temporarily affecting the quality of administration in OASDI.

My point is that Social Security, in expanding to meet the needs and desires of the American people, has successfully met a series of administrative crises, and most importantly that these crises have been met with high morale by the best field organization in the public service.

Social Security has come a long way since early 1939 and is an established and well-accepted part of American life. Not that there should be any complacency. Social Security has become so big and so important in the last 15 years or so that everyone is paying attention to it and everyone, correctly, expects more of it than when it was just starting out.

I remember just before Medicare, in 1963, making a series of speeches to managers around the country that stressed the difference between the administration of a mature program compared with the administration of a program in its youth. A few of the points I made were:

1. The program had become very important to everyone. One in ten in the population (now one in seven) were beneficiaries and that most of the other nine would be. Members of Congress received more mail, questions, and complaints about Social Security than about anything else. Trustees of a major institution could expect to be asked for an accounting. We were under the spotlight—a situation very different from, say, 10 or 15 years earlier.

2. People are paying a lot and expecting a lot. We had no reason to expect people to be grateful for Social Security benefits or for the services that we were rendering in the district offices. Unlike the early days of the program, when people were paying in $30 a year, they were now paying high Social Security contributions, and would be paying more, and correctly expected good service and equitable benefits for those payments.

3. Individual payments are worth a lot. For the first time, Social Security benefit payments had become substantial, and the goal of making sure everyone got what he was entitled to and no one got more was now doubly important because so much in the way of benefit payments was at stake. And this required continual study of claims policy matters, developmental requirements, adequacy of proofs, quality of adjudication, accuracy rate, etc. My point was that as compared with the program when it was in its early stages, this was no longer just our interest but the interest of the Congress, the General Accounting Office, and the public, who would increasingly want assurances that the very substantial amounts of money being spent were spent as intended.

4. The sheer volume of our work, I said, meant (a) the increasing importance of our methods—the application of scientific methods to the problems of production, operations research, data processing, etc. There was so much at stake we couldn't afford to make administrative decisions on anything less than the best facts and policy analysis, and we put a lot of money into methods work and policy. And it meant (b) a large staff—35,000 people then (now 80,000)—which made management problems a bit different than when the organization consisted of a few thousand.

We had to become somewhat more formal in promotion plans, in dealing with unions, in making sure practices were fair in regard to race, religion, and sex. We had to be a model of fairness and set an example in dealing with our own employees. Size also meant that we had to guard against the diseases of large bureaucracies, such as (a) the hardening of organizational lines and sticking to narrow responsibilities; (b) failure to represent the whole organization to the public—passing the buck; (c) callousness to the individual case—danger of averages; at that time an error of one-hundredth of 1 percent in checks meant an error affecting 1,500 beneficiaries, and that was enough to ruin the organization's reputation; (d) the need for individualized service for those who need it; (e) the idea that the claims manual is a minimum and that we should be alert for exceptional cases that did not fit the rules reasonably; (f) and, above all, to avoid the design of procedures and practices set up for the convenience of the organization rather than the public it served; (g) that we needed more than ever to look at everything in terms of a concept of a trust, a public trust.

I repeat some of these things here because they still seem to me to be applicable and to be part of the tradition of the Social Security Administration. But let me turn from these musings about the past and the tradition of administration as a service to the state of the Social Security program today.

I am just completing service on the latest statutory Advisory Council on Social Security. This is a good council, and I believe it will produce a constructive and useful report. There is a good blend of new thinkers and traditionalists among the public members, and both the employer and labor members are very knowledgeable and reasonable people. The chairman is Henry Aaron, an economist from the Brookings Institution and former Assistant Secretary for Planning in the Department of Health, Education and Welfare in this [Carter] administration. He and fellow panel member Joe Pechman, also of Brookings, were co-authors in 1967, along with another economist, Mike Taussig, of a comprehensive and somewhat critical book on Social Security. Gardner Ackley, a former Chairman of the Council of Economic Advisers in President Johnson's administration, is also a professional economist, as is Eveline Burns, another public member who has written several important books on Social Security, going back as far as the 1930s. I am the other public member with previous Social Security experience. Then there are two other public members to whom Social Security issues are relatively new: Grace Davis, the Deputy Mayor of Los Angeles, and John Porter. The actuary this time is Morton Miller, Vice Chairman of the Board of Equitable Life Insurance Company, and the two other employer members are Mary Falvy, who did not have previous experience with the Social Security program, and Jerry Van Gorkom, who was one of the leading employer members on the 1975 Advisory Council and who by now knows a lot about Social Security. The three employee members are Bert Seidman, in charge of the Social Security department of the AFL-CIO;

Mel Glasser, in charge of the Social Security department of the United Auto Workers; and Velma Hill.

In spite of some rather basic differences in points of view, this council has been able to come to a large number of important decisions by lopsided majorities, and sometimes even unanimously. A few items, but not necessarily the most important ones, have been decided by a vote or two. It has been very interesting to me to compare the current issues and problems before this council with those of the first advisory council in which I had a major role: the 1948 council, of which I was the staff director. The differences in the issues show how far Social Security has come in its effectiveness and in building a solid foundation in the very structure of life in this country.

In 1948 the basic issues about Social Security were really issues of survival. Social Security had started out with great promise in 1935, and was improved by the amendments of 1939. However, it was designed largely as a program for the future—a promise in the next generation to those who contributed today. A relatively small proportion of the aged in the first few years could be expected to draw benefits—about 15 percent by the time the 1948 Advisory Council looked at the program; only 60 percent of the jobs in the country were covered at any one time; and benefit amounts in the early years were very low and were constructed to get larger as people contributed longer. In 1948 the system had not had any significant amendments for 10 years and it was not doing a very effective job. Benefits averaged about $22 a month, substantially less valuable than when the program began because of wartime inflation. The [old-age] assistance program was paying several times as many old people as Social Security was. Many people were seriously advocating flat benefit programs, pensions from general funds, and other substitutes for Social Security as it was set up.

If wage-related, contributory social insurance was to become the basic approach in the United States to meeting income loss in old age and on the death of the wage earner, it was clear that major changes had to be made. That advisory council recommended extension of coverage to just about all of those previously left out; greatly liberalized the insured status provisions for those already old; considerably liberalized benefits to those retiring in the early years—dropping the increment idea; recommended a permanent and total disability insurance program; recommended paying benefits at a younger age for women, particularly widows, liberalizing the retirement test, and other changes. In a series of sweeping amendments over the next 10 years these recommendations were put into effect, and then the recommendations of later councils were also largely embraced by Congress. So the 1978–79 Advisory Council had a very different job. This council examined a highly successful system. The issues are hardly those of survival, as they were in 1948. The problems confronting this council were problems related to an effective, fully functioning system, and the questions were primarily those of how can it be designed to do an even better job for society in preventing poverty and promoting economic security.

The council's findings and recommendations are conveniently divided into seven areas:

1. The reaffirmation of the most important provisions and basic principles of present law after a thorough discussion and consideration of alternatives.

2. A series of changes in the benefit structure.

3. Some findings and relatively minor changes in disability insurance.

4. Proposals for gradual extension of coverage to presently excluded government employees.

5. Equity questions dealing with the treatment of women and minority groups.

6. The relationship between Social Security and the related programs of private pensions and Supplementary Security Income and financing.

7. Administration.

First let me say what the council has reaffirmed. There have been so many attacks on Social Security recently that it seemed to many of us almost as valuable to make a strong defense of the principles, objectives, and nature of the present system as to make recommendations for improvement. Some of the more important findings by the council in this area of reaffirmation are:

a. Future Social Security beneficiaries can count on receiving their benefits, and the program is fully financed under present law over the next 50 years according to cost estimates that have been carefully examined and found to be reasonable in assumption and in methodology. [*Author's note:* This council was the first to establish a technical advisory group of economists, actuaries, and other professionals to advise the council in difficult technical areas. In recent years this has become standard practice.]

b. The program should continue on into the future to be based on the principle of providing replacement rates that are the same in the long run as they are in the near future, and the best way to bring this about is through wage-indexing and the updating of the brackets in the formula.

c. There should be no change (some council members would insert "at this time") in the age at which full benefits are first paid.

d. The major source (some members would say "only") of financing cash benefits under the program should be contributions from workers' earnings and payroll taxes on employers.

e. The council looked at the retirement test, and while recommending that the test for those under 65 be made the same as for those over 65, it did not recommend any changes in the over-65 test. Throughout the report there is strong support for the method of contributory, wage-related social insurance as the basic way to meet the risks insured against by the program, with a reaffirmation of the traditional approach of supplementation by private pensions, individual voluntary savings, and an improved means-tested program.

f. The council reaffirmed the design of the trust funds as limited to the purpose of the contingency reserve and explicitly turned down proposals for a rapid buildup in the reserves as an aid to capital formation.

g. The council also examined the value-added tax and unanimously recommended against it for any part of the financing of Social Security.

The council was asked by President Carter to evaluate the series of budget recommendations that were included in last year's budget message. All of these Social Security cuts were turned down by a majority of the council, although in some cases by a narrow margin. The council was overwhelmingly in favor of retaining students' benefits, currently-insured status, narrowly rejected dropping the lump-sum benefit and instead recommended that it be increased to a maximum of $500, narrowly rejected any change in the minimum benefit from present law, and proposed a much more liberal cap on family disability benefits than that included in the budget recommendations.

On financing, the council has tentatively agreed to a major change. Medicare would be entirely financed from a specially earmarked portion of the individual income tax matched by an equal amount derived from the corporation income tax. It is believed by the majority, and I am one of them, that the showing on the individual income tax return that an individual is specifically contributing toward Medicare will prevent the later introduction of a means test and major reductions in benefits, both of which might be threats if the entire program were financed from undifferentiated general revenues. It is also believed that this approach retains the fiscal discipline that is involved in the need to raise visible taxes when benefits are increased. As you all know, there is a strong interest on the part of economists to reduce the size of the overall collections from employers' payrolls because such taxes add to the cost of doing business, which puts pressure on prices and probably prevents the employment of some people who would otherwise be hired. With this change in the way Medicare is financed, it is possible to accommodate these economic goals while at the same time actually improving both the short- and long-range financing of the cash benefit program under Social Security. Specifically, instead of a 6.13 percent contribution rate in 1980, covering both Social Security and Medicare, the proposal would be to have a 5.6 percent rate for cash benefits alone and then hold this rate throughout the rest of the century. (On a pay-as-you-go basis, 5.6 percent is enough to fund the program until about the year 2005.)

At the same time it would be possible to avoid, of course, any increase now scheduled in the 1981 overall rate and to actually rescind the ad hoc increases in the maximum earnings base scheduled for 1980 and 1981. Moreover, since the funds for the cash benefit program would be building much more rapidly than under present law between now and 1985, this would address the uneasiness that now exists about whether the 1984 situation could, under conditions of a severe recession, cause a cash flow problem in the OASI part of the system. [*Author's note:* This advisory council proposal was not adopted. Rather, the financing of the system during the 1980s was assured by a different set of recommendations developed by the 1982–83 Greenspan Commission and adopted by Congress in 1983. These are discussed in Chapter 14, "Majority Recommendations of the Greenspan Commission."]

Finally, the council would call for a balancing rate of 7.3 percent to be put in the law for possible implementation in about 2005. This would be enough under present estimates to carry the program through the full 75 years under which the actuarial cost estimates are made. Nobody expects that the rate of 7.3 would actually be charged in 2005. It might turn out to be too low or, in my judgment, more likely too high, but in any event it would undoubtedly be spread out on a pay-as-you-go basis when the time actually came. The purpose of showing it in the law, however, would be to indicate to people both that there may well be higher costs in the next century but also that they are of manageable size even without some of the changes that have been talked about, like extending the retirement age or reducing replacement rates.

The council also made a series of other financing recommendations of lesser importance such as recommending against President Carter's 1977 proposal to have general revenues make limited payments to make up for revenues lost due to high unemployment.

The council also suggests a limited kind of borrowing authority from general revenues, and the merger of the disability insurance and old-age and survivors insurance trust funds.

On cash benefits, the council is proposing a different benefit formula: a two-step formula which would have the objective of making sure that workers who were under the program for at least 30 years and worked at approximately the federal minimum wage, or somewhat less, would get a benefit equal to at least the poverty level and that, of course, workers who earn higher amounts would get more, and also that workers now young who earned high wages throughout their lives would get a larger return than provided by present law. The adjusted formula is 61 percent of the first $422 of average indexed monthly earnings, and 27 percent above that, as compared to the present formula of 90 percent of the first $180, and 32 percent of the next $905, and 15 percent above $1,085. Both of these objectives seem to me important ones to carry out the purpose of the program and to hold the loyalty of young, higher-paid persons.

The council recommended that automatic adjustments in benefits tied to the cost of living should be made twice a year as in the case of civil service retirement rather than only once a year as is now the case.

Regarding gradual extension of coverage to government employees not now covered and to the employees of nonprofit organizations not now covered, the majority felt that the goal of universal coverage was very important both from the standpoint of making sure that employees of now excluded employers would always get at least as much protection as those covered by Social Security and also to eliminate windfall benefits payable to those who qualify under Social Security after relatively short periods of employment and get the advantage of the weighted benefit formula.

The council is recommending in the state and local and nonprofit area that all new hires be covered compulsorily by Social Security at some future specified date, and that all states be covered by the divided retirement system provisions of the present act. These two actions, the council believes, would give the states and localities opportunity to adjust to the new situation of universal coverage gradually and with the greatest possible flexibility while still accomplishing the objective.

In the case of federal employees, the council takes the position that either a similar provision or some kind of exchange of credit plan, perhaps modeled after the Railroad Retirement System, would be equally workable.

In other coverage areas, the council endorsed the long-standing recommendations for the coverage of first dollar earnings if a farm operator has expenditures of $2,500 annually for farm labor; and that employers should pay the full employer tax on tips reported by their employees.

*　　*　　*

A final note: Let me congratulate you for preserving the image of the Social Security district office as the efficient, friendly, and helpful organization it has always been. No other federal government organization comes in contact with so many people in such a meaningful way. You *are* "Uncle Sam" in community after community in the

United States. How you perform your work will help determine importantly how people feel about their government. It is a great responsibility.

You are engaged in a great cause—contributing to the abolition of poverty in the United States and the provision of economic security. I know you will always perform in a way worthy of so high a trust.

17

CONTRIBUTION RATES AND
FUNDING SOURCES

President Clinton's proposal to use part of the projected surplus in general revenues to help finance Social Security has renewed an old argument over whether or not the program should be financed entirely by earmarked contributions. This article examines various rationales for a government contribution.

The immediate practical problem facing the Congress in the financing of old-age and survivors insurance is the determination of a schedule of contribution rates. To date the rates charged under the program have not been based on the adoption of any particular plan of financing. Rather, they have been frozen each year at the original rate (1 percent for employer and 1 percent for employee), and the adoption of a long-range plan has been postponed. It is the purpose of this paper to suggest a plan and to indicate the major alternatives to that plan.

THE NATURE OF OLD-AGE AND SURVIVORS INSURANCE

The old-age and survivors insurance program is not one program but two, each with very different financial problems. It is an old-age retirement program, and it is also a form of life insurance that provides monthly income for survivors. The survivors or life insurance part of the program is susceptible of the usual insurance technique of giving full protection for a limited period of time after the payment of small initial premiums. In general, as in term insurance, the contributions

From "What Contribution Rate for Old-Age and Survivors Insurance?" in the *Social Security Bulletin,* July 1949, pp. 2–8.

paid by covered workers each year meet the cost of the protection afforded during that year, and the contributions collected should roughly equal the benefits paid out.[1]

The benefit in the retirement part of the program is essentially an annuity, and the contribution is primarily a way of accumulating a capital sum over a period of many years. By the time a worker retires, this capital sum plus interest should be sufficient to pay benefits at the desired level for his life expectancy.

THE CENTRAL PROBLEM IN FINANCING

Financing the old-age and survivors insurance program presents difficulties largely because persons retiring in the first 5, 10, 15, or even 20 years of the program cannot be expected to contribute at a high enough rate to accumulate a sum that would provide reasonably adequate benefits. Yet for sound social reasons we are not willing to postpone adequate payments under the social insurance program to the time when the amounts accumulated would cover the cost of such payments. This is a problem that all new retirement systems face. In private pension plans the usual solution is to give past-service credits to the older worker, with the employer paying the whole cost of these credits.

Most social insurance programs also give to the workers retiring in the early years of the program benefits that are much greater than can be bought by the contributions paid for their age group. This was true of the old-age benefit program under the original Social Security Act, passed in 1935; and in the 1939 amendments, older workers were given even larger benefits in relation to their contributions. Today, in the midst of a race between the effort to make contributory social insurance more effective immediately and a renewed drive to establish noncontributory pensions from general taxation, it is more important than ever that workers who are now old be paid insurance benefits which are socially adequate, but which therefore are much greater than can be paid for by their contributions and those of their employers.

The financial problem presented by the clear necessity to pay substantial benefits immediately is how to make up for the deficit in the contribution of older workers. One solution to this problem suggested by the Committee on Economic Security in its report preceding the passage of the 1935 Social Security Act was that the government bear this cost of getting the system started, just as employers bear it in private plans. The reasoning of the committee in making this suggestion was outlined in the report as follows:

> The plan outlined above contemplates that workers who enter the system after the maximum contribution rate has become effective will receive annuities which have been paid for entirely by their own contributions and the matching contributions of their employers. Workers now middle aged or older will receive annuities which are substantially larger than could be purchased by their own and matching contributions, although considerably less than the annuities which will be paid to workers who contribute for longer periods. Larger annuities than on a strictly earned basis would seem desirable because annuities build up only very slowly—for instance, a 4-percent contribution rate on a wage of $100 per month will produce at age 65 an annuity of only $2.58 per month if contributions were made for 5 years beginning at 60 years; $5.95 after 10 years, contributions beginning at 55; and $10.19 after 15 years, contributions beginning at age 50.
>
> The allowance of larger annuities than are warranted by their contributions and the matching contributions of their employers to the workers who are brought into the system at the outset, will involve a cost to the Federal Government which if payments are begun immediately will total approximately $500,000,000 per year. Under the plan suggested, however, no payments will actually be made by the Federal Government until 1965, and will, of course, be greater than they would be if paid as incurred, by the amount of the compound interest on the above sum.[2]

In some foreign systems the deficit of contribution of persons brought into insurance late in life has also been considered an important reason for financing the system partly out of a government contribution. In Great Britain, for example, the government contribution consists of two items—one to cover this deficit and another to cover part of the cost of benefits for those under the program for a full working lifetime.

These two distinct types of government subsidy are separately provided for in Britain's National Insurance Act of 1946. Section 2(3)(b) provides for "an annual payment fixed on a rising scale for a period of years of such amount as will meet the estimated cost of accepting entrants of all ages into insurance under the scheme on the same terms as entrants at age 16," while section (3)(a) provides for "a supplementary payment in respect of each contribution paid by insured persons and employers."

In Appendix A of the Beveridge Report of 1942, the Government Actuary gives the reasoning underlying these provisions:

> For the purpose of this analysis the view adopted on similar occasions in the past has been followed, namely, that for assessing the rate of contribution which can equitably be charged in a compulsory scheme of Social Insurance a fair basis is obtained by expressing the value of the future benefits to a new entrant at the minimum age of 16 in terms of the contribution, payable throughout working lifetime, which should be made to insure the benefits on an actuarial basis; this is commonly termed the *actuarial contribution*. . . .
>
> If a contribution on [this] basis were charged, new entrants at age 16 would be self-supporting in the sense that, if they could be isolated as a class and their contributions accumulated in a separate fund to meet the future cost of their benefits, no State subsidy would be required in respect of them since their pensions, for example, would be met out of the reserves accumulated during the working lifetime of each year's new entrants, which, on the assumptions made, would be exhausted on the death of the last pensioner. . . .
>
> Looking at the matter in another way, there is a deficiency because [older] persons have not paid the contribution at the new rates continuously in the past from age 16. The resulting excess in the cost of benefits over the income from contributions has to be met from the Exchequer. . . .
>
> In the Social Security Plan it is proposed that in addition to the subsidy provided by admitting the bulk of the existing population over age 16 at the flat rate of contribution without reduction of benefits . . . the Exchequer should provide a further subsidy by undertaking the liability for a proportion of the cost for future entrants at the initial age.[3]

THE ACTUARIAL RATE

The Committee on Economic Security contemplated a government contribution for the American program sufficient to cover the deficit arising from paying annuities larger than could be bought by the combined employer-employee contributions for individuals covered at the outset. The maximum combined contribution rate for employers and employees was to be the rate necessary to yield the proper capital accumulation for a generation of workers under the program for a full working lifetime. This is the rate referred to above by the Government Actuary of Great Britain as the actuarial contribution. Under the British flat-benefit scheme, the actuarial rate expresses the value of the benefits to the individual. Under the American program with its graduated benefit formula (now 40 percent of the first $50 of average monthly wage plus 10 percent of the next $200) the actuarial rate is a group rate. Low-wage earners get larger benefits in relation to their contribution than do high wage earners, and the actuarial rate represents the average value of the benefits for persons in each age group that has the opportunity to contribute over a working lifetime.

The actuarial rate for the present program in the United States is estimated to be within the range of 2 to 3.5 percent. A greatly liberalized system such as that proposed by the 1948 Advisory Council can be financed for those who spend a working lifetime under the program through contribution rates of approximately 2 percent for the employer and 2 percent for the employee.[4] (The council estimated a combined rate of from 3 to 5 percent.) The proposals of the Social Security Administration (exclusive of disability benefits) might require a slightly higher rate, since costs under this program would be somewhat greater in later years. (The combined actuarial rate for these recommendations is estimated to be within the range of 3.5 to 6 percent.)[5]

If under the actuarial plan the government share were to be paid into the trust funds from the beginning on a level-premium basis, the employer, employee, and government would pay in equal shares. If the government contribution is deferred, however, as suggested by the Committee on Economic Security, it would amount eventually to about one-half of annual disbursements. This is equivalent to the deficit of contribution of those who do not pay the actuarial rate over a working lifetime.[6] Such support from general tax resources is justified in part by the decrease in public assistance expenditures that would result from paying higher benefits in the early years than could be bought by the contributions of retired persons alone, and in part by the fact that old-age and survivors insurance, although not yet universal, is very broad in its coverage and serves the general welfare.

It is not essential to the theory of the actuarial rate that employers and employees must pay the full rate from the beginning of the program; it may also be thought of as a maximum rate, to be reached in one or two step-ups during the first decade or so of operation. Postponement of the effective date of the full actuarial rate, however, means that the eventual government contribution must be increased somewhat and will go partly to pay some of the cost of benefits for young persons who enter the system during the early years.

The Level-premium Rate

In this country in recent years the controversy over the rates to charge employers and employees has centered largely around two alternatives to the actuarial rate—the so-called level-premium rate and a schedule of contributions under a "pay-as-you-go" plan. Like the actuarial rate, these alternatives would provide for equal employer and employee contributions, but they would not provide for a government contribution.

The level-premium rate is the rate that will cover the full cost of the system if charged from the beginning and in perpetuity. It is considerably higher than the actuarial rate, because it includes the cost of the benefits for workers who do not have the opportunity to contribute to the system over a working lifetime. The advisory council estimated, for example, that for its proposals the level-premium rate would be from 4.9 to 7.3 percent of payroll as compared with 3 to 5 percent for the actuarial rate. Comparable figures for the Social Security Administration proposals (exclusive of disability benefits) would be 5.2 to 8.2 percent for the level-premium rate as compared with 3.5 to 6 percent for the actuarial rate.

Charging the level-premium rate would make reliance on other sources of revenue unnecessary. In the early years of the system, when few persons aged 65 and over are eligible for benefits, imposition of the level-premium rate would result in the building up of a large reserve. Later, when the income from contributions would not be sufficient to meet benefit costs, the interest income from this fund would make up the deficit.

This method of financing requires a combined contribution rate in excess of the actuarial value of benefits for younger workers, although the rate paid by the worker alone would seldom be in excess of the value received.[7] The deficit of contribution of older workers, under this system, is usually thought of as coming from the employer contribution, with many younger workers paying the full cost of their own benefits.

There has been considerable opposition on both economic and political grounds to a plan that would result in such a large excess of income over outgo in the early years of the program. It has been opposed on economic grounds largely because during the first few decades of operation the excess of contributions over benefits might result in a decrease in the money available for consumer purchases and have a deflationary effect on the general economy, an effect which during certain phases of the business cycle is undesirable. This effect, it is true, may be offset by other fiscal activities of government; taken as an isolated phenomenon, however, charging employers and employees the level-premium rate would be deflationary for some time.[8]

It has also been argued that a reserve as large as would be developed if the level-premium rate were charged (perhaps as much as $200 billion under current proposals) would create strong political pressure for liberalization of the program beyond what it could afford. Other opponents feel that a long-continued excess of income over outgo would encourage extravagant federal expenditures by providing a ready source of funds which the Treasury could borrow for general purposes. The proponents of building up a large reserve, whether through this plan or through a government contribution paid into the trust funds from the beginning of the program, argue that such a reserve is the best way to make sure that the benefits will be paid when due.

Although there are differences of opinion over whether a large reserve is desirable, there is general agreement that in a government program full-reserve financing is not necessary. In private insurance, because there is no guarantee of the continuous sale of new policies for a particular company, reserves are required in an amount sufficient to cover liabilities at all times. If the company stops writing new business, the protection for which people have already paid can be provided from these reserves. In social insurance a full reserve of this sort is not needed since it is not necessary to sell policies to new people to keep going. The entrance of new people into the system is guaranteed by the mandatory nature of the program, and the guarantee of solvency is in the taxing power of the government. The level-premium-rate plan places considerable reliance on a large reserve but would not result in a full reserve sufficient to cover all liabilities.

PAY-AS-YOU-GO

The other widely discussed alternative is a plan with contribution schedules based on the idea of "pay-as-you-go." Under this plan the contribution rate is not related to the value of the protection afforded. It is set at the point at which contributions will meet disbursements in a given year or over a period of a few years.

The pay-as-you-go method, which equates income from contributions and short-term expenditures, would result in rates that are relatively very low in the early years of the program and that increase gradually over the first half century of operation. When the system is just starting, only a very few workers aged 65 and over are able to meet the requirement of a certain minimum amount of employment after the beginning date. As the program matures, however, a larger and larger proportion of those attaining age 65 will have had an opportunity to earn wage credits and to qualify for benefits.

Not only will there be a great increase in the *proportion* of those over age 65 who will be entitled to benefits, but the *total number* of those aged 65 and over is expected to increase by roughly 75 percent during the next 25 to 30 years. These two factors taken together explain why the annual cost of old-age benefits will increase each year from now until the end of the century and beyond.

Combined contribution rates under a pay-as-you-go system would look like this if the low-cost estimates for the Social Security Administration proposals (exclusive of disability benefits) were taken: 1950, 1.0; 1960, 2.9; 1970, 4.4; 1980, 5.6; 1990, 6.5; 2000 and thereafter, 6.6. If the high-cost estimates were taken the rates would be like this: 1950, 1.5; 1960, 4.1; 1970, 6.0; 1980, 8.0; 1990, 9.9; 2000 and thereafter, 11.2.

A pay-as-you-go system financed exclusively from payroll contributions makes little sense in an old-age retirement program. From the standpoint of persons who spend a working lifetime under the program, it seems somewhat absurd to charge first a combined employer-employee rate of only 1.0 or 1.5 percent and then gradually to increase the rate to perhaps as much as 11 percent. For social insurance just as for private annuities, it is much easier for both workers and employers to pay a more or less level rate over a working lifetime.

Even more important, under a pay-as-you-go system financed entirely by employee-employer contributions, a large proportion of those who come into the system after the top rate is reached would pay more in earmarked Social Security taxes than would be necessary to cover the cost of the protection that they would receive. Because, in this system, the rates would be kept below the actuarial value of the benefits for many years, the resulting deficit of contribution would be too large to be met entirely by the employer. Therefore, part of the contributions made by employees of the next and future generations would have to be used as well.

To charge employees a contribution rate in excess of the value of the benefits in order to finance this deficit will certainly be considered unfair. Because of its regressive nature (a flat tax levied on only the first $3,000 or $4,800 of income), the payroll tax is a doubtful way of raising general funds; its justification rests on the quid pro quo arrangements of a genuine contributory system of insurance benefits.

OTHER POSSIBILITIES

Certain modifications of these three basic plans have been suggested from time to time and deserve mention.[9] For example, the rate—instead of being based on a strict pay-as-you-go plan—might be increased at regular intervals, say every 10 years, with the goal of keeping the system on an approximately current-cost basis. This modification does not, of course, remove the basic objections to the pay-as-you-go idea.

Another possibility, a modification of the actuarial-rate plan, is the British practice of a government contribution covering more than the deficit of contribution of older workers and resulting in a subsidy for young entrants as well. In the American system with its graduated benefit formula the additional amount would be a subsidy for low-paid workers. Under the actuarial-rate plan as described above, the contribution of low-paid workers and their employers does not cover the cost of benefits even in the long run. If the actuarial rate is charged, part of the employer contribution paid on the wage of high-paid workers is shifted to pay for the benefits of low-paid workers.

(The high-paid worker gets more than the value of his own contribution but not the full value of the combined contribution.) With an additional subsidy, such as that provided in the British system, part of the deficit of contribution of low-paid workers as well as the deficit of contribution of older workers would come from general revenues rather than entirely from the employer contribution. Since the deficit of contribution of older workers alone, however, is as much as one-third of total costs on a level-premium basis—or roughly one-half of eventual annual disbursements if the government contribution is deferred for several decades—it is probably the maximum that general revenues should now be committed to support.

Still another possibility would be to provide for an eventual government subsidy less than sufficient to cover the full deficit of contribution of older workers. Under one such plan, the maximum employee rate would be set at a point which would be intended roughly to equal the value of old-age and survivor protection for young, high-paid workers, and a part of the employer contribution as well as a government subsidy would go to meet the benefit cost for older workers. The maximum employee rate, to be reached in a series of step-ups, would be about half the level-premium rate or the same rate as would be charged employees from the beginning under the level-premium plan.

This approach differs from the actuarial-rate plan in permitting a combined employer and employee rate in excess of the value of the benefits to a generation of workers continuously under the program. If the self-employed are to be charged even as much as one and one-half times the employee rate, many of those under the program for a working lifetime would under this plan pay more than the value of the protection that they receive.

The 1948 Advisory Council suggested that the maximum combined contribution rate should be set arbitrarily at a point that would result eventually in an equal division of annual contributions among employers, employees, and government. The council based its recommendation in large part on the rationale of the actuarial rate but was reluctant to commit government revenues to as large a share in meeting future costs as the actuarial-rate plan would require. The council said in part:

> The old-age and survivors insurance program starts with an accrued liability resulting from the fact that, on retirement,

the present members of the labor force will not have contributed toward their benefits over a full working lifetime. Furthermore, with the postponement of the full rate of contributions recommended above, even young people who enter the labor force during the next decade will not pay the full rate over a working lifetime. If the cost of this accrued liability is met from the contributions of workers and their employers alone, those who enter the system after the full rate is imposed will obviously have to pay with their employers more than is necessary to finance their own protection. In our opinion, the cost of financing the accrued liability should not be met solely from the payroll contributions of employers and employees. We believe that this burden would more properly be borne, at least in part, by the general revenues of the Government.

Old-age and survivors insurance benefits should be planned on the assumption that general taxation will eventually share more or less equally with employer and employee contributions in financing future benefit outlays and administrative costs. The timing and exact proportion of this contribution, however, cannot be decided finally now.[10]

Most of the plans that provide for a government contribution may be considered variations of either the reserve financing of the level-premium-rate plan or the current-cost financing of the pay-as-you-go approach. If the full employer-employee rate selected as desirable is paid from the beginning of the program or shortly thereafter and the government contribution is paid into the trust funds from the beginning, the combined rates, including the government contribution, equal the level-premium rate. If, on the other hand, the desirable employer-employee rate is considered an ultimate rate to be reached gradually as costs increase and the government contribution is introduced only when benefit disbursements exceed contribution income, the combined rates, including the government contribution, equal the rates under a pay-as-you-go plan. It is also possible, of course, to adopt a middle ground between reserve and current-cost financing. The actuarial rate plan, for example, results in reserve financing, current-cost financing, or something in between, depending on when the government contribution is introduced and when the full actuarial rate is imposed.

WHICH PLAN?

For the reasons suggested above, neither the level-premium rate nor the strict pay-as-you-go plan seems completely acceptable as a basis for determining the employer-employee rate. Moreover, the various modifications of these plans offer little in the way of rationale that is convincing to the general public or the proponents of one or the other of the major alternatives.

The actuarial rate might well, however, offer a reasonable ground for agreement. It is as firmly based in sound annuity and actuarial principles as is the level-premium rate. In fact, it is the level-premium rate for those who have an opportunity to pay over a working lifetime and provides for them a completely self-financing system. Yet the actuarial rate, considered as the maximum employer-employee rate to be arrived at gradually over the first decade of operation and assuming that the government contribution will be postponed as suggested by the Committee on Economic Security, largely avoids the disadvantages and misunderstandings associated with a huge reserve. Unlike the pay-as-you-go plan, it maintains the principle that the direct contribution should not exceed the value of the benefits.

Perhaps most important of all in a program of contributory social insurance, the actuarial rate maintains over the long run a close relationship between the value of the protection and the rate of contribution; each generation after the first pays its own way but no more. The social cost of paying full-rate or nearly full-rate benefits in the early years of the program—a cost unrelated to the value of the protection for those who come later—is borne by general taxation, which is relatively progressive and relates the amount of tax much more closely to "ability to pay" than does the payroll tax. Under the pay-as-you-go or the level-premium plan or the various modifications of these plans, part or all of this cost is borne by the regressive employee contribution or by the employer payroll tax, which in large part may be shifted either to the consuming public or to wage earners.

A NEW SCHEDULE OF CONTRIBUTION RATES

If Congress were to accept the actuarial rate as the desirable combined employer-employee rate for the long run, it would also be necessary to decide how soon this ultimate rate should be imposed and when the government should start paying its share of the costs of the program.

In the opinion of the writer the most practical form of the actuarial rate plan is somewhere between reserve and current-cost financing. It is important that the ultimate rate be reached gradually, as this results in less disturbance to business and industry than imposition of the ultimate rate at the very beginning of the program. Furthermore, as suggested earlier, it is now desirable to minimize the deflationary effects resulting from an excess of income over outgo during the early years. On the other hand, there is no need to increase the future burden on general revenues to the extent required by strict current-cost financing and the postponement of all increases in the tax rate until actually needed to meet benefit costs.

It is probably most acceptable to time the first increase in rates with a substantial increase in benefits. An increase to 1.5 percent for employees and 1.5 percent for employers should therefore take place on the effective date of the new benefit amounts. Such an increase in contribution rates in 1950 is already provided for in the present act.

On the assumption that improvements in the program will approximate the cost of the recommendations made by the advisory council, a further rise to 2 percent would be needed to reach the actuarial rate.[11] Determining how soon it would be wise to impose this maximum rate is a matter of balancing broad fiscal and political considerations against the internal requirements of the social insurance system. If the present contribution schedule in the act were allowed to stand, the full actuarial rate for the cost equivalent of the advisory council plan would be reached at the beginning of 1952. From the standpoint of the insurance system alone, this would be the most desirable course. Postponing the imposition of the full rate means postponement of the time when benefits for younger workers entering the system would be completely self-financed and thus increases the eventual burden on general revenues.

On the other hand, if it is considered desirable on broad economic or political grounds to keep down the excess of income over outgo in the early years, the 1.5 percent rate might be kept until, as recommended by the advisory council, the income from this rate "plus interest on investments of the trust fund is insufficient to meet current benefit outlays and administrative costs." The council estimated that this would be likely to occur in 1957.

Whether the full actuarial rate were imposed in 1952 or five years later, it would be an important clarifying step to have it recognized as the proper rate that should be charged for the long run and reached as soon as practicable.

Under this method of financing, the generation reaching age 65 after paying the actuarial rate for a lifetime under the program will, with their employers, have paid enough to finance their own benefits. The payment from general revenues will be replacing the contributions of younger workers and the interest thereon which were used in the early years to pay the benefits of those who did not contribute long enough or at a high enough rate to pay their own way.

This government contribution would in all likelihood be introduced at the time when contributions based on the actuarial rate, plus interest on the trust funds, prove insufficient to meet benefit disbursements and administrative expenses. In this way the trust funds would be maintained at their highest point, and the greatest benefit would be derived from the interest earnings on the funds. Under this plan the government contribution would first be needed about 1965. It would be small in the beginning but would grow eventually to about one-half of annual disbursements.[12]

KEEPING THE BENEFITS CURRENT AS WAGES INCREASE

In addition to the problem of financing the deficit of contribution of older workers, there is one other problem which must be solved in establishing a satisfactory contribution schedule. Over the past 150 years there has been a tendency for wages to increase substantially, and there is good reason to expect this long-range trend to continue. The advance will, of course, include periods of decline in the future as it has in the past, but the long-run course of development is quite clear.

The problem created for the retirement program by increasing wages is this: dollar amounts that seem satisfactory as benefits in 1949 are very likely to be much too low by 1980. Because of the higher wages then current, reflecting probably both greater productivity and higher prices, any level of benefits established now will probably appear quite inadequate when younger workers now contributing are ready to retire. A retirement payment which was intended to be, say, a 30 percent replacement of previous wages turns out to be a 20 percent replacement or less.[13]

As indicated by the advisory council, "in setting contribution rates for the system, the essential question is probably not 'What percentage of payroll would be required at some distant time to pay benefits equal to the money amount provided in the Council's recommendation?' Rather it is 'What percentage of payroll will be required to pay benefits representing about the same proportion of future monthly earnings that the benefits recommended by the Council represent of present monthly earnings?'"[14]

The rates quoted throughout this paper are intended to answer this second type of question. If the rates quoted are put into effect and, as is likely, wages rise over the long-range future, benefits may be constantly liberalized without changing the contribution rates. This is possible because as wages go up the same contribution rate brings in more dollar income, and the effect of increasing wages on benefit amounts under the formulas proposed is not as great as the increase in this dollar income. The estimates used here are based on the idea, therefore, that in the long run the formula in the Social Security Act will be revised as wages go up, to provide benefits which on the average represent a constant percentage of average wages under the program. If wages rise and benefits are not liberalized, the contribution rates discussed here are higher than necessary.

Putting the problem a different way, it may be said that the benefit formulas proposed by both the administration and the advisory council could be financed, in all probability, with lower contribution rates than suggested in this paper, because, in the estimates used, wages were assumed to remain constant. It seems prudent, however, to charge the higher rates and allow for liberalizations in the formulas since, as wages increase, the benefits resulting from the formulas as now written will seem inadequate.

CONCLUSION

Lack of a plan for the long-range financing of the old-age and survivors insurance program is at present a source of doubt and confusion about that program. It is important to public confidence that a clear plan be adopted and that a schedule of contribution rates be included in the law and adhered to. In the opinion of the writer, the actuarial rate should be the maximum employer-employee rate and should be so figured as to allow liberalization in the benefit formula as wages increase over the long-run future. This rate should be arrived at gradually, the first step-up to come when benefits are liberalized and the second no later than the estimated time (about 1957) when a continuation of the old rate would result in a reduction in the trust funds. The government contribution should be introduced when the income from the actuarial rate plus interest on the fund is insufficient to cover current disbursements. The government's obligation to eventually make up the deficit of contribution of older workers and those who in the early years contribute at less than the actuarial rate should be explicitly stated in the legislation.

18

SUPPORTING SOCIAL SECURITY FROM GENERAL REVENUES

President Clinton's proposal to partially support the system from the projected surplus in general revenues has its roots in the original discussions on how to finance a contributory social insurance program.

I love to study the early days of our social insurance system. I find it interesting to see how persistent the problems of such a system turned out to be and what the founders of the system proposed for dealing with the problems. I am amazed at how much they anticipated.

When the system started, few people other than the founders themselves and the representatives of labor and employers who had been on advisory groups understood what the program was all about. However, the founders and their supporters were confident that the public and politicians would come in time to support the principles in which they devoutly believed. Roosevelt from the beginning had a vision of an insurance policy issued at birth to cover the major risks of life "from the cradle to the grave." (And he resented it when this phrase was popularly attributed to Lord Beveridge rather than to him!)[1] Of the nine major principles identified today with the current Old-Age Survivors and Disability Insurance program—universal, earned right, wage related, contributory and self-financed, redistributive, not means tested, wage indexed, inflation protected,

From remarks delivered at the 1999 Annual Conference of the National Academy of Social Insurance, Washington, D.C., January 27, 1999; published in Sheila Burke, Eric R. Kingson, and Uwe Reinhardt, eds., *Social Security and Medicare: Individual vs. Collective Risk and Responsibility* (Washington, D.C.: Brookings Institution Press, 2000), pp. 62–68.

and compulsory—all applied to the Old-Age Benefits Program in 1935 and to subsequent amendments. The fact that during a transition period the founders supported reliance on a means-tested assistance program, for example, did not indicate any confusion about the nature of social insurance. The issue, rather, became whether the insurance program based on these clear principles from the beginning should be kept.

In 1947–48, as staff director of an advisory council to the Senate Finance Committee, I worried a lot about whether Congress might not drop the whole thing because it was so ineffective, with only about 16 percent of the elderly eligible for benefits and the benefits averaging only about $25 a month, much less than Old-Age Assistance was paying. I think the council and the Social Security Administration saved the program at that time by recommending the extensions of coverage, the increase in benefits, and the liberalization of eligibility requirements that were adopted in the 1950 amendments. But the principles of social insurance were always clear; they were not being invented. The question was whether the country was to keep a program with such principles or reject it in the late 1940s as being ineffective. The case for a system of flat payments paid for from general revenues, which would be immediately effective, was pressed from many quarters from the days of the Townsend plan on, and the double-decker idea—a flat benefit for all, plus an upper deck related to wages—was quite popular.

I want to focus on one of the nine principles about which there was disagreement then as there is now. A *totally* self-financed system was not a universally accepted Social Security principle in 1935. When the staff-prepared proposal on old-age benefits was about to go to Capitol Hill (Roosevelt had announced that it would be transmitted the next day), the president stopped it and sent it back for a rewrite. In so doing he highlighted differences of view on the use of general revenues for Social Security that will probably surface again in the developing debate over President Bill Clinton's current Social Security proposals.

In recommending an eventual government contribution from general revenues, the Committee on Economic Security's three-member staff on old-age benefits thought they had the answer to a basic dilemma that arose in getting the insurance system started. The staff members on old age (certainly influential among the founders) were Barbara Nachtrieb Armstrong, the leader of the group, a professor of law at the University of California; Doug Brown, director of the

Industrial Relations Section at Princeton; and Murray Latimer, an expert on industrial pension plans and the first chairman of the Railroad Retirement Board. They knew that for this program to be acceptable, it would have to pay benefits in the first generation that would exceed what the first generation of workers and their employers paid in.

The problem was that most workers were already well advanced in their careers. There were middle-aged and older workers to whom benefits would need to be paid but who did not have a full career remaining over which their contributions could be accumulated. To give them only what their contributions could have paid for would have meant a very unsatisfactory benefit level for all but the very young and a long postponement of any help that old-age insurance might be in solving the problem of old-age security. Few would have voted for such a proposal.

So the plan paid much higher benefits to the first generation of Social Security recipients than their contributions justified. In doing so the staff recognized that they were creating a permanent accrued liability for the system, and that concerned them. They feared that those starting to pay in the 1960s and beyond would complain about not getting their "money's worth" if the full cost of the earlier liability was to be paid from earmarked Social Security contributions—the payroll tax. Doug Brown described their reasoning in a 1972 book, *An American Philosophy of Social Security:*

> The staff members of the Committee on Economic Security responsible for the planning of the old-age insurance system were convinced that eventual government contributions would be necessary. To provide a reasonable level of benefits for those retiring in the early years of the system would require paying more in benefits to the retired worker than the worker and his employer had contributed. The difference, drawn from the contributions of younger workers, would need to be reimbursed to the system as these younger workers became old. . . . In private insurance terms, the system assumed an accrued liability in paying adequate benefits to those retiring in the early years of the system. . . . It was the conviction of the staff that the accrued liability within the system was a proper charge upon the government. Millions of aged workers who would otherwise require needs-tested

old-age pensions, entirely financed by the state and federal governments, would be receiving benefits instead from the contributory social insurance system. It seemed entirely reasonable to ask the government to reimburse the system the amount it would save through reduced old-age assistance payments.[2]

The staff suggested that the government contribution should be paid when it was needed and not before, and estimated that under their approach the first government contribution would begin in 1962.

The chair of the Committee on Economic Security, Secretary of Labor Frances Perkins, and the executive director, Edwin Witte (along with then-assistant secretary of labor Arthur J. Altmeyer, the other important member of the founders' group), went along with this reasoning, but Perkins and Witte were not nearly as interested in the old-age provision as they were in unemployment insurance. At the last minute Roosevelt intervened, probably at the instigation of Secretary of the Treasury Henry Morgenthau, and said "no," the program should be completely self-financed in the sense that the earmarked contributions had to cover the whole cost down the road—not just at the beginning. Roosevelt wanted to avoid any burden on the general treasury. The only way he would let the staff plan go forward was to say that this was just one possible approach. Later the administration submitted a plan without general revenue, and this is how the bill passed.[3]

But those concerned about the payroll taxes going "too high" and the program becoming unpopular unless there was some general revenue to meet the cost of the accrued liability did not give up. Doug Brown chaired the advisory council in 1937–38 and was a member of the 1947–48 council, and many others after that. He never changed his mind and kept pushing for eventual general revenue support. Both the 1937–38 and the 1947–48 advisory councils and most Social Security experts agreed with him.

I did, for example. I wrote an article for the July 1949 issue of the *Social Security Bulletin* [see Chapter 17] in which I argued that workers should pay a contribution rate matched by employers that was estimated to pay for the benefits of their generation—what the Government Actuary in the United Kingdom called the "actuarial rate"—and that the cost of the accrued liability was fairly borne by the general taxpayer.

Support for a general revenue contribution slacked off in the late 1950s, although I kept advocating it as late as 1978, in a book I published that year. But then I changed my mind. I just could not see a commissioner of Social Security, as I had been, successfully arguing before Congress for the huge amounts of general revenue that the accrued liability rationale required. Moreover, because the general revenue contribution has been postponed, the rationale would no longer have led to one-third financing from employees, one-third from employers, and one-third from the government. Instead, it would have shifted financing to about one-fourth from the employees, one-fourth from the employer, and one-half from the general taxpayer, and would have been in competition with all the other demands for federal financing. Considering the great resistance on the part of the public to general taxes, I was fearful that sufficient general revenue would not be voted. On the other hand, the public generally seemed quite willing to pay a hefty tax earmarked for Social Security, so I and most other experts gave up on general revenue financing and adopted the "self-financed" principle.

But times have changed. President Clinton has proposed $2.7 trillion for Social Security out of general taxes down the road, in addition to the roughly $2.7 trillion excess in Social Security taxes plus interest over benefits estimated for the next 15 years under present law. This is only about one-third of what Doug Brown's rationale would call for, but it is certainly a major commitment in this direction.

I am astounded at this, after some 30 years of advocating such a policy and then abandoning it, but I am pleased—I think. The pledge for later general support will be backed by gradually placing interest-bearing bonds in the trust funds over the period of the next 15 years, except that about one-fifth of this $2.7 trillion infusion devoted to Social Security from general revenues will be used to buy equities up to a maximum of 15 percent of the Social Security funds. This is being done with the full support of Treasury Secretary Robert E. Rubin, who is looked to on Wall Street with at least as much deference as Federal Reserve chairman Alan Greenspan, who opposes this move. I could not be more pleased than I am about the breakthrough on equity investment, which is new and has no historical precedent. [*Author's note:* The plan described was the president's first proposal. In October 1999 he submitted a substitute designed to gain more support in the hope of getting a quick agreement with Congress. The new proposal did not include investments in stocks (although the 2001 budget, presumably expressing the administration's preferred position, does so) and proposed an annual general revenue contribution beginning in 2011. For the years 2011 through 2016, the contribution would be the estimated amount of interest saved in those years on the publicly held debt because of reduction made in that debt beginning in the year 2000 as the growing Social Security surpluses were used to buy back debt from the public. From 2016 on, the amount of the annual payment would be fixed at the 2016 level. The payments would end with 2044, the estimated exhaustion date (as of 1999) for the non–Social Security budget surplus. It should be noted that in 2000 the estimated non–Social Security surplus was very substantially increased, providing further room for larger general-revenue infusions into Social Security.]

There are other rationales for government contribution than the one urged by Doug Brown. Some have argued that the cost of modifying the equity principle of quid pro quo to carry out a social purpose—the weighted benefit formula, for example—ought to be carried by the general taxpayer, not solely by the better-off contributors. Some have just left the argument at the point that Social Security is an extremely important institution in American life and the government should pay part of the cost, leading to a somewhat more progressive way of raising the funds, while still keeping strong reliance on the contributory principle.

So far the Clinton administration has not taken the risk of leaning on any particular rationale. The administration seems to be saying, rather (in my words), "We anticipate these large surpluses in the unified budget over the next 15 years, let's use a large part of it to pay down the debt held in private hands and increase the debt held by Social Security and Medicare—more bonds in these trust funds to be cashed later as needed. Let's just give a big part of these anticipated surpluses to Social Security and Medicare, thus avoiding much of the need for substantial Social Security benefit cuts or Social Security tax increases." No particular rationale is offered or apparently needed.

Reducing the size of the federal debt held in private hands and instead increasing the size of the debt held by Social Security will give the Treasury more flexibility in meeting future Social Security and Medicare obligations. For example, the bonds could be paid off by increased general taxes or by borrowing from private lenders once again. (It is necessary, of course, that future general revenues to the amount of the promise—$2.7 trillion or its equivalent in percent of payroll—be actually committed to Social Security, with bonds and stocks representing the commitment put in the trust funds. The actuaries could hardly be expected to estimate the ability of the system to pay full benefits until 2055 instead of 2032, as under present law, on a vague commitment of 62 percent of whatever the unified budget surplus turns out to be over the next 15 years!)

Eventually everything comes around again. Clinton's proposal for U.S. government annuities supplementary to Social Security was part of Roosevelt's plan in 1935, although bargained away in the negotiations over the 1935 bill. The Clinton plan is in somewhat different form with more appeal to conservatives. The proposal in 1935 looked like a competitive threat to insurance companies and other private sellers. The Clinton plan looks more like an incentive for middle-income workers to put more into private investments.

In an interesting informal comment, Arthur Altmeyer, the second chairman of the Social Security Board and the first commissioner for Social Security (and perhaps the most influential father of all the founding mothers and fathers of Social Security), actually proposed to the Republican leader on Social Security, Senator Arthur Vandenberg, that because of his opposition to a big fund buildup he might want to put some Social Security money in stocks, but Altmeyer never pursued the idea.[4]

Further debate is needed. To get rid of the entire long-range 2.19 percent of payroll deficit reported by the trustees in 1998 we need changes beyond the Clinton proposal, amounting to about 0.85 to 0.90 percent of payroll more when the interaction among proposals is taken into account. [*Author's note:* In the Trustees' Report for the year 2000, the deficit was estimated to be 1.89 percent of payroll, and the change needed beyond the Clinton proposal of June 20, 2000, was estimated to equal 0.75 percent of payroll.] One big step in that direction would be to raise the maximum earnings base to where it makes taxable about 90 percent of earnings in covered employment as it used to, instead of 86 percent as at present. This would result in a 0.58 percent payroll reduction in the Social Security deficit. (Under the assumptions in the 1999 Trustees' Report, this change alone is just about enough on top of the president's proposal to eliminate the entire 75-year deficit.)

We do not have to invent everything all over again. There were a lot of good ideas developed in the past that are applicable today. What seems clear is that we need to know enough history to preserve what is good, but we must also be willing to embrace new ideas like equity investment as they come along and are shown to be useful.

19

A PUBLIC-PRIVATE
INVESTMENT STRATEGY

The 1994–96 Advisory Council was unable to arrive at a consensus about the future of Social Security. Some members, myself included, argued for strengthening the existing program and maintaining it as a defined-benefit system. Others advocated moving the program toward a defined-contribution system by redirecting a percentage of workers' contributions into personal savings accounts. I was the principal author of the recommendations to strengthen the existing program. The following excerpt makes the case for considering investment of a portion of Social Security's trust funds in stocks. On this point, particularly, Thomas W. Jones, at that time president of TIAA-CREF and a member of the advisory council, made many important contributions.

When Social Security was on a pay-as-you-go basis and had only a relatively small contingency reserve, how that reserve was invested did not make much difference. But as the system shifts toward partial advance funding and builds up a significant reserve against future costs, how the accumulating funds are invested becomes important, and a departure from tradition may be warranted.

In Social Security, the government is the administrator and fund manager of an enormous pension and group insurance plan. It collects

From "Social Security for the 21st Century: A Strategy to Maintain Benefits and Strengthen America's Family Protection Plan," in the *Report* of the 1994–96 Advisory Council on Social Security. The other members supporting this plan were Edith V. Fierst, Gloria T. Johnson, Thomas W. Jones, George Kourpias, and Gerald M. Shea.

dedicated taxes which are the equivalent of the premiums in a private insurance plan and the payments into the defined-benefit pension plans of a private corporation or state retirement system. And it administers benefits which, like the dedicated tax contributions, are spelled out in detail in the law. There are, of course, important differences between Social Security's defined-benefit plan and the defined-benefit plans managed by the private sector and the states, but the broad characteristics are similar.

Currently it can be argued that the government is not adequately performing its role as fund manager for Social Security—not because of any failure on the part of those managing the system but because Social Security by law is allowed to invest only in the most conservative of investments: long-term, low-yield government bonds. Trustees of private pension systems, and managers of state pension systems, who have the authority to invest much more broadly, would surely be castigated if they pursued such an ultra-conservative investment policy, and it can be argued that Social Security should have the same freedom to invest part of its funds in the broad equities market representing practically the entire American economy. The higher rate of return from such investment would make Social Security more attractive as a savings vehicle, particularly for younger workers, and the increased revenues would help eliminate the system's anticipated long-term deficit.[1]

The plan we propose for consideration would gradually invest up to 40 percent of Social Security's accumulated funds in private equities (reaching the 40 percent range in about 2015), with the balance to be invested in long-term government obligations as before.[2] [*Author's note:* President Clinton in 2000 proposed investing 15 percent of Social Security's accumulating surplus in stocks. Coupled with his proposal for a contribution to the system from general revenues, this would reduce the anticipated 75-year deficit from 1.89 percent of payroll to 0.48 percent of payroll, and the trust fund exhaustion date would be extended to 2063.]

Investments would be indexed to the broad market, and the objective of investment neutrality would be established in law by requiring investment solely for the economic benefit of Social Security participants and not for any other economic, social, or political objective. As in the case of the Federal Retirement Thrift Investment Board, which administers the Federal Employees Thrift Savings Plan (TSP), an expert investment board would be established. It would have three functions:

- First, it would select an appropriate passive market index (such as the Russell 3000 or the Wilshire 5000) to govern Social Security's equity investments.

- Second, it would select, through bidding, several of the leading passive equity index portfolio managers with experience in managing large institutional accounts. In addition to managing the portfolio, the managers would be responsible for maintaining the investment ratio of Social Security's accumulated funds at roughly 40 percent in stocks.

- Third, it would monitor portfolio management and establish mechanisms to impartially review the overall operation of the plan, report to the Congress and the public, and periodically consider changes in the index or in portfolio managers as appropriate.

The investment of Social Security funds would have only a limited effect on the market. Although Social Security represents a large part of the government's total operations, it does not represent a large part of the entire $7.5 trillion U.S. economy. Social Security's annual stock transactions would involve less than 1 percent of the value of U.S. equities, and, even at the peak in 2014, would probably account for considerably less than 5 percent of the value of all stocks.

In addition to pursuing a policy of investment neutrality, it is important to ensure that Social Security's holdings have a neutral effect on stockholder voting on company policy. It may be sufficient to simply prohibit, by law, the voting of any stocks held by Social Security. Alternatively, it might be desirable for the voting of Social Security stocks to automatically be scored in the same proportion as other stockholder votes, or the exercise of proxy voting could be delegated to the portfolio managers, as is the case with the federal Thrift Savings Plan. Whatever the approach, the point is that it is entirely feasible to ensure the neutrality of Social Security investments in matters of corporate policy.

Some critics of this investment strategy argue that politicians would be tempted to tamper with the index of government investments in order to steer investments toward preferred social objectives. In reality this is unlikely to be a problem. Once the objective of investment neutrality is set, we can be reasonably confident that our competitive political system will furnish the necessary checks and balances to protect this principle. Efforts by one party to undermine neutrality would provide a major point of attack for the other party, with the result that future Congresses would be reluctant to interfere with an established investment arrangement in which nearly every American family would have a stake. (The same principle of political balance has thus far protected Social Security from radical change.)

Social Security would be the largest but not the first federal defined benefit retirement system to invest a significant proportion of its assets in the stock market. In 1995 the Tennessee Valley Authority had about 40 percent of its $3.8 billion in assets invested in stocks; the Federal Reserve System had about two-thirds of its $2.9 billion in assets in stocks; and the systems covering the Army/Air Force exchanges had about 80 percent of their $1.9 billion in assets in stocks.

None of these federal systems has been politically influenced in selecting investments. Nor has the Federal Retirement Thrift Investment Board. In 1986 the Congress authorized the board to make indexed stock investments. As Francis X. Cavanaugh, a former high-ranking Treasury official and first executive director (1986–94) of the board, has stated:

> I encountered no significant problems as we selected an index (the S&P 500), obtained competitive bids from large index fund managers, and established a highly efficient stock fund with minimal administrative expenses. By 1996, 1 million federal employees had elected to invest $13 billion in the Board's stock index fund. I see no reason why the Social Security trust fund should not have the same stock investment advantage as the Thrift Savings Plan.[3]

Coupled with the other changes previously described, investment of part of Social Security's accumulated funds in the stock market has the great advantage of leaving the essential principles of the system undisturbed while restoring long-term balance and offering Social Security participants the same stock investment benefits that are enjoyed by participants in other large retirement plans—state, local, and private. The investment risk is kept manageable and affordable by investing as a group rather than as individuals, and the administrative costs are, of course, very low in comparison to buying stocks and mutual funds at retail and managing millions of relatively small individual accounts (not to mention regulating these accounts and reporting them to the

Internal Revenue Service). And any lingering concerns about what might go wrong with a centrally managed fund should be balanced against considerations of what might go wrong in a partial-privatization plan requiring more than 127 million compulsory individual savings accounts.[4]

It is very important not to confuse the idea of investing in an indexed, passively managed portfolio of equities with proposals to move toward a system in which workers are either required or encouraged to divert part of their Social Security contribution to individual savings accounts. Under the first approach, Social Security remains a defined-*benefit* plan; under the second it is converted in part to a defined-*contribution* plan, with benefits determined not by law but by individual experiences with investment.

Investment in stocks by a defined-benefit plan is not, of course, a new idea, nor does it fundamentally alter the nature of a public plan. State retirement systems with defined benefits invest heavily in stocks—but are still public plans. As Social Security's trust funds build up in anticipation of future costs, it simply makes good sense to consider investing part of the buildup in stocks in order to obtain a higher return than is possible under a policy of investing only in low-yield government obligations. And this approach to restoring long-term balance to the program, unlike payroll tax increases and benefit cuts, greatly improves Social Security's "money's worth" for younger workers.

Increasing the return on Social Security funds can also be justified on the grounds that large-scale investment of Social Security funds in government bonds results in more of a return to the nation's economic well-being than Social Security is now receiving. When Social Security invests a dollar in government bonds, it frees a dollar for investment in the private sector. Thus, a full reflection of Social Security's contribution would be closer to the real return on all private capital (roughly 6 percent) than to the government long-term bond rate. Although investing 40 percent of Social Security accumulations in the stock market nearly doubles the real rate of return on the total of Social Security accumulated funds—raising it from an estimated 2.3 percent on long-term government bonds after inflation to 4.2 percent after inflation—it properly goes only part of the way toward what might theoretically be justified.

We reiterate that except for this change in investment policy, Social Security's principles and structure would remain unchanged under this approach. Social Security continues as a defined-benefit plan, with the amount of benefits and the conditions under which they are paid still determined by law rather than by individual invest-ments. In contrast, the plans proposed by other advisory council members establish compulsory savings plans, with workers investing their savings individually and, in retirement, getting back whatever their investments may yield. These are fundamentally different approaches.

Risk for individuals investing on their own is quite a different matter from the shared risk of investing through the Social Security system or indeed via any other system. We do not believe that the nation's basic retirement system should require everyone to bear investment risk as isolated individuals, as would be the case with a system of compulsory savings plans. A central fund broadly indexed to the stock market and investing regularly in good times and bad is at far less risk. With Social Security's investments tied to the perfor-mance of the entire U.S. economy, there would be ups and downs in returns, but only very long-range trends would matter. And the assumed rate of return, while important, would be secondary to the fact that benefits would remain defined by law rather than by the relative uncertainty of individual investment decisions.

There is no denying that Social Security funds could be earning a higher return than is possible under present law, and that doing so would help stabilize the program for the long run while making it a better investment for younger workers in terms of "money's worth" criteria. If changes in investment philosophy are to be considered, the approach outlined above would appear to have many advantages over the much more radical change that the partial-privatization pro-posals call for.

Some members of the advisory council have argued that our proposal to invest part of the Social Security funds in the private capital market would have a destabilizing effect on the market even if such investments were passive and representative of the broad market. The proposal we have offered for further study would grad-ually build to a 40 percent passive indexed equity asset allocation over a 15-year period from 2000 through 2014 (that is, approxi-mately 2.67 percent of trust fund assets reallocated to passive indexed equities each year). This would total approximately $1 tril-lion by 2015. In comparison, approximately $600 billion was invest-ed in passive equity index portfolios in the U.S. market at the end of

1995, and this would increase to approximately $5 trillion in 2015 at a 12 percent compound rate of growth (combined total return and new funds allocated to passive equity index strategies). Total U.S. equity market valuation of approximately $8 trillion in 1996 will increase to roughly $60 trillion in 20 years at a compound annual growth rate of 10 percent (combined total return and new funds committed to equity investment).

Why does $1 trillion in Social Security Trust Fund investments destabilize the market when it follows the same strategy with the same investment advisors as $5 trillion in non–trust fund passive equity index assets? If trust fund passive equity index assets were spread, say, among the top 20 or 25 private-sector passive equity index managers, trust fund equity assets would be seamlessly integrated into the broad pool of indexed assets in the market. Trust fund equity assets would not be disruptive, nor would they be a disproportionate share of the market. Further, the proposed trust fund passive equity asset allocation of 40 percent is a less severe shift away from the current Treasury debt investment policy than would be experienced with individual accounts, which are expected to hold at least 50 percent of assets in equities. If asset reallocation under individual account proposals would not be disruptive to U.S. debt and equity markets, there is little reason to believe that a more moderate asset reallocation by the trust funds would be destabilizing.

As to the question of which investment approach is more efficient— individual accounts or central management—expenses and transaction costs are likely to erode substantially the investment performance of individual accounts, particularly for low- and moderate-income workers. Consider a $30,000-per-year worker contributing 2 percent to an individual account. The $600 contribution will be eroded by flat dollar account maintenance fees ($30 per year is typical of charges levied for IRAs and Keoghs), sales charges on mutual funds (often 3 percent or more), and expense charges on mutual funds (often 1.5 percent or more for equity mutual funds). This worker's investment selections would have to outperform the market by 5 to 9 percent before expenses in order to equal the market after expenses.

Some argue that competition will lower these expenses to more reasonable levels. This certainly has not been the experience in the mutual fund marketplace. Individuals continue to pay hefty sales charges along with operating and investment advisory expenses for funds which usually fail to outperform the market. This apparent irrational behavior may suggest that many investors don't understand the total expenses they are paying, or how poorly their mutual funds are performing relative to the market.

In contrast, Social Security investment in equities could be done very efficiently on a portfolio basis by contracting with private sector passive equity index managers. For example, the federal Thrift Savings Plan pays one basis point investment advisory fees to an equity index manager to manage an $18 billion S&P-500 passive portfolio, and two basis points to manage a $3 billion passive indexed bond fund.

Can a hands-off equity index fund principle be maintained? The ultimate guarantor against political intervention in what we describe as a kind of "blind trust" arrangement for Social Security's investment in private stock is our competitive political system. Once the policy of nonintervention is established in law and policy, it is unlikely that the political cost of advocating change would be lightly undertaken. Social Security in the past and in the future involves the interests of just about every American family, and for one party or faction to advocate change that is seen as damaging to the institution creates a major opportunity for the other political party. It is the competitiveness of our political system that has protected Social Security from radical change for 60 years.

We believe that this democratic control is more powerful than the theoretical risk that anything one Congress sets up another can change. There is tremendous protection for settled policy in a contributory, nearly universal system such as Social Security, once the policy has been agreed to and enunciated in law. The uncertainty of future congressional activity is much more of a real threat to proposals which start out without substantial support, as would be true of the proposal to cut back Social Security to a flat benefit program of interest and usefulness for only those of low income. The substantially reduced protection of the government portion of the proposed plan for individual accounts also has this problem: If "money's worth" analysis raises questions of young workers' loyalty to the present system, how much more is this likely to be the case for a system collecting as much in taxes but over time cutting the average benefit by 30 percent?

Can a reasonable distinction be drawn between financing Social Security partly through equity investment as compared to other government programs? We believe the answer is yes. Social Security is a huge group insurance and pension fund which is administered by the federal government as a public utility for the participants. Its investment arrangements can follow those of state retirement systems and private pension systems without logically needing to allow federal programs in general to be financed by equity investment. Thus, as in the case of the Thrift Savings Plan, investment in stocks should be seen as uniquely suited for retirement income, not as a way of financing the general activities of government.

20

THE MYTH OF
MEANS TESTING

This op-ed, co-authored with Henry J. Aaron of the Brookings Institution, was written in response to efforts by the Concord Coalition and others to means test Social Security—a perennial issue.

Everyone *knows* that rising Social Security expenditures are boosting the federal budget deficit. Right? Everyone *knows* that cutting Social Security expenditures is the key to lowering the deficit. Right? And common sense tells us that the fairest way to cut benefits would be by means testing them so that benefits only of the well-to-do elderly are cut. Right?

"Yes, yes, and yes," says Peter G. Peterson, president of the Concord Coalition, founded by former senators Warren B. Rudman and Paul E. Tsongas. Peterson is everywhere with his message. TV interviews galore, an *Atlantic Monthly* article, a new book, and the Coalition's September report, "The Zero Deficit Plan." But in fact the correct responses to the three statements above are "wrong, wrong, and wrong again." Here's why:

Far from increasing the deficit, Social Security is now reducing the deficit. In 1993 Social Security revenues will exceed outlays by $46 billion. If it weren't for Social Security, the federal deficit would be that much larger.

That contribution to deficit reduction will continue to grow for many years. Without Social Security, the federal deficit in the year

From the *Washington Post*, November 14, 1993.

2000 would be $97 billion larger than the already frightening $251 billion projected by the Congressional Budget Office. [*Author's note:* Given the surpluses that have developed in the relatively short time since CBO made the projection cited in this op-ed, this is a useful illustration of how difficult it is for even the most sophisticated actuaries and economists to accurately forecast the course of the U.S. economy—a cautionary lesson for lawmakers, media commentators, and others to keep in mind when reacting to forecasts that Social Security's revenues and expenditures may fall moderately out of balance over a 75-year period.]

Falsehoods repeated often enough come to be accepted by many as true. In this fashion, the statement that Social Security costs are a major factor in pushing up the federal deficit has gained currency. But it is still false.

Cutting Social Security benefits would almost certainly not lower the deficit. That's because any change that would increase the excess of payroll tax revenues over current benefit payments would make it virtually impossible to resist calls for cutting payroll taxes in tandem. Why, it would be asked, should even more of the proceeds from a regressive tax on earnings—justified only because it pays for a progressive benefit structure, also linked to earnings—be used to offset deficits generated by the failure to pay for other government operations?

Last year Congress seriously considered, and the Senate only narrowly rejected, a proposal to cut payroll taxes enough to eliminate any excess of Social Security revenues over expenditures. A substantial cut in benefits would surely prompt Congress to action. Of course, if Congress cut benefits and taxes in parallel, the deficit would not fall.

Means testing Social Security—the denial of benefits to people whose income or wealth exceeds a stipulated level—would be unfair and undermine support for our universal pension system, by far the most effective anti-poverty program we have ever had. The Social Security system includes a simple but subtle principle that is very important in protecting the families of low-wage earners against poverty when such workers retire, become disabled, or die. Everyone pays taxes at the same rate on earnings up to a limit, so that everyone can claim a pension in return, as a matter of right and without the stigma of welfare. But the benefit paid low earners replaces a larger share of their past earnings than does the benefit paid to high earners. As a result, Social Security is keeping about 15 million people from poverty and millions more from sinking to near-poverty.

What makes it possible to pay benefits to workers with low earnings histories sufficient to keep them out of poverty is Social Security's weighted benefit formula. That formula rewards low earners more generously for each dollar of past contributions than it pays workers with high earnings histories. High earners in fact sometimes complain that they could get more privately for the taxes they and their employers pay. This claim is debatable, as Social Security has valuable insurance features no private pension can claim, such as complete protection from price inflation and safety from loss from business failure, industry decline, or poor investment results. Still, making major reductions in the benefits of high earners and making uncertain the receipt of all but a tiny benefit, as in the Concord Coalition plan, would generate massive pressures to permit higher-paid people to opt out of Social Security.

Given the weighted benefit formula, the system could not survive if substantial numbers of higher-paid earners opted out. Moreover, without such a formula, millions of elderly and disabled beneficiaries would find Social Security benefits to be way too low to support them and would have to turn to welfare for help. Welfare would then determine the maximum income of such households, and past contributions to Social Security would be meaningless for them.

The succession of events arising from the introduction of a means test could well destroy the Social Security system, which is now of critical importance not only to the 6 out of 10 workers in private industry for whom Social Security is the only pension, but also for the vast majority of those who have a supplementary private pension built on top of Social Security. Social Security is not intended to be just a poverty program, successful as it is at that task. It is also meant to be a base upon which people can add income from pensions and savings.

The United States has taken 50 years to develop a four-tier system of retirement protection, consisting of a universal and compulsory Social Security system, supplementary private and government pensions, individual savings, and a safety net—Supplemental Security Income (SSI)—that guarantees everyone some income during retirement or disability, albeit at a level below the poverty line. The four tiers are complementary. Changing one will force changes in the others.

Means testing Social Security, for example, would produce perverse effects in private pensions. Many companies with plans that guarantee pensioners a defined level of benefits are already having difficulty keeping up with funding requirements. If Social Security benefits were cut, or made uncertain, they would have to increase their plans' funding or announce reductions in total retirement protection for their employees. Others would drop their pension plans rather than incur added expense.

Paradoxically and perversely, the biggest losers from means testing Social Security might not be the intended target—the wealthy. The real losers might well be middle-income workers now fortunate enough to receive both Social Security and a private pension. And, of course, if Social Security disappeared, as well it might, the SSI welfare rolls for the elderly would grow 10 to 15 times their present size.

Social Security is family protection for everyone against loss of income from disability, death, or retirement. It would be tragic if myopic deficit cutters put at risk this most widely supported of federal programs through measures that would not even cut the deficit.

21

GETTING THE FACTS STRAIGHT

One of the major problems with the ongoing debate about the future of Social Security is that there is so much misinformation in circulation. This piece discusses three critically important points of confusion: Social Security's financing; how to interpret the 75-year forecasts used in estimating Social Security's incomes and expenses; and what would happen if Social Security were to be partially privatized.

1. MISUNDERSTANDINGS ABOUT SOCIAL SECURITY'S FINANCING

Much of the public concern about the future of Social Security stems from widespread misinformation about the financing of the present system—misinformation reported so often that it has become part of the conventional wisdom. More than anything else, this accounts for the growing lack of confidence in the system, particularly among younger Americans. Four main areas of confusion about the financing of Social Security need to be addressed:

• the meaning of trust fund exhaustion;

• the significance of the declining number of workers per retiree;

• the impact of Social Security on the federal budget; and

• Social Security as an entitlement.

From *Straight Talk about Social Security*, with Thomas N. Bethell (New York: Century Foundation Press, 1998), pp. 1–5, 33–39, and 41–58.

WHAT HAPPENS WHEN THE TRUST FUNDS ARE "EXHAUSTED"?

When the trustees report that the Social Security Trust Funds will be exhausted in about 2030, as they have each year for the past several years, this is widely interpreted as meaning that from 2030 on there will be no money to pay benefits. This is not the case.

Under present law, income from Social Security Trust Fund investments plays a relatively small part in financing benefit payments. Most of the financing comes directly from the income from Social Security taxes on employers and employees, and this source of support is ongoing. The income from the Social Security tax rates now being charged would be sufficient to fund about 70 percent of Social Security's expenses for decades after 2030—even with those expenses increasing—and would still meet two-thirds of the cost 75 years from now.

In other words, Social Security is not "going broke." Far from it. What the system will be facing in 2030 or thereabouts (*if* no corrective steps are taken in the meantime) is a *shortfall*. This problem should be addressed—and sooner rather than later—but the point is that we are facing only a shortfall; the major part of benefit costs is already financed.

WHAT IS THE SIGNIFICANCE OF THE DECLINING NUMBER OF WORKERS PER RETIREE?

Another point about Social Security financing that is broadly misunderstood concerns the declining ratio of workers (those paying in) to the number of beneficiaries (those taking out).

In starting up a new contributory retirement system in which eligibility for benefits depends upon contributions and work in covered employment, no one is eligible at first because no one has worked in covered employment or paid contributions. Most of those who are elderly have stopped working and will never be eligible for benefits, so the proportion of the elderly receiving benefits goes up slowly and only as younger workers who have worked within the system reach retirement age. Although contributions to Social Security started in 1937, as late as 1949 only 16 percent of the elderly were eligible for benefits.

On the other hand, those working under the system were contributing regardless of age, with the result that in the mid-1940s there were 42 contributing workers per beneficiary. By 1950 the ratio had dropped to 16 workers per beneficiary, while today the ratio is approaching 3 to 1, and eventually it will drop to about 2 to 1. The inevitability of the decline has long been evident *and has been anticipated in financing the program.* But this fact is often misunderstood by commentators, who treat the changing ratio of workers to beneficiaries as if it were a recently discovered phenomenon that throws the future financing of Social Security into doubt.

Confusion about the meaning of a declining worker/beneficiary ratio in Social Security is linked to confusion about the trend in the even more fundamental ratio of workers to nonworkers of all ages whose support must come from the total volume of goods and services that workers produce. Are workers in the future faced with the dismal prospect of carrying the burden of support for more and more nonworkers? That is the impression created by depictions of baby-boomer retirement, beginning about 2010, as a back-breaking load for workers. But this is not the whole story.

It is true that the ratio of those age 65 and older to those aged 20–64 will climb rapidly once the baby boomers enter old age, going from 0.214 in 2010 to an estimated 0.370 for 2035 and to somewhat over 0.400 in 2065. But what is left out of this picture is that the trend within the other big group of nonworkers—children—has been going the other way, and the combined ratio of *all* dependents to workers is not expected to be as high again at any time in the entire 75 years of Social Security forecasting as it was, for example, in the decade from 1960 to 1970. At that time the ratio averaged over 0.900—in other words, very close to one nonworker per worker—while in 1995 it was only 0.710. Looking ahead, even with the increases in the number and longevity of the elderly, the ratio as projected will not reach 0.800 until 2050 and will not reach 0.846 until 2075. [*Author's note:* These numbers have been updated to reflect the 2000 Trustees' Report.]

The basic economic point is unmistakable: The picture of future workers staggering under an increasing and intolerable load of dependents is inaccurate. Relative to those of working age, there will be more elderly but fewer children.

WHAT ABOUT SOCIAL SECURITY AND THE FEDERAL DEFICIT?

It has also become part of conventional wisdom that Social Security has been a major cause of federal budget deficits. This is not so. Since 1937, when Social Security taxes were first collected, Social Security has taken in approximately $6.8 trillion and paid out approximately $5.9 trillion, leaving a balance of about $900 billion in a contingency reserve. Clearly that doesn't add to the deficit. In fact, speaking in terms of the "unified budget"—as budget negotiators do in spite of the fact that the law has put Social Security off-budget—Social Security has been a major contributor to reaching a balanced budget. Under present law, Social Security income is expected to exceed expenditures by $80 billion in 1997, by $133 billion in 2000, and by $211 billion in 2006. Without Social Security, the government would have to find these additional amounts elsewhere in order to be able to present the same unified budget balances for these years. [*Author's note:* These numbers have been updated to reflect the 2000 Trustees' Report.]

Is Social Security a "Runaway Entitlement"?

The false notion that Social Security has been part of the deficit problem gets expressed most forcefully in attacks on "runaway entitlements." Social Security is, of course, an entitlement program—and rightly so. The concept is of great importance to the future economic security of those covered by Social Security. "Entitlement," in the context of Social Security, means that all people without distinction of sex, race, or income are *entitled* to receive benefits in an amount specified by law once they have met the objective criteria of having worked in employment covered by the program for a specified period of time and have met other objective qualifications—for example, by reaching age 62 for reduced retirement benefits, or by having a total disability estimated to last for a long and indefinite period, or by being the widow, widower, or child of an insured worker.

"Entitlement" means that Congress has set the conditions of eligibility in law, and the administrators of the system have no discretion beyond evaluating the proof of whether an applicant meets those conditions. If an applicant for Social Security benefits feels that eligibility has been wrongfully denied or that the amount of the benefit has been incorrectly computed, he or she can, after an administrative hearing, appeal to the federal courts, all the way to the Supreme Court. Social Security is very explicitly an entitlement—and it is a good thing that it is. We need to rehabilitate the term.

The opposite of an entitlement is a discretionary payment, which if applied to Social Security could mean—as in some programs—that eligibility conditions and benefit levels would be determined not by long-term considerations but by the exigencies of short-term budget cycles in which various programs compete against one another for funding. For Social Security, with its uniquely long-term commitments, this approach would clearly be unworkable. Social Security should, of course, be subject to periodic review and its value should be assessed, just as with other programs, but not as part of the annual budget cycle.

In the case of Social Security and Medicare, as distinct from certain other entitlement programs such as food stamps, there is not only a legal entitlement but also, since the benefits grow out of past earnings and contributions, the benefits are looked upon as an *earned* entitlement. Thus, although the Supreme Court has ruled that benefits and conditions for payment may be changed by law if the changes affect a broad category of participants in ways that are reasonable and nondiscriminatory, there is considerable reluctance on the part of lawmakers to substantially reduce protection or make any radical changes. There is good reason for this. Social Security commitments are very long-term. People are contributing now toward benefits that may not be due for some 40 years in the future, and a high degree of stability in both contribution rates and benefit levels is a valued part of the Social Security tradition.

2. UNDERSTANDING SOCIAL SECURITY'S 75-YEAR COST ESTIMATES

There are several issues related to relying on 75-year estimates as the measure of long-term balance that need discussion. These include an evaluation of what can be expected of 75-year estimates and why such a long period is chosen in the first place; why, in spite of the length of the period we need, nevertheless, to think *beyond* any particular set of 75-year estimates; and why we need a fail-safe provision in the law to deal with the possibility that changed assumptions in the future may move the long-range balance either way—up or down.

One reason for the erosion of public confidence in Social Security is that several times over the past 30 years the long-range estimates have changed substantially and, in each case, after modifications have been made in the system to meet the revised estimates of cost, the public has been assured that now the system is soundly financed for the long run—only to discover within a few years that the estimates have been changed again and a new deficit is being predicted.

After the 1972 amendments were enacted, the program was said to be soundly financed for 75 years, but in a short time the trustees reported it to be out of balance because of the unexpectedly high inflation caused by the first oil crisis and related changes in long-range economic assumptions. Important changes in financing were enacted in 1977, after which the program was said to be in financial balance for the next 50 years. But the even higher rates of inflation triggered by the second oil crisis in 1979 undermined that financing plan, and a highly publicized rescue mission was conducted by the National Commission on Social Security Reform (the Greenspan Commission), culminating in the 1983 amendments. At that time President Reagan, members of the commission, and both liberal and conservative congressmen and senators once again pronounced the system in balance for the traditional 75-year period. But within little more than a decade the trustees were reporting, once more, that the program faces a long-term deficit. It is not surprising that as people now look at various proposals to bring the system into balance, some ask, "Why should we believe you've got it right *this* time?"

Maintaining long-range balance has not always been a problem. Prior to the 1972 amendments, which introduced automatic cost-of-living increases and several other automatic provisions, the long-range cost estimates had a major built-in safety factor. Specific assumptions were made, as they are today, about future fertility rates, mortality rates, marriage rates, and many other demographic factors that affect cost, but no attempt was made to predict the future movement of wages and prices.

For the purpose of estimating, it was assumed that wages and prices would remain unchanged indefinitely—in other words, that there would be no real growth in wages. No one really expected this to be the case, of course, but the assumption was a good hedge. When, in fact, wages did increase faster than prices, as they generally have, the old cost estimates proved to be too conservative, and a surplus was reported. This surplus was first used to absorb any changes in cost resulting from any less favorable assumptions that might have been substituted for earlier assumptions, and then any remaining surplus was used to update benefit levels to help keep them abreast of the increases in wages and prices.

For many years this process was repeated without triggering any widespread public concern about long-range costs. However, after the law was changed so that benefits and many other program features moved automatically in relation to increasing prices and wages, there was no longer a rationale for basing estimates on an assumption that wages and prices would remain level. Indeed, the estimates needed to incorporate assumptions about their future movements. Thus the estimating safety factor was lost. We need something to take its place.

Of course, future trends may have the effect of making the system less expensive than currently estimated. Over the past two decades, the assumptions upon which the estimates are based have become increasingly conservative as a reflection of the dramatic decline in real wage growth (going from an assumption of real wage growth of 2.5 percent annually to 1.5 percent and now to 0.9 percent). If this trend is reversed over the next 75 years, program revenues would be higher than currently estimated. And there are many other factors that could move either way—fertility rates, mortality rates, and immigration rates being among the most important. [*Author's note:* The 2000 Trustees' Report assumes real wage growth of 1.0 percent annually.]

The one certainty is that *a 75-year estimate can never get it exactly right.* Think how things would have turned out if, in 1923, during the administration of President Harding, experts had tried to forecast population growth and the movement of wages and prices up to 1998. Among other things, they could not have anticipated—let alone quantified—the impact of the Depression, the Second World War, and the Cold War.

The fact is that there is no way to make anything like an accurate prediction of costs and income over a 75-year span. Indeed, the trustees do not really attempt such a forecast. They make, first, high-cost and low-cost estimates, which differ greatly over the 75-year period and either of which could turn out to be close to reality or far off, and then they turn to a middle-range estimate—a best-guess estimate—and use it, for all practical purposes, as if it were the only estimate. They really have no other choice. In a self-financed, contributory program, a particular set of estimates has to be selected as a basis for establishing contribution rates. The best-guess estimates are used for this purpose and then become the basis for just about all discussions of costs.

Unfortunately, a misleading sense of precision is conveyed by the process because the estimates are, of necessity, carried out to two decimal points. For example, the trustees' current best-guess estimate is that Social Security will be out of balance by an average of 2.23 percent of payroll over the 75-year period, and proposals to bring it into balance add up, one by one, to precisely reach this seemingly exact figure. But again there isn't any real choice. To assign a long-run saving or cost to a change of any magnitude quickly requires getting into two decimal points. Sophisticated observers realize that these long-range cost estimates can be only the roughest kind of a comparison of income and outgo over such a long period of time, but the media and the public are left with an unrealistic impression of exactitude, which then makes the public-confidence problem that much worse when these seemingly precise calculations turn out to be only best-guesses that periodically have to be revised.

So why make 75-year estimates at all, if they can't be relied on as accurate predictors? There are three reasons:

First, they are an expression of the nation's intent to continue Social Security as a self-supporting system. There is no other way for Congress to make this point so convincingly as to plan ahead, including in the law contribution rates intended to make the program self-supporting over a span of time that roughly encompasses the entire working life and retirement of young people just entering the labor market.

Second, many current provisions—and virtually all proposals for change—require decades before they are fully phased in, so long-range estimates are needed to get any kind of feel for the full cost of proposed changes. To make changes based on assumptions about what will happen only during the next decade or two could be grossly misleading.

Third, this approach has the advantage of anticipating problems before they arrive and alerting policymakers to the need for action when it is easiest to make adjustments. Even though long-range estimates cannot ever be exactly on target except by the wildest of coincidences, they can warn us of developing problems.

So great care is taken to make the estimates as reasonable as possible and to report on them fully to Congress and the public. The trustees report annually and in great detail, and their conclusions, particularly if they point to problems ahead, receive major press attention. Other groups, including official advisory councils and various unofficial organizations, also frequently report on Social Security long-range financing, generating additional media coverage. The pattern has been that, as assumptions about long-range trends and the trustees' estimates change, the system is widely reported to be in or out of balance or to have increasing or decreasing deficits; Congress takes notice; and adjustments are made, ideally decades before they are actually needed. There are no last-minute surprises in Social Security financing, and this is as it should be in a program that has been correctly called "the largest trusteeship in the history of the world." (Canada excepted, no other national system of social insurance uses such long-range estimates. This has consequences. Several nations have had to struggle with serious financial imbalances that overtook their systems without much warning.)

We need to continue to make 75-year estimates just as in the past, but they should be presented with more emphasis on the process of constantly reassessing the assumptions and bringing them up to date with the latest information as it develops, so that the media and the public understand that Social Security costs, just like those of any public or private program with long-range consequences, are subject to change—a process that should not, in and of itself, cause undue anxiety, especially once a fail-safe provision is included in the law to accommodate any long-term imbalance that might develop.

At the risk of complicating this discussion, we must also recognize that a complete solution for the long-term financing of Social Security requires that the program be balanced not only over the 75-year period immediately ahead but that it remain in balance for *successive* 75-year periods—that is, 75-year estimates made next year, or five years hence, or 25 years from now. Rightly or not, it is currently assumed that life expectancies will continue to rise indefinitely. That being the case, in the "out years" of each new 75-year period over which estimates are successively made the estimates will show more and more longer-living, elderly beneficiaries receiving benefits, while the number of wage earners paying into the program will not keep pace. This assumption alone, unless offset by changes in other assumptions, produces a slight but regular increase in estimated costs for each successive 75-year estimating period. Consequently, with present funding arrangements the program may be in balance for the 75 years following 1998, say, but not for the 75 years from 2010 to 2085 or from 2025 to 2100. Unless the program is financed so that the trust funds are increasing rather than declining at the end of a given 75-year period, the trustees will soon be reporting once again that Social Security over the long run has insufficient funds to continue to pay full benefits on time.

Various options can restore Social Security to long-term balance—that is, within the current 75-year estimating period. To make sure that the trust funds are building up at the end of 75 years, however, it will be necessary in conjunction with these proposals to schedule a tax increase toward the end of the period. Otherwise the packages described would show declining trust funds at the end of the 75-year period. I would suggest, therefore, that consideration be given to scheduling, in addition to any contribution-rate increases chosen from among the available alternatives, an increase, effective in 2050, of 0.80 percent of earnings for employees matched by employers. This increase would not be put into effect unless cost estimates made as the effective date approaches show a need for it, but if the need is there, the law will have provided a solution.

Finally, we need a safety factor—a hedge like the old level-wage assumption—to accommodate any future changes in the estimates. The 2050 rate increase described above can serve this purpose. If, as 2050 approaches, the program appears likely to cost *less* than is now being estimated, the scheduled increase could be moved further into the future. Conversely, if the system is estimated to be more expensive than previously thought, the 2050 increase could be moved up to an earlier year.

With the 2050 rate increase serving the dual function of providing a fail-safe and making sure that the trust funds are increasing at the end of the 75-year period, the system would under almost all foreseeable circumstances stay in balance over the whole 75 years, requiring only an adjustment in the effective date of the tax-rate increase already provided for. We would avoid the erosion of public confidence that now follows virtually any statement by the trustees to the effect that the system requires substantial shoring up, because this possibility would already have been taken into account and written into the law in the form of a rate increase scheduled far in advance. Of course, in the unlikely event that the estimated long-range costs increased so much that they could not be met in this way, Congress would have to decide whether to enact further tax increases and/or benefit cuts.

One other aspect of Social Security's long-range financing requires attention. Although in practice Social Security has been largely pay-as-you-go, collecting only enough to pay current benefits and maintain a contingency reserve, the law in the past has contained scheduled future rate increases that would have resulted in partial advance funding had they been allowed to go into effect. Thus the system, while charging only a current pay-as-you-go rate, has been able to project a long-range balance because of a contribution schedule that later on would have produced a large fund with substantial earnings.

No clear-cut policy decision has ever been made regarding whether to stay indefinitely with pay-as-you-go in practice or move to partial advance funding by building an earnings reserve larger than a contingency fund—that is, a reserve large enough to make a significant contribution to long-range financing. A decision to stay with pay-as-you-go while still requiring full self-financing for the program would have meant a big increase in the ultimate rate in the law. In effect, we have been following a pay-as-you-go policy without facing up to the long-range consequences of continuing with such a policy. This ad hoc approach has been expedient, perhaps, but it has also been misleading. I believe that we should explicitly adopt a set policy of partial advance funding.

3. PARTIAL PRIVATIZATION OF SOCIAL SECURITY: THE DRAWBACKS OF INDIVIDUAL ACCOUNTS

Many proposals to privatize Social Security have been put forward. Some would substitute private savings accounts for the entire Social Security system. Another approach, exemplified by the Personal Security Accounts (PSA) plan proposed by five members of the 1994–96 Social Security Advisory Council, would reduce the government-operated program eventually to the payment of low flat benefits, substituting a compulsory savings program with individual accounts for the rest of what we know as Social Security today. These are radical proposals that appear to have little chance of enactment.

More likely, serious consideration will be given to proposals that would shrink the present Social Security system to make room for a plan of individual savings accounts—leaving the core system *looking* much like the present program, but reduced. These partial-privatization schemes may appear to be reasonable compromises. They really are not.

In order to bring the residual Social Security program into long-range balance while at the same time funding the new system of individual accounts, they have to reduce benefits under the residual program—by about 30 percent on average. In other words, they replace nearly a third of Social Security's defined-benefit protection with a defined-contribution scheme—compulsory in some proposals, voluntary in others—and thus weaken the foundation of our national retirement income system.

Take, for example, the Individual Accounts (IA) plan proposed by the chairman of the 1994–96 Advisory Council. This plan sets up a system of individual savings accounts. Workers and employers would continue to contribute to the present system at the current level of deductions from workers' earnings (6.2 percent), with their contributions matched by employers. However, since the income produced at this combined contribution rate of 12.4 percent of payroll would not be sufficient to maintain the present program in balance over the long run, Social Security benefits would be gradually scaled back—ultimately by 30 percent for the average worker, 22 percent for the lower-paid, and 32 percent for the higher-paid. In addition to contributing 6.2 percent of their earnings to the present system, workers would have an additional 1.6 percent of their earnings deducted (with no employer match) to fund their individual accounts. The goal would be for the earnings from investing these accounts to offset, *on average*, the reduction in Social Security benefits.

Under this approach, in other words, workers would be required to set aside more of their earnings than at present to fund a two-part system in which the ultimate level of combined benefits is determined not by law but by the investment earnings from the funds they select. Behind the IA plan is a political calculation—that workers would *not* accept a tax increase to strengthen the present Social Security system but *would* accept an increase in deductions from their wages as long as it is earmarked for an individual account that they see as their own (notwithstanding the strict rules that would be necessary to prevent access to the account before reaching retirement age).

The IA plan also assumes that workers would prefer to rely to some extent on their own investment skills (choosing from a menu of government-overseen investment options) rather than continue to rely on a defined-benefit retirement program in which it is the government's responsibility to see that benefits defined by law are paid. Risk is present in either situation, of course, but in Social Security the risk is very broadly shared, while in individual accounts the risk is borne by the individual. Behind the IA plan, in short, is an untested assumption that wage earners setting aside funds for retirement would prefer to bear part of the risk individually rather than share risk in a system for which all of the participants are collectively responsible.

Proponents argue that the IA approach will, *on average*, protect present benefit levels for Social Security participants by bringing the combined benefits of the reduced Social Security system and the new savings plan up to the level currently provided for—but not fully funded by—the present Social Security system. But, averages being averages, many participants would receive less than average returns on their investments, so their combined benefits would be less than under present law.[1]

The inescapable fact is that the IA plan would reduce Social Security's defined benefit in the long run by 30 percent for the average worker, replacing the diminished benefit with the *hope* that the *average* return on savings in individual accounts would make up for the loss. But even if this turned out to be the case on *average,* many participants, particularly the lower-paid, would fall below the average. As the late Herbert Stein, who chaired the Council of Economic Advisers during the Nixon years, observed: "It is not sufficient to say that some people who are very smart or very lucky in the management of their funds will have high incomes and those who are not will have low incomes and everything will average out."[2]

There are other problems with the IA approach:

The plan puts workers at increased risk. A major objection to replacing part of Social Security with individual accounts is that it increases risk for the individual—which, while appropriate for supplementary protection, is questionable policy for Social Security, the basic floor of retirement protection. In addition to the general risk of picking funds that perform poorly, workers would also be exposed to a timing risk—the risk of beginning or ending an investment period in a bad market. They would have little control over this. They would have to start investing when they first become employed and then convert to a benefit when they retire. They would be able to choose equities or bonds and make transfers between the two, but they would not know ahead of time when to invest in equities and when to get out of the market (although, of course, they might choose to increase their bond holdings as they neared retirement). Market fluctuations would be beyond their control.

Calculations by Gary Burtless of the Brookings Institution based on historical stock market prices and dividends show the enormous variation in replacement rates (the percentage of past earnings that a pension represents) that could result solely because of the timing of retirement within very brief periods of time—with replacement rates going, for example, from 47 percent in 1980 to 68 percent in 1981, then back down to 42 percent in 1993, then back up to 72 percent in 1997.

Variations of this magnitude would represent a serious problem for workers, whose expectations of retirement income could be abruptly thrown off track. This is made clear by looking at Burtless's historical data and assuming that an IA-type system had been in effect at the time. A 58-year-old worker in 1970, seeing the 90 percent replacement rate going to a 65-year-old retiree in that year, would be shocked to discover seven years later that his own pension would be pegged at a replacement rate of 41 percent—less than half as much as expected. There would be little he could do about it: settle for much less retirement income than anticipated or keep working in hopes that replacement rates would rise. His situation would be even worse if, in 1969, Congress had looked at the 104 percent replacement rate made possible by the then bull market and opted to cut back on contributions to these accounts. By 1977, with replacement rates plummeting, elected officials would be inundated with complaints about hardship among the elderly and pleas to fill in the gap. Looking at this illustration of what might have been, it seems clear that dissatisfaction with the vagaries of a system of individual accounts could have wide-ranging and long-lasting repercussions.

The plan promises more than it can deliver. Even on average, the individual-accounts plan would be unlikely to achieve the goal of adequate retirement income because it seems inevitable that over time the savings account holders would be allowed access to their accounts for purposes unrelated to retirement, with the result that many would spend much of the money in the account prior to retirement. After all, a major selling point for personal savings accounts is that the money "belongs" to the individual. Account-holders facing health emergencies, tuition payments, or other major expenses would want access to their "personal" funds in such situations. Based on experience with IRAs and 401(k) plans, it can be confidently predicted that political leaders would acquiesce. Once early access is permitted, however, many personal savings accounts would be much smaller than anticipated by the time the account-holder reaches retirement.

Public support for Social Security could be undermined. Under the IA approach the residual Social Security system would produce lower and lower benefits as time went on, while individual reports on investment returns would show growing accumulations (even in those cases where the returns would actually be quite low), reinforcing the impression that IAs were outperforming Social Security. Many workers might press to change the law in order to allow more of their contributions to be shifted from Social Security into private accounts. If that were to happen, the redistributional capabilities of the present system would be lost. The weighted Social Security benefit formula favoring the low-paid, which has been so successful in reducing poverty and near-poverty among the elderly, is unsustainable in a system made up largely of individual accounts. (On the other hand, a parallel government system of flat benefits high enough to make a major impact on poverty is likely to be means tested, regardless of the specifications proposed by sponsors, with the result that, like all means-tested programs, it would have limited political support.)

The plan would reduce the living standard of low-wage earners. Proponents of compulsory individual savings account plans argue that this kind of plan would increase national savings, but most of the increase would come from the lower paid. Present savers—mostly above-average earners—would tend to decrease the saving that they had been doing voluntarily, to offset the new requirements. It is difficult to judge how much net additional saving would come from them. Most of the increase would probably come from low-wage workers who are not saving now; this is where the new compulsion hits, and there is no relief. Is it really desirable to force more saving from the lower paid for the purpose of increasing their cash income in retirement even beyond the level of promised Social Security benefits? Probably not. Many lower-paid workers live from payday to payday and have more immediate needs for their funds—for health insurance, or to pay for even more basic needs such as adequate shelter, food, and clothing—than to set aside more earnings exclusively for retirement.

The IA approach makes solving Medicare's financial problems harder by preempting increases in compulsory deductions from workers' earnings for retirement savings rather than for health care. Putting this another way, if a significant additional deduction from earnings of the kind required by the IA plan were to be seriously considered by

Congress, there would be a more immediate need to direct at least part of the income to Medicare or to health insurance generally rather than to retirement income alone.

The individual-accounts approach weakens our three-tier retirement system. Social Security, as the foundation of that system—augmented by supplementary private pensions and individual savings—is, as it should be, a defined-benefit plan with benefits determined by law rather than by the risks and unpredictability of individual investments. Partial privatization would shift Social Security toward becoming a defined-*contribution* plan, in which the level of benefits depends on how successfully contributions are invested. This is a particularly bad idea now, since private pension plans are increasingly of the defined-contribution type, such as 401(k) plans. Taking risks with supplementary protection is reasonable only if the base is secure. If Social Security is not itself maintained as a wholly defined-benefit plan, a worker's entire retirement package becomes subject to the risk of unfavorable market returns.

The plan weakens disability protection even more than retirement protection. Changing the benefit formula from 90 percent, 32 percent, and 15 percent of average indexed earnings to 90 percent, 22.4 percent, and 10.5 percent, as the IA plan calls for, would have a disproportionate impact on the disabled, because as a general rule the disabled have lower incomes than retirees. They are less likely to have private pensions or insurance benefits to augment Social Security and are less likely to be able to get and keep part-time work, so they must rely on Social Security to provide a relatively large share of their total income.

Further, disabled workers typically have much smaller asset holdings than retirees. This reflects two of the realities experienced by disabled workers: Their careers are cut short before they have accumulated savings to supplement Social Security, and they face new disability-related expenses. Unlike retirees, whose regular living expenses may decline when their working years–related expenses decline, living costs for persons with disabilities may rise after they leave the labor force. Over time disability benefits, like retirement benefits, are cut 30 percent for the average worker but the compulsory saving plan is much less likely to make up for the loss. For workers who are disabled while young the compulsory saving plan is just about useless.

The plan could lead to new labor relations problems. Cutting Social Security's defined benefits would likely cause friction between employers and employees. Virtually all private and public pension plans are built on the assumption that the retiree will also receive Social Security. And pension arrangements, at least at large firms, have usually been worked out over the years with employee representatives; pensions are part of the overall compensation bargaining process. What would happen to these plans if the basic Social Security benefit were to be gradually cut by an average of 30 percent? At the very least, we could expect a long period of uncertainty and unrest. Would private plans have to make up the difference—particularly for older workers—as Social Security is scaled back? Unions would certainly want to protect workers by retaining the equivalent of present Social Security promises in defined pension benefits, and employers would just as certainly resist. The stakes would be high. Moreover, all the pension integration rules would have to be changed, since the effect of the weighted benefit formula would be reduced, and these changes could result in significant increases in private pension costs.

No doubt many workers would find it appealing, at least initially, to have their own accounts—particularly because of the widespread misconception that major cuts in benefits and/or major increases in taxes are necessary to put the present Social Security system back into balance. But many presumably would not want to bother with individual accounts if they were more confident of the long-term stability of the present Social Security system. Some of those initially attracted to individual accounts would feel less enthusiastic as they learned of the trade-offs—in essence, a stronger sense of personal "ownership" versus the risk of ending up with less security—and particularly as they learn more about their personal stake in the present system.

Thanks to an amendment sponsored by Senator Moynihan some years ago, workers are already becoming better informed about what they can expect from Social Security. The Social Security Administration has distributed Personal Earnings and Benefit Statements (PEBES) to millions of workers (starting with those nearing retirement age and working down from there), and beginning in 1999 will send annual statements to all workers over 25 for whom mailing addresses are available—expected to be about 122 million people out of the expected 140 million workers in covered employment. This represents a huge step forward in the dissemination of important information to Social Security participants. Suddenly, the benefits of the present system are becoming more tangible.

ADMINISTERING INDIVIDUAL ACCOUNTS: A MAJOR CHALLENGE FOR EMPLOYERS AND GOVERNMENT

In assessing the pros and cons of partial privatization, it is also important to focus on what has been perhaps the least closely examined aspect of this approach: the difficulties that employers and the government would face in administering such a plan.

The administrative challenges are substantial. At a minimum, employers would need to deduct the additional 1.6 percent from earnings each payday and forward the amounts to the government identified in such a way that they could be correctly deposited to an individual's account in one or more of the approved funds. Information about the choices available would need to be furnished to employees and their fund choices communicated to the government. Individual records would need to be kept of all deposits and their earnings and reported to employees, who would also need to be given opportunities to periodically change their allocation of investments. And it would be necessary to correct reporting errors and to reconcile differences between employers' reports and employees' claims of errors. The government at a minimum would need to see that all this happens—and, in addition, to ensure that funds deposited in individual accounts are retained to retirement and then converted to annuities.

The numbers initially involved would be very large: about 6 million employers and more than 140 million individual accounts—approximately 133 million for employees and 8 million for the self-employed. Nothing comparable to the IA plan has ever been undertaken by any retirement income plan. In comparison, when the federal Thrift Savings Plan (TSP) was started, about 3 million federal employees needed to be informed of their eligibility to participate and advised about their TSP investment options. And TIAA-CREF, one of the largest managers of private defined-contribution plans with participant-directed accounts, works with only about 6,000 employers and 1.5 million participating employees. These are very small undertakings in comparison to the scope of the IA and other partial privatization proposals.

How the necessary tasks described above are parceled out among employers and government is of enormous importance to the parties involved and could well determine both the political viability of the plan and its success or failure in actual operation. What should employers be required to do? Their participation in helping inform their employees could be of great help to government, but would they resist such a requirement? And, of particular importance, would they be willing to make more frequent reports than are now required? Employers now pay Social Security taxes and transmit withheld income tax continually throughout the year, but only the annual W-2 statement individualizes these taxes. In the case of voluntary 401(k) payroll-deduction savings plans, employers are required to deposit funds withheld in any given month no later than the fifteenth business day of the next month. Contributions by federal employees participating in the TSP must be deposited every two weeks or on payday. Are employers now going to be required to follow similar rules and identify by payday or on a monthly basis how much has been withheld from a particular worker so that the funds can be promptly allocated and invested in order to start earning returns as soon as possible? More frequent reporting would be a major increase in responsibility for many employers over what they now do for Social Security.

In the past, employers were required to provide information for Social Security purposes on individual employees on a quarterly basis, but widespread employer dissatisfaction with this requirement eventually prompted Congress to change many Social Security provisions in order to accommodate a system of annual reporting. Employers already administering 401(k) plans might not have major objections to more frequent reporting, but the much larger number of employers who do not offer such plans—particularly small employers—could find such new reporting requirements burdensome and expensive. Would employers also be expected to explain investment choices to employees and be involved in their decisions? What happens if the information provided by employers is inaccurate? What happens if the employer is late or makes mistakes in reporting and the employee loses investment earnings as a result? Will employers be held responsible? And how will the costs of administration by government be covered?

Most employers are small. Although employers are encouraged to report W-2s to Social Security electronically (and are required to do so if they employ 250 or more employees), about 5 million of the slightly more than 6 million employers paying Social Security taxes still compile and file their W-2 reports on paper. Many, if not most, of the employers in this category might be expected to object to adding substantially to what they have to do now under the annual reporting system.

It thus seems likely that to avoid employer opposition the IA plan would be modified to permit annual reporting to continue. This could be done, but not without loss for employees. One approach would be to have all the deductions from workers' earnings invested for a year in a single "default" fund (probably a fund investing only in low-yield but safe long-term government bonds) without employee designation. The employee's designated investment choice could then be followed for future deductions and the original investment redirected as the employee wished. (It can also be assumed that some employees would not make designations promptly, if ever, in which case deductions from their wages could go to the same safe but low-return fund.) But whenever the employee wanted to make a change in the allocation among funds there would be the same lag before the change could be carried out. This annualized approach might make the plan more acceptable to employers, but employees would lose some control over their investments, would earn less investment income on average, and would be faced with the loss of earnings for a period on changing investment designations.

Another possibility might be to do what the British do with their voluntary system: Have the government collect the withholding each payday but invest in a designated fund only once a year. The government benefits from the float, and rationalizes it as a way of meeting its administrative expenses.

These adjustments can be made, but there is no way to avoid putting responsibility on employers for accurately reporting employee deductions, participating in the process of correcting errors, and responding to what employees believe to be errors. And the standard for accuracy will be higher than in the case of the present Social Security system because every dollar deducted from an employee's wages will "belong" to that individual—whereas in Social Security, where the benefit is based on averaging the highest 35 years of earnings, a single error in wage reporting may have little, if any, effect.

Long experience with reporting to Social Security suggests that the burden of correcting errors will be disproportionately borne by smaller employers and that error rates will be significant. In Social Security, error rates are higher for W-2s compiled on paper than for W-2s prepared electronically. The annual combined error rate—that is, the percentage of wage items that cannot be credited to an account—is initially about 3 percent. Each year some 6 million W-2s cannot be promptly processed and credited to individual earnings records because of errors in reporting names and Social Security numbers. The Social Security Administration, after contacting employers and/or employees, is able to reduce the error rate to about 2 percent. This still represents nearly 5 million unresolved cases, which largely carry over and accumulate from year to year. And these error rates do not include errors resulting from failure to file or from misreporting the amounts withheld. Many of these additional mistakes are likely to develop into investigations as employees find wage items missing from the Social Security reports they are now receiving as a result of the Moynihan amendment, or as taxpayers seek W-2s to support their income tax returns.

Although correcting errors would, of course, be important to beneficiaries, in many cases the exercise would not be cost-effective because the amounts at stake would be so small. Error rates are likely to be highest among the lowest-paid workers, simply because they typically work for smaller employers who are more likely than major employers to misreport withholding. For workers with annual taxable earnings at or below, say, $8,400 a year (about 42 million workers, a third of all workers currently covered by Social Security) the 1.6 percent IA set-aside would, at most, amount to $134 annually, or $11.15 per month. An error rate of 3 percent would mean that at any given moment the IA accounts of more than 1.2 million workers within the lowest-paid category would be subject to adjustment, but because their IA set-asides are so small, the average administrative cost of correcting an IA withholding error for them could easily be much greater than the amount in dispute.

This raises a related issue. In weighing the administrative burdens of partial privatization, a major unaddressed question is whether the benefits paid by the savings plan will seem worthwhile to a large number of the employees involved. The amounts going into individual accounts in most cases would be quite small. Among workers covered by Social Security, 56 percent have annual taxable earnings of $18,000 or less, for which the annual IA contribution, at 1.6 percent, would be $288 or less. Average annual earnings among all workers covered are about $26,000, producing a deduction of $416 at 1.6 percent.

At the same time, many higher-paid workers familiar with 401(k) plans might compare the returns, restrictions, and limitations of their

IAs unfavorably with their 401(k)s. Contributions to 401(k) plans are voluntary; employees can drop out or defer payments; employers often make matching contributions; many 401(k) plans can be borrowed against; and 401(k) funds can be withdrawn when an employee changes jobs or decides to use the funds for purposes other than retirement, such as medical emergencies or tuition payments (subject to a 10 percent tax penalty). Although few if any of these features are envisioned for IA accounts, it seems likely that employees would agitate for them—particularly for the right to have access to their IA funds in emergencies—and that, as suggested earlier, policymakers would sooner or later acquiesce. In that case, of course, administration of the funds would become more complex and the income stream in retirement would be reduced as more workers withdrew funds for other purposes.

There are additional IA administrative costs that should be examined. Looking narrowly at start-up costs, it can be assumed that a major effort would have to be made to familiarize workers with their investment options, an effort that would need to be ongoing in order to respond to employees' questions and to reach employees newly entering the labor market. How much would employers be asked to do? If employers were not expected to help employees understand the plan and their choices, and this job were assigned entirely to Social Security, for example, the cost for its district offices could be large and hard to predict. The first wave of inquiries presumably could be dealt with by setting up and staffing an 800 number, but many people would want to talk things over in person—and that goes double, at least at first, for questions about the IA status reports that would be periodically sent to each employee. Many would come to Social Security seeking clarification.

Of course, major employers might elect to help their employees whether required to do so or not. It is common now for personnel departments of major employers to take responsibility for helping employees with the requirements of Social Security claims filing and income tax withholding, and there would be a price to pay in good will if employers just turned off inquiries about a government-required savings plan. But giving advice also carries a cost when the employee thinks the advice has been bad.

Most small employers would want to avoid taking on any additional administrative responsibilities, but regardless of whether they were expected to help employees navigate the IA plan, they would have to report and correct errors, and thus would inevitably find themselves involved with their employees and with government on another broad front. And overall the government (or private contractors paid by the government) would have to continually report on and update the status of millions of small individual IAs—a task that would automatically result in the creation of a huge and potentially controversial database of information on individuals' investments.

Only the government agencies involved are in a position to say how all of these operational difficulties might be addressed. It seems clear, however, that decisions about whether or not to advocate such a plan should not be made solely on the basis of broad goals. The agencies that would be held responsible for the successful operation of the plan should have an opportunity to determine the feasibility of doing the job *before,* not after, the political decision is made. There would be little tolerance by the public for errors in administering a plan in which each dollar deducted from earnings is seen as belonging to a particular individual. And there is ample opportunity for error in carrying out all the necessary tasks.

Perhaps most problematic for the administration in charge of implementing the plan would be the public's assessment of whether it is going well. Headlines after three or four years of implementation to the effect that millions of items cannot be assigned to any individual and that so many hundreds of millions of dollars of deductions from workers' earnings cannot be identified and credited to IAs could cause serious political repercussions—even though the government would not really be at fault, since the problem would have originated with inaccurate reporting.

An administration could suffer politically if the public perceived that implementation of the plan was not going smoothly and fairly. When just about every income-earning, tax-paying citizen is affected, negative perceptions whether accurate or not can be detrimental to public trust and difficult to dispel, as the Postal Service and the Internal Revenue Service can testify. And it doesn't take a lot of mistakes to create a bad impression. In the case of tax collection, many Americans may not particularly value a high degree of accuracy, and political leaders by and large would rather live with errors and lost revenue than invite taxpayer unrest by deploying more IRS agents to improve the accuracy of reporting. But administration of a savings plan is something else. People will want to receive—and to be confident that they will *always* receive—full credit for their deductions from earnings. Government better get this one right, and in advance.

Is the IA plan worth all the trouble? The plan relies on higher deductions from workers' earnings to buy higher benefits for some participants (those with above-average returns from investments) at the cost of lower benefits for others, along with less certainty for all participants about which group they might end up in—the group that gets little more than the basic Social Security benefit (30 percent lower on average than under present law) or the group that gets more than under present law because of successful investments. In total, of course, the greater deductions buy higher benefits on a group basis (although the greater administrative costs of individual accounts need to be factored in). For individuals, however, the amount of retirement income will inevitably be uncertain, since so much depends on the movement of the stock market and the timing of one's entry into, and retirement from, the labor market.

Social Security policy should be conservative, in the sense of retaining what works best for most people. This argues for keeping Social Security as the basic part of a three-tier retirement system, maintained as a fully defined-benefit plan governed by the same major principles that have traditionally governed and still govern the program. With the foundation of a multi-tier system secure, supplementary private pensions and savings investments may more reasonably take chances with the level of future benefits (although I believe that ordinarily the first part of a private pension system should also be a defined-benefit plan, with the riskier provision of 401[k]s and IRAs supplementary to that).

I see little reason to compromise on individual accounts. On the contrary, I believe that a public education campaign could build strong support for strengthening the present Social Security system by adopting alternatives that spread the cost of bringing the system into balance among current and future beneficiaries and present and future workers without imposing intolerable costs on anyone and without taking on the problems associated with individual accounts. And investing part of the accumulating Social Security funds in equities would make the task of achieving long-range balance relatively easy.

It is possible, of course, that no consensus will emerge from bipartisan consideration of possible Social Security changes. Even so, there could still be progress. If it had been their objective, a majority of the 1994–96 Advisory Council could quite easily have agreed on a plan that would have postponed trust fund exhaustion from about 2030 to 2050 and reduced the average deficit over the 75-year estimating period from 2.23 percent of payroll to 0.72 percent of payroll, a figure within the meaning of "close actuarial balance." I would much prefer taking steps now to eliminate the full 75-year deficit and to put the program in a sustainable position for the even longer run, and I would hope we could all agree to pursue this goal. But if that degree of unanimity is presently unattainable, I believe that most Americans, once the trade-offs are understood, would prefer to take the really quite modest steps that are needed to bring the system into full balance over 50 years and into close actuarial balance over 75 years—postponing for now the goal of arriving at exact balance over the full 75-year period—rather than drastically curtailing Social Security to make room for privatization.

22

A PROGRAM FOR THE FUTURE

The final chapter of my 1978 book, Social Security Today and Tomorrow, *outlined a series of propositions expressing my beliefs about the program and how protection for American families should be improved. Since then there have indeed been improvements, but many of these propositions remain unaddressed.*

1. *Workers have a common interest with the retired, disabled, and surviving families of deceased workers in sound planning for income insurance.*

Everyone who is fortunate enough to live until retirement will need a regular, permanent income to replace the earnings that were previously their main source of support. Moreover, any worker may become totally disabled before retirement, or may die and leave surviving dependents. This is why most workers strongly support the concept of social insurance and are willing to make substantial contributions toward Social Security protection, and it is why they push for supplementary protection through pension plans based on the place of employment.

Useful as it is for many kinds of economic analysis, a one-time, cross-sectional look at who is paying and who is getting is not the most useful way of illuminating the policy issues in Social Security. Planning for income security is not primarily a matter in which those at work help those who are not. It is a matter of all of us planning for a continuing income for ourselves and our families during periods when earnings stop or are greatly reduced. Continuing income when one is unable to work is a universal need. The basic issue in income insurance is how much to give up while at work in return for how much income security when one is not at work.

2. *The self-help principle of contributory social insurance has roots deep in the past and appeals to people everywhere.*

It is apparently puzzling to some tax experts that in country after country, flat-rate deductions from earnings for the support of social insurance have been increasing, with the result that if the tax structure is viewed as including Social Security contributions, the structure has become less "progressive."[1] This should not be puzzling. The Social Security contributions are not an ordinary tax. They are based on the benefit principle of taxation—a payment for a specific purpose by those who will benefit. They are a "users' tax." They are like insurance premiums. The premiums are "regressive" when viewed solely as a tax in the same way that payments for food or clothing would be regressive if viewed as a tax.

Most people want the security that comes from an insurance arrangement, in which their right to benefits is earned and the payment is not simply a grant from the government. Most people like the idea that their contribution has created an obligation on the part of government, and, as a result, government is not at liberty to change eligibility conditions and the amount of the payment from year to year without restriction. This preference is not the result of a failure to understand economic principles or just plain wrongheadedness; rather it has grown up on the basis of hundreds of years of experience with the two major approaches to income security—needs-tested assistance and self-help insurance programs.

The self-help principle is important. The fact that Social Security is "income insurance," provided under government auspices but operated as a utility for the contributors, sharply distinguishes it from the usual government-financed programs which are correctly in competition with each other for financing year by year. In Social Security the social insurance institution is the insurer, guaranteeing specific benefits in return for specific contributions. The object is to prevent poverty and economic insecurity by insuring against a loss of earnings.

3. *It would add significantly to public understanding of the trustee character of Social Security as a retirement and group insurance plan if the program were administered by a separate government*

*corporation or board and if its financial transactions were kept com-
pletely separate from other government income and expenditures.*

[*Author's note:* Since 1995, the Social Security Administration has
been an independent agency directed by a commissioner reporting
directly to the president. As for financing, since 1999 both parties
have agreed that Social Security's financial transactions are to be kept
entirely separate from other government income and expenditures.]

This would be similar to the way it used to be. Social Security
was at first administered by a separate board reporting directly to
the president, but in 1939 it was put into the newly established
Federal Security Agency, the predecessor of the Department of Health,
Education, and Welfare [predecessor in turn of the Department of
Health and Human Services]. In 1946 the board was abolished.

Whatever justification there may have been in 1939 for grouping
Social Security with other programs, today a separate organization is
fully justified on administrative grounds alone. But even more important, administration of Social Security by a separate government corporation or board would underline the trustee character of this social
insurance system.

Until the fiscal year 1969 budget, the financial transactions of the
Social Security system were kept entirely separate from general revenue income and expenditures, except for purposes of economic
analysis. Today, they are a part of a unified budget, which lumps
together general revenue income and expenditures and the separately financed Social Security system. This is leading to confusion about
just how separate from other government programs Social Security
really is. Recommendations to change Social Security benefit provisions in ways that are completely unacceptable in terms of social
insurance policy are often made by the executive branch solely to
conform to short-term budget policy.[2] In the interest of protecting
Social Security's long-term commitments, the separateness of Social
Security financing should be made unmistakably clear.

4.   *In spite of what is sometimes said, there have been no major depar-
     tures from the original purposes of the Social Security system.*

Over the years the cash benefit program has been greatly improved,
principally by extensions of coverage, the addition of disability insurance,
the addition of the automatic provisions, the shift to a wage-indexed

system, and substantial increases in benefit levels. But the key elements of the present program were present in the amendments of 1939, passed just four years after the original Social Security Act and prior to the first monthly payments under the program. The concept of dependents benefits and survivors benefits, the weighted benefit formula favoring lower-paid individuals, and the payment of sizable benefits to those who had little opportunity to contribute because they were already old were all in the 1939 Act. The annual reports of the Social Security Board and the Advisory Council reports also show that the goal of universal coverage and the addition of disability insurance were present in the minds of those who developed the 1939 structure.

The system has not in recent years become less of an insurance system and more of a welfare system. Actually, benefits are more closely related to contributions today than they were at the beginning of the program, and as people pay over a longer period of time, at the current, much-higher-than-the-original rates, the protection will be even more closely related to contributions.

5.   *For a majority of the retired aged—but by no means all—an inadequate income is still the number one problem.*

The adequacy of retirement income should not be tested against an across-the-board abstract minimum like the "poverty level," a "near poor" level, the welfare level in a given state, or some other budgetary measure such as those put out by the Department of Labor. For most people, retirement income will seem inadequate if it is substantially below what is required to maintain the level of living they are used to.

Thus, many retired people who are not "poor" find the lack of an adequate income their principal problem—one that brings with it a host of other problems: inadequate housing, inadequate nutrition, inadequate opportunity to participate in community and recreational activities, inadequate health care, and the lack of the amenities and comforts that many of them were used to while working.

6.   *Permanent retirement money income of from 65 percent to 80 percent of previous wage income will produce for the elderly who are in good health an ability to live independently at a level roughly comparable to what they had attained while working.*

The needed wage replacement ratio will differ among retirees. Some differences between their money income needs and those of workers exist for almost all the retired group—for example, differences in tax payments, absence of expenses of working, and the ability to partly substitute one's own labor for purchased goods and services. Other differences exist for a high proportion of the elderly but are not universal—for example, lower housing costs because of home ownership [80.3 percent of the elderly own their own homes in 2000], fewer persons dependent on the family income, and decreased need to buy house furnishings, durable consumer goods, and new clothing.

Other differences exist for only a minority of the retired elderly, and therefore are not useful in helping to determine the ratio of retirement income to previous earnings that is generally desirable. For example, it was no help to the half of the elderly couples and the four-fifths of those living alone who had no earnings at all during 1975 that a minority of elderly people had a total of about $20 billion in earnings. The fact that many of the younger elderly have not retired and have regular full-time earnings of substantial amounts is hardly relevant to judging the needs of those who have retired.

None of the needs-tested programs would seem to be relevant to this purpose either. They are, by definition, residual and fill in when regular retirement money income is inadequate. Although needs-tested programs obviously improve the well-being of those who receive help, they are a measure of the inadequacy of retirement income rather than a reason for changing the measure of what retirement income should be. Thus, Supplemental Security Income, veterans' pensions, food stamps, Medicaid, public housing, and charitable contributions should not be considered in determining the proper ratio of retirement income to past earnings. This is true, too, for intra-family transfers—if the elderly person is to retain a sense of independence and a sense of carrying his own weight, he must have enough retirement income to live on his own if he wants to.

7. *The goal for retirement income should be to provide in retirement a level of living roughly comparable to that earned while working. To achieve this goal, we should work toward: (1) a universal contributory social insurance system adequate in itself for those who earn less than average wages and work regularly under the system; (2) supplementary pensions which, together with*

Social Security, do the same for most of those with average and above-average earnings; (3) individual voluntary savings, which, while useful for all, can be expected to provide a significant part of the retirement income only for the 10 to 15 percent of earners who have the highest incomes; and (4) an improved Supplemental Security Income (SSI) program designed to keep anyone from falling below the poverty level.[3]

Private pension plans and government career plans tend to be available largely to those who have above-average earnings. Many older persons, particularly women, have little or no benefit from such arrangements. Even in the long run, 50 percent or more of America's elderly will have very little other than Social Security for retirement income. It is necessary, therefore, that Social Security be designed so that in itself it is sufficient for the below-average earner who works regularly under the program.

Because Social Security provides protection which follows the worker from job to job, is underwritten by the government, has very low administrative costs, and can deal more readily than private pension plans with the problem of inflation, we should also provide through Social Security the basic amount of protection that we want to be sure is available to all regular workers. Social Security, however, should not be asked to guarantee an adequate level of living for people who contribute to the system only occasionally or not at all. A minimum guarantee for everyone including irregular and part-time workers can best be supplied by SSI, which is income-tested and financed from general revenues.

Private pensions and government career plans form an important supplement to Social Security for those workers with such protection, mostly those with above-average earnings. It is doubtful, however, whether subsidies in the form of income tax advantages should be available to provide full replacement incomes to the highest paid. Individual voluntary savings can be important to workers at all earnings levels, but it should be expected that savings will be sufficient to provide significant annuities in old age only for those who are the best-off.

8.   *The federal government should take responsibility for seeing that the totally disabled and all persons 65 or over have the right to a level of living equal, at least, to the poverty level as defined by the federal government.*

Through SSI, it would be a simple matter for the federal government to raise the 14 percent [10.5 percent in 1998] of the elderly now below poverty up to at least that level. (State supplementation would still be required where living costs were above average or where a state wished to guarantee a level of living above this standard.) The improved standard should apply, of course, not just to the elderly but to the needy disabled and the needy blind.

The total federal cost of this change would be in the range of $8 billion to $10 billion a year [approximately $15 billion estimated in 2000], with some offsetting savings to the states. Over time, the proportion of elderly and disabled persons eligible for SSI under the improved standards should gradually decline, since newly eligible Social Security beneficiaries as a group will, for several reasons, receive higher benefits than are received by the group now eligible. Not only will the benefits of these new eligibles for Social Security have been kept up to date with the rising level of living of the community—which may or may not be true of SSI payments—but also Social Security benefits will be higher in the future because coverage is now nearly universal, and those retiring in the future will not so frequently have worked part of their lives in noncovered employment.

9.   *Those who are not eligible for SSI but who also should be excused from work outside the home (mothers with young children) should be guaranteed payments at the federal poverty standard. For those with marketable skills, the emphasis should be on jobs—in private employment if possible, in public service jobs if necessary. Those without marketable skills should have access to training, with adequate support payments during the learning process.*

The cornerstone of any good welfare policy is a commitment to the provision of jobs, in the private sector to the extent possible, and through pinpointed training programs and public service jobs for those for whom private employment is not immediately available. Welfare payments should be limited to those who are unable to work (or excused from work because they must care for others) and for those who remain in need after there has been a vigorous pursuit of the alternative of work. We must face up to the tough problems involved in providing opportunity and not accept a permanent underclass condemned to live on welfare payments when they could be equipped to share in society's responsibilities and rewards.

The most promising approach to an economical and humane welfare program requires dealing differently with two groups now in poverty: those who have work potential and those who should not be required to work for pay. Those not required to work would be eligible for a benefit at least equal (if they had no other income) to the federal poverty standard. Those with work potential would be either in training, at work, or in the process of getting a job. Those in training would receive a stipend equal to or above the poverty level. If, over time, no work could be found for a particular individual and further training was considered unlikely to be helpful, he or she would be treated as a person excused from paid work.

It is impossible to overemphasize that the most helpful policy for poor people with work potential is a general economic policy supporting full employment. No combination of social programs can be as helpful as a tight labor market in which employers are looking for workers.

10. *Although Social Security will continue to provide the major part of retirement income for most workers, private pension plans are an important supplement to Social Security and should be improved. On the other hand, the government subsidy now paid to private plans should not be available to plans which, when combined with Social Security, provide a replacement of past wages at the time of retirement more than sufficient to buy the level of living enjoyed by workers when still employed. It is more important that private plans put money into assuring that the level provided at retirement continues throughout retirement.*

Even with improvements in the Social Security that I have suggested, private pension plans will continue to be important. A greater degree of vesting should be required by the federal tax laws, automatic adjustments in benefits to changes in prices up to some annual limit should be encouraged, and survivors benefits should be improved.

At the same time, the outside limit of tax-favored retirement income at the time of retirement—Social Security plus private pensions—ought to total no more than 80 percent of recent earnings, kept up to date with the rising standard of living of the community. Given that private pension plans are tax-subsidized, they should be designed so that initial payments under such plans plus those under Social Security do not exceed this percentage. Future liberalizations in private plans ought to go in the direction of adequate vesting and the protection of the purchasing power of the retired person, rather than toward higher and higher replacement rates at the time of retirement.

11. The next steps in Social Security development should not be further across-the-board benefit increases for everyone, but selected changes for those persons regularly under the program who are the worst-off and selected changes to improve the equity and acceptability of the program.

Social Security has been greatly improved in recent years and now contains automatic provisions to keep the benefits up to date with wages and prices. It will in the future provide a base on which the average worker can build adequate retirement income by adding relatively small amounts of additional income from private savings and private pensions. At the same time, scheduled contribution rates— although far below those being paid in many foreign systems—are considered by many Americans, perhaps the majority, to be quite high. Consequently, each change in the program that costs money should be carefully scrutinized in terms of its relative priority. The changes which seem to me to be of the greatest importance are listed in the several propositions immediately below.

12. Social Security coverage should be extended to all state and local employees, and the staff systems covering such employees should be modified to take Social Security coverage into account.

The situation today in which some government retirement plans are still uncoordinated with Social Security should be changed. This lack of coordination makes it possible for government employees covered by such plans to gain eligibility for Social Security in nongovernment jobs at bargain rates and in some instances to get excessive retirement income. There are other situations in which government employees may contribute to two or more plans but, by failing to qualify under one of them, may get inadequate protection. And there are still

others in which a combined Social Security and state or local system
would provide much better protection than the present arrangement.

In a few systems it is possible to reach a level of retirement pay at
retirement which, when combined with Social Security, is in excess of
past earnings. Such situations are unreasonable and will be increasingly attacked. It would be wise for state and local employees to take
the initiative and, while building toward adequate retirement income
in all cases, avoid such excessive payments. Coverage under Social
Security, with consequent modification of government plans, is the
key to solving this problem, which occurs also for some specialized
employees who may also get retirement or disability benefits from
military service.

One way of improving the situation in those systems that are over-
ly generous because of early retirement provisions, or for whatever reason, would be to modify the arrangement for new employees only. This
would avoid the problems involved in reducing protection for people
who may reasonably consider the level of protection now promised to
be part of the agreed-upon conditions of their employment.

13. *In the long run, the general revenues of the federal government
    should bear part of the cost of the weighting in the Social Security
    benefit formula and dependents benefits.*

Although high-paid workers under Social Security have enjoyed significant bargains even when their employers' contributions as well
as their own are taken into account, in the long run this may not be
the case under a completely self-financed system. It would be desirable
to have dependents benefits and the cost of the weighting in the benefit formula borne by the more progressive sources of general revenue rather than being shifted entirely to the contributions of
higher-paid workers and their employers. A taxpayer benefits under
Social Security by the reduction of the general tax burden of assistance
programs and by the contribution that Social Security makes to the
general welfare. Social Security should be financed in part by deductions from workers' earnings, by contributions of employers, and by
general revenues. [*Author's note:* See Chapter 17, "Contribution Rates
and Funding Sources," for a discussion of other rationales for a general revenue contribution, now supported by President Clinton and
Vice President Gore. Such a contribution is also now supported by

many conservatives as a way to finance some of the transition to partial privatization.]

14. For the long run, a policy that encourages early retirement will not make sense, either for the economy or for the individual.

For a long time, fewer and fewer older people have been working. If in the next century there turns out to be, as now expected, a large increase in the proportion of people over 65, it would make sense economically for more older people to have the opportunity to work.

It would not be desirable, however, to raise the age of first eligibility for full Social Security benefits, as the 1975 Advisory Council on Social Security suggested might later be considered. Not only would such a change violate the compact between the contributor and the insured in Social Security, but it could also result in great hardship for those who were not successful in holding onto or getting jobs—and, of course, many wouldn't be able to. If the elderly are to eventually increase their participation in the labor force, the primary effort will need to go toward changing some union and employer attitudes, although worker motivation is also important.

15. Social Security benefits for single workers and for widows should be increased.

Specifically, I would propose that the rate for retirement benefits be increased by 7 percent, but that the spouse's benefit be reduced from one-half of the retirement benefit to 40 percent. As a result, couples in which only one person worked would get the same replacement percentage of previous earnings as in present law, but single workers would get more, and couples in which both persons worked would get more; widows and children would also get more.

This is an expensive proposal and may have to be approached gradually. It would require an increase in the combined employer-employee contribution rate of about 0.75 percent of payroll [as of 2000], but it would greatly increase the equity and effectiveness of the program. If Social Security is to do a better job of contributing to income security in the later years, improvements need to be made in benefit levels for elderly people living alone—particularly women.

The proposed change in the benefit arrangements would also mean that when a man and wife both worked and had benefits on the basis of their own earnings records, their combined benefits would much more often than at present be higher than when only one member of the family worked. And much more often under this proposal than today, a married woman who went to work would get benefits entirely in her own right rather than partially as a dependent of her husband. In almost all cases, if she worked regularly under the program for a substantial period of time, her own benefit would exceed the 40 percent of her husband's benefit that she could get as a dependent.

16. *Several steps should be taken to improve the administration of the disability insurance program and to control its cost.*

I believe that federalizing the disability determination process might well lead to better and more uniform disability determinations; state agencies under contract are just not as amenable to direction as are integral parts of the Social Security Administration.

Equally important, it would be desirable to strengthen incentives for work by applying the overall Social Security–workmen's compensation 80 percent rule to a combination of Social Security and any other disability benefit either paid for or subsidized by the federal government, such as private pensions, veterans' benefits, and black lung benefits. It would also improve work incentives if a graduated earnings test were adopted in place of the present sharp cutoff of all benefits when earnings reach the level defined as "substantial, gainful activity." The rehabilitation of more disabled workers should also result from the earlier contact with the rehabilitation process which would result from reducing the waiting period (see Proposition 17).

17. *The disability insurance program should be improved by reducing the waiting period before benefits are payable from five months to two, by liberalizing the definition of disability for older workers, and by paying benefits regardless of age to disabled widows and widowers.*

Most foreign social insurance systems pay benefits in the event of short-term total disability (usually called "sickness insurance"). In the United States we have such a provision in only five states. The best way to make this protection universal is to add it to our federal disability insurance program. I would propose that we pay a disability benefit after a waiting period of two months, instead of five as at present (to get a benefit one must be disabled for six months, but a benefit is paid for the sixth month). Moreover, payments should be made even though the disability might not be expected to last for 12 months, as must be the case under present law.

Although the present very strict definition of disability—inability to engage in any substantial gainful activity—seems reasonable in the case of younger people, it is not realistic for the older worker. Benefits should he paid to all disabled persons after 55 if they meet the definition now used for blind workers—that is, if the person is unable to engage in substantial gainful activity *requiring skills or abilities comparable to those of any gainful activity in which he has previously engaged with some regularity and over a substantial period of time.*

Disabled widows and widowers are now paid partial benefits beginning at age 50 on the assumption that their disability makes it impossible for them to support themselves. Such an assumption, however, argues for eliminating the age requirement.

18. *Taxation of Social Security benefits should approximate the approach that is taken in the taxation of private pensions and benefits paid by other government retirement systems.*

Although the detailed rules on taxation of these other plans can become quite complicated, the general theory is that in retirement the employee should include for income tax purposes that part of the retirement benefit that exceeds his own previous contributions.

19. *Special tax treatment of the elderly and subsidized prices for various public and private services the elderly receive do not make sense over the long run. The double exemption in the federal income tax for those 65 and over should be dropped.* [Author's note: *The double exemption has since been dropped.*]

We now have a large and growing number of subsidies based solely on age, which apply to federal and state taxation and to a variety of special services: bus fares, tickets to various kinds of entertainment, lower fees for adult education, and so on.

People 65 and over are not a homogeneous group. Some are poor and sick, but some are decidedly better-off economically than when they were younger. Increasingly, if we improve the Social Security system and private pension plans, the majority will have reasonably adequate retirement income and many will be able to maintain a level of living in retirement that is close to the level they had attained while working full-time. It is not desirable to identify older people as a class apart who need help simply because they are over 65. Our goal should be for the elderly to have adequate retirement income so that they can pay their own way.

20. *There needs to be early improvement in the national health insurance system for the elderly and the disabled (Medicare) as part of the plan to improve retirement income security.*

The subject of health insurance generally is one for a book of its own, but some mention is necessary here since the adequacy of money income in retirement and during total disability depends in part on the adequacy of health insurance.

Here is what I would propose for improvements in Medicare:

- In addition to the protection now provided, the program should cover catastrophic situations. Although very long hospital stays are required in only a small percent of cases (about 5 percent of the hospital stays of older people are for more than 60 days), in those few cases cost-sharing provisions are now introduced just when the burden gets greatest. Under hospital insurance, full costs of all needed hospital care should be paid for under Medicare once the deductible has been met.

    There should also be a limit on the total amount of deductibles and coinsurance to be paid under the physician coverage part of the plan (Part B). Once the part the patient paid reached some absolute dollar amount in a year, then the plan should pay full costs.

- Also, if the physician wishes the advantage of having the plan pay him directly, he should be required to abide by the reasonable-charge determinations of Medicare in all cases. A physician who does not wish to join the plan should be required to take his chances on billing and collecting from his patients in all cases.

[*Author's note:* Medicare now reimburses physicians according to a relative-value fee schedule based on resources used in each procedure (known as the Resource Based Relative Value Scale, or RBRVS), and physicians are allowed to collect only up to 115 percent of the Medicare schedule.]

- Supplementary Medical Insurance, the program covering the cost of physician services, should be combined with the hospital insurance program (Part A), and the combined protection should be financed partly by a contribution paid by the worker and his employers throughout his working career and partly by a government contribution.

- Medicare should be broadened to cover prescription drugs.

- Disabled beneficiaries should be covered under Medicare when they become eligible for cash benefits, rather than having to wait two years as under present law.

21. *We need greatly improved services for the very old and the elderly who are chronically ill, including more and better nursing homes, emphasis upon rehabilitation for self-care, and services that help elderly people remain in their own homes if they wish to. To make such improved services available, the federal government should finance a long-term-care benefit for elderly people, and it should be available without a test of need.*

In the over-65 group, the number of the very old is increasing more rapidly than the number of the less elderly. In 1977 there were about 2 million persons over 85 [4.5 million in 2000]. And at some point even a reasonably adequate retirement income is not by itself sufficient to supply the kind of help needed by those with severe limitations because of chronic illness or advanced age.

Many services needed by the functionally dependent elderly— if they are to continue to live in the community rather than being institutionalized—are best supplied and organized at the local level. There is no good reason to have national administration of telephone reassurance services, meals-on-wheels, handy-man services, shopping services, etc. On the other hand, there is good reason for the federal government to stimulate the provision of such services and to see that they are available.

The federal government should finance a long-term-care benefit without a test of need in any community that has established three qualifying services:

- an assessment program designed to determine the functional capacity of the older person (physically, mentally, and socially) and to determine the most appropriate services and levels of care needed;

- the availability in the community of a minimum number of home-based services;

- the availability of a variety of institutional care services of different levels of intensity within reach of the members of the community.

With an assessment program serving as the gateway to services, and with the assurance of the availability of alternatives to institutional care, such a program would hold the promise of being as economical as, and more effective than, the present widespread use of institutional care. [*Author's note:* See Chapter 15, "A System for Mutual Support," for a further discussion of long-term care. In 1989, I developed a plan for long-term care insurance as a branch of federal social insurance (described in *Because We're All in This Together*, with Thomas N. Bethell, Families USA Foundation, Washington, D.C., 1989).]

22. *There should be an automatic increase in the Social Security benefit upon the attainment of advanced age, say, 85.*

The person reaching 85 has typically been receiving Social Security benefits for 20 years or more and having them updated only in accord with increases in purchasing power. Nevertheless, two things have undoubtedly happened in this period of time. The level of living of the community as a whole has risen, and some increase in the Social Security benefit should he made in recognition of this fact; in addition, the needs of the older person are likely to have increased because of the additional handicaps of old age. Moreover, in many instances, it would have been necessary for the older person to have used up some of his private resources, if any, to meet the emergency situations that would likely have occurred during his 20-plus years of retirement. I would therefore propose phasing in an increase in the benefit level beginning at age 85.

23. *It would be desirable to partly offset the Social Security contributions paid by low-income people by expanding the earnings credit in the income tax law and making it permanent.*

[*Author's note:* This proposal has been adopted. In fact, the entire amount of what low-wage earners are required to pay for Social Security may now be offset in this way.]

The earnings credit should not apply only to workers with children, as it does now, but to all earners. In this way, a considerable part of what low-wage earners are required to pay for Social Security would be offset. Yet, under the Social Security program, they would be treated the same as everyone else and their earned right to the benefits would be backed by a contribution paid on their behalf.

24. *Social Security benefits should continue to be weighted in favor of those with low wages, and benefits for dependents should be retained.*

Some have argued that Social Security benefits should have a more direct relationship to past earnings, a position which at the extreme would result in all retirees getting the same percentage of past earnings, and single workers getting the same as those with dependents. The argument is that Social Security should not try to do two things at once. If Social Security is a wage replacement system—so the argument goes—it should stick to that; the relationship of benefits to wages should not be modified in order to pay more to those who are presumptively in greater need.

There is a delicate balance to be maintained on this issue. On the one hand, as in private group insurance, if the departure from strict equity (defined in this instance as the direct relationship of benefit protection to past earnings) is perceived to be unfair by a large number of people who are covered, the system risks rejection. On the other hand, a major purpose of Social Security from the beginning has been to provide security for low-wage earners, as well as average earners, and it is quite clear that to attain this objective at reasonable cost the system must pay a higher proportion of past earnings to low-wage earners than to higher-wage earners, and pay more to those with dependents than to those without dependents.

There is nothing inherently wrong in having one system accomplish two good purposes instead of one. The only proper question seems to me to be whether the financing of departures from a strict benefit-contribution relationship is fair. With the addition of a government contribution as outlined in Proposition 13, the system will more clearly meet this test of fairness.

Under a system which paid the same percentage of past wages at all earnings levels, Social Security benefits just wouldn't be high enough to meet the minimum needs of the low paid unless, of course, benefits were made much higher for the highest-paid workers. Therefore, if the weighted benefit formula were dropped, either the system would have to be a much more costly one or low-wage earners would be required to pay contributions for a lifetime and still end up having to rely on the income-tested SSI program.

[*Author's note:* If this chapter had been written in 2000 instead of 1978, it would certainly have included a strong warning against privatization schemes based on diverting some of Social Security's financing to private accounts, and would also have argued for Social Security's seeking a higher return on its accumulating funds by changing the law to allow direct investment in stocks. Instead of repeating the arguments in an addendum here, however, let me direct the reader particularly to Chapter 21, "Getting the Facts Straight," and Chapter 19, "A Public-Private Investment Strategy."]

CONCLUSION

Providing a decent measure of economic security to the retired, the disabled, and widows and motherless and fatherless children is a hugely expensive undertaking. This is true no matter what the method chosen—fringe benefits earned through private arrangements while employed, needs-tested programs of assistance, or social insurance. The portion of our population that is working must, in one way or another, support the portion that is not working and that does not have enough resources to meet living costs. Most nonworking spouses and children are supported, in normal course, by family breadwinners. However, the retired and the disabled, the widows and children, commonly have neither family support nor savings sufficient to maintain a minimally adequate standard of living, and some arrangement is essential if they are not to go hungry.

The nation has chosen contributory social insurance as the primary mechanism, and those who would radically change that system must be prepared to substitute some form of noncontributory aid to those groups in the population which would otherwise be eligible for Social Security benefits.

A 100-percent noncontributory system, lacking the compact between government and contributors that is built into Social Security, could offer no comparable assurance to working people, or even to those already on the rolls, that the promised benefits would not be curtailed in times of budgetary stringency. The hard reality is that a noncontributory system would almost inevitably come to rest upon a means test, so that no one would receive benefits until after poverty had overtaken him. The experience with welfare augurs ill for the willingness of taxpayers to help their fellow citizens who are thought, rightly or wrongly, to be able in one way or another to support themselves. It is not likely that taxpayers would be willing, or that Congress would be willing to compel them, to provide noncontributory benefits at a level comparable in adequacy to Social Security. It is much more likely that noncontributory benefits would be conditioned on a means test.

Social Security benefits are earned rights based on the beneficiaries' past work and contributions, or on those of family members, thus reflecting the beneficiaries' previous levels of living and serving in some measure as a reward for diligence. The benefits are payable without scrutiny of individual means and needs and so permit supplementation by anything the recipient has been able to save. Because they are payable as an earned right, the benefits accord with the self-respect of people accustomed to providing for themselves. It is small wonder that the Congress and the people have preferred contributory social insurance to a system benefiting only those who can show themselves to be destitute.

Social Security has been thought by some to be an infringement of liberty, requiring the worker to take out insurance that he may not want or need and interfering with the free disposition of what he has earned. This is not, however, a view ordinarily taken by workers themselves. The Social Security system has given them, rather, a mechanism to assure both their security and their freedom. In our society there is little freedom without money. Social Security enlarges the choices and the opportunities of those who, without the system, would be among the most deprived groups in our society: the retired elderly, the totally disabled, widows, and motherless and fatherless children.

Social Security is America's most successful program of social reform. Built on the conservative principles of self-help, with the protection growing out of the work that people perform, it has nevertheless created a revolution, transforming life for millions of our people from poverty and insecurity to relative economic well-being. An America without Social Security is almost unimaginable today. But there remains the question of how much security. American workers need to ask themselves what kind of society they want to live in—not only in terms of the level of living provided today's Social Security beneficiaries but in terms of the level of protection they want for their families and themselves and others of their generation. To what extent does it make sense to them to reduce a current level of living while at work in order to build protection against the loss of earnings because of old age, disability, and death? Since the decision is so determining of the quality of our civilization, it cannot be made by each individual alone; it must be a collective decision.

NOTES

CHAPTER 2

1. Germany set up the first old-age, survivors, and disability insurance program in 1889, and well before 1935, when the U.S. Social Security system was established, governments were providing protection against these risks, in one form or another, in Austria, Belgium, Bulgaria, Czechoslovakia, Denmark, France, Hungary, Ireland, Italy, Luxembourg, the Netherlands, Poland, Romania, Russia, Spain, Sweden, and the United Kingdom. There also were systems in place in many countries outside Europe. Social Security Administration, *Social Security Programs throughout the World—1983*, Research Report No. 59 (Washington, D.C.: Government Printing Office, 1983), p. 19.

2. In the staff reports to the Committee on Economic Security, the cabinet committee responsible for making the original recommendations for a Social Security program, the foreign experience is carefully described. See *Social Security in America, The Factual Background of the Social Security Act as Summarized from Staff Reports to the Committee on Economic Security* (Washington, D.C.: Government Printing Office, 1937). Also, the staff working on what was to become the old-age benefits section of the Social Security Act were fully familiar with the European precedents. One staff member, Barbara Nachtrieb Armstrong, had produced a major work on social insurance: *Insuring the Essentials: Minimum Wage, Plus Social Insurance* (New York: Macmillan, 1932). The other two professionals working on this part of the study were economics professor J. Douglas Brown of Princeton, an industrial relations expert, and Murray W. Latimer, who had written the monumental study of private pensions, *Industrial Pension Systems in the United States and Canada,* 2 vols. (New York: Industrial Relations Counselors, 1932).

3. For example, the Gild of the Blessed Virgin Mary founded in 1357 at Kingston-upon-Hull in England collected annually two shillings and twopence in silver from each married couple and from each single man and woman. Benefits are described as follows:

> If it happen that any of the gild becomes infirm, bowed, blind, dumb, deaf, maimed, or sick whether with some lasting or only

temporary sickness, and whether in old age or in youth, or be so borne down by any other mishap that he has not the means of living, then, for kindness' sake, and for the souls' sake of the founders, it is ordained that each shall have, out of the goods of the gild, at the hands of the wardens, sevenpence every week, and every one so being infirm, bowed, blind, dumb, deaf, maimed or sick, shall have the sevenpence every week as long as he lives. If any of these poor and infirm folks should get so low in the world that he cannot pay the before-named yearly charge of two shillings and twopence, and has no goods on which it may be levied, then part of the weekly payment of sevenpence shall be set aside, so that the quarterly payments towards the two shillings and twopence shall be fully made, and so that on no account shall that yearly payment be released.

—Toulmin Smith, *English Gilds*, published for the Early English Text Society (London: N. Trubner & Co., 1870), pp. 155–57.

4. For a brief, authoritative account of the forerunners of social insurance, see John Graham Brooks, *Compulsory Insurance in Germany, Fourth Special Report of the Commissioner of Labor* (Washington, D.C.: Government Printing Office, 1895), pp. 29–44.

5. For a considerable discussion of the origin and nature of these orders and societies in England and the United States, see Terence O'Donnell, *History of Life Insurance in Its Formative Years* (Chicago: American Conservation Co., 1936), pp. 612–77.

6. Ibid.

7. In 1932, Murray Latimer estimated that there were about 160,000 recipients of private industrial pensions, to which must be added civil service and military retirees, ministers, and teachers. Latimer, *Industrial Pension Systems in the United States and Canada*, p. 852.

8. See Abraham Epstein, *Insecurity: A Challenge to America* (New York: Harrison Smith and Robert Haas, 1933).

9. From the March 1985 *Current Population Survey* of the Bureau of the Census, quoted in A. Ycas Martynas and Susan Grad, "Incomes of Retirement-Aged Persons in the United States," paper delivered at a meeting of the International Social Security Association, Baltimore, May 6–8, 1986.

10. *Committee on Economic Security, Report to the President* (Washington, D.C.: Government Printing Office, 1935). This report, along with other basic Social Security documents, was reprinted at the time of the fiftieth anniversary of the Social Security Act as *The 50th Anniversary Edition of the Report of the Committee on Economic Security of 1935* (Washington, D.C.: National Conference on Social Welfare, 1985).

11. The detailed provisions of the Old-Age, Survivors, and Disability Insurance program can be traced in summary form from the original act through all successive amendments by reference to *The Social Security Bulletin, Annual Statistical Supplement, 1984–85* (Washington, D.C.: Government Printing Office, 1985), pp. 2–34. [*Author's note:* The annual statistical supplement continues this practice year after year.]

12. Advisory Council on Social Security of 1937–38, *Final Report* (Washington, D.C.: Government Printing Office, 1939).

13. Advisory Council on Social Security of 1947–49, *Recommendations for Social Security Legislation, Reports to the Senate Committee on Finance* (Washington, D.C.: Government Printing Office, 1949).

14. Consultants on Social Security, *A Report to the Secretary of HEW on Extension of OASI to Additional Groups of Current Workers* (Washington, D.C.: Government Printing Office, 1953).

15. Advisory Council on Social Security Financing, *Financing Old-Age, Survivors and Disability Insurance, A Report* (Washington, D.C.: Government Printing Office, 1959).

16. Advisory Council on Social Security of 1965, *The Status of the Social Security Program and Recommendations for Its Improvement* (Washington, D.C.: Government Printing Office, 1965).

17. Advisory Council on Social Security of 1971, *Reports of the 1971 Council on Social Security* (Washington, D.C.: Government Printing Office, 1971).

18. Quadrennial Advisory Council on Social Security, *Report of the Council* (Washington, D.C.: Government Printing Office, 1975).

19. Advisory Council on Social Security of 1979–80, *Report of the Council* (Washington, D.C.: Government Printing Office, 1980).

20. National Commission on Social Security Reform, *Report of the Commission* (Washington, D.C.: Government Printing Office, 1983).

21. Ibid., chap. 2, p. 2.

22. Much of the material that follows is based on the author's essay, "The 1939 Amendments to the Social Security Act and What Followed," in *The Report of the Committee on Economic Security of 1935 and Other Basic Documents Relating to the Developments of the Social Security Act, Fiftieth Anniversary Edition,* ed. Alan Pifer and Forrest Chisman (Washington, D.C.: National Conference on Social Welfare, 1985), pp. 161–72. See also Robert M. Ball, *Social Security: Today and Tomorrow* (New York: Columbia University Press, 1978).

23. Arthur M. Schlesinger, Jr., *The Age of Roosevelt: The Politics of Upheaval* (Cambridge, Mass.: Riverside Press, 1960), p. 613.

24. Ibid., p. 636.

25. Supreme Court, 837 and 910, October term, 1936.

26. Made up of six representatives each from labor and industry and thirteen representatives from the general public, the council was chaired by

Professor J. Douglas Brown of Princeton. As a staff member of the Committee on Economic Security, Brown had a major role in the development of the 1935 Old-Age Benefits program.

27. This is a common misstatement. See, for example, Michael J. Boskin, *Too Many Promises: The Uncertain Future of Social Security* (Homewood, Ill.: Dow Jones-Irwin, 1986), p. 7.

28. Robert J. Myers, *Social Security*, 3d ed. (Homewood, Ill.: Richard D. Irwin, 1985), App. 3-5: 233. *[Author's note:* The figures were the same in the year 2000.]

29. Advisory Council of 1937–38, *Final Report*, p. 15.

30. *1986 Annual Report of the Federal Old-Age and Survivors Insurance and Disability Insurance Trust Funds* (Washington, D.C.: Government Printing Office, 1986), p. 82, Table A1.

31. For example, the Portland, Maine, *Press Herald* for February 5, 1982, quoted Deputy Commissioner of Social Security Paul B. Simmons as follows: "Overriding all other difficulties—unemployment, inflation, benefit changes—it's a demographic problem. In 1950, 16 workers were paying taxes for each beneficiary. Today the ratio is 3.3 workers per beneficiary. By the turn of the century, the ratio could drop to 2:1 because the population grows increasingly older."

32. Advisory Council of 1947–49, *Recommendations for Social Security Legislation.*

33. Ibid., p. 1.

34. Ibid.

35. Under the 1939 law, a worker reaching age 65 in early 1955 would have had to have earnings in 36 calendar quarters to be eligible for retirement benefits (one-half the calendar quarters elapsing after 1936 and prior to the quarter in which the worker reached age 65). After the 1950 amendments, such a worker needed earnings in only eight quarters earned after 1936 (a number equal to one-half the calendar quarters elapsing after 1950 up to the quarter in which the worker reached age 65). Under the 1939 act, wages on which the benefit was based were averaged from 1936 up to the quarter in which the individual became 65; but after 1950, the averaging period was from 1950 on, if that produced a higher benefit, as it usually would, since the low wages of the past were eliminated from the average.

36. For example, benefits for surviving children of a married female worker were made generally available for the first time, as were benefits for dependent husbands and widowers. Also, for the first time benefits were paid to the wives of retired workers, regardless of age, if they were caring for the worker's child under age eighteen. Benefits for surviving divorced wives caring for eligible children were added as well.

37. Advisory Council of 1947–49, *Recommendations for Social Security Legislation*, pp. 69–93.

38. The early days of the Eisenhower administration were a period of considerable uncertainty for Social Security. Democrats had been in office for twenty years, and the new administration, understandably, approached all New Deal programs and their administrators with skepticism. A Republican Congress was conducting a hostile investigation of Social Security under a Subcommittee of Ways and Means whose chairman favored scrapping OASI and substituting noncontributory flat benefits for all elderly people. See U.S. Congress, House Committee on Ways and Means, *Analysis of the Social Security System: Hearings*, 83d Cong., 1st sess., 1953.

Gradually, however, after a thorough investigation involving a group of outside consultants (*A Report to the Secretary of HEW*) and after an investigation by an associate of Under Secretary Nelson Rockefeller, Roswell B. Perkins, who later became an assistant secretary of HEW, the administration endorsed Social Security.

The influence of some Social Security supporters in the administration also was of great importance. Marion B. Folsom, first under secretary of the Treasury and later secretary of HEW, was particularly important. As an official of Eastman Kodak he had been a member of the advisory councils of 1935, 1937–38, and 1947–49 and was a strong supporter of the system, as was Arthur Larson, the under secretary of labor.

39. For a summary of the arguments then made against such a program, see "Memorandum of Dissent by Two Members," Advisory Council of 1947–49, *Recommendations for Social Security Legislation*, p. 85.

40. For discussion see U.S. Congress, House Subcommittee on the Administration of the Social Security Laws, *Hearing on the Administration of the Social Security Insurance Program*, 86th Cong., 1st sess., 1959.

41. Prior to the adoption of the automatic provisions in 1972, the contribution rates were based on long-range cost estimates using level-earnings assumptions. According to the chief actuary of the Social Security Administration, the chief purpose of basing the contribution rates on estimates using such assumptions was to allow for future benefit increases "to keep the benefits up to date in the event of rising earnings levels." Myers, *Social Security*, p. 392.

42. The Reagan administration in May 1981 proposed benefit cuts which, when added to the cuts the administration had earlier proposed in its budget, would have amounted to a reduction of one-fourth in the future level of Social Security protection. The proposals were presented as necessary to save the system. Although the proposals were overwhelmingly rejected by the Congress, the administration continued to argue throughout 1981–82 that cuts of this magnitude were needed to solve the system's financial problems. Save Our Security (SOS)—a liberal coalition of labor organizations, organizations representing retired and disabled persons, social welfare organizations and churches—argued, on the other hand, that the difficulty was temporary (beginning in

1990 the actuarial cost estimates showed large annual surpluses for many decades) and that the program should be allowed to borrow from the general fund to tide it over. Throughout the period various groups, experts, and congressional committees joined in the argument with a variety of plans and proposals, and the newspapers, radio, and television were full of stories of impending doom. For further discussion of the factual background of the problem and some of the proposals made during this period see Robert M. Ball, "Social Security Today and Tomorrow," testimony before the Task Force on Entitlements, Uncontrollables and Indexing, U.S. Congress, House Committee on the Budget, 97th Cong., 2d sess., March 1, 1982.

43. National Commission on Social Security Reform, *Report.*

44. For a description of the National Commission's recommendations and the 1983 amendments see Myers, *Social Security*, pp. 282–98. Annual surpluses for OASDI under the intermediate cost estimates are projected to be $16 billion in 1987, $31 billion in 1988, $41 billion in 1989, $55 billion in 1990, $61 billion in 1991, $93 billion by 1995, with the trust funds building from $44 billion at the end of 1984 to $1.3 trillion by the year 2000 and to $12.7 trillion by 2030 before starting to decline. "Long-Range Estimates of Social Security Trust Fund Operations in Dollars," Actuarial Note no. 127, Social Security Administration, Baltimore, 1986.

45. A trust fund equal to about one and a half times the following year's outgo would be sufficient to weather a severe recession such as the one in 1981–82 and still have sufficient funds available to provide a safety margin during the early stages of recovery. [*Author's note:* The trust funds are already beyond this point, and the system is committed to at least some earnings-reserve financing.]

46. These goals can be accomplished, for example, by increasing the PIA by 7 percent and reducing the spouse's benefit from 50 percent to 40 percent of the PIA. Such a change would add 0.75 percent of payroll to the 75-year cost of the program.

47. The view that, in general, the remaining needs of low-income persons can be met better through SSI improvements is widely held. The distinction here is that some would not change Social Security to meet even part of the remaining problem.

48. The author believes in a mixed system that keeps a careful eye on equity considerations while also moving toward the goal of adequate benefits for regular, full-time, low-paid earners. How to maintain the desirable balance between the two principles of equity and adequacy so that goals are met and political support is maintained is a matter for compromise and judgment.

49. For example, see Congressman Roybal's proposal in 1986 that high-salaried persons pay Social Security taxes on their full salaries so that lower-paid workers could pay lower rates than scheduled, thus tilting the system still further away from a direct relationship between benefits and contributions.

50. The numbers in this paragraph and the next two, with the exception of the last sentence of the second paragraph, are from the Bureau of the Census. Reported in Lynette Rawlings, "Poverty and Income Trends: 1998," Center on Budget and Policy Priorities, Washington, D.C., March 2000, pp. 29, 30.

51. Kathryn H. Porter, Kathy Laran, and Wendell Primus, "Social Security and Poverty among the Elderly," Center on Budget and Policy Priorities, Washington, D.C., 1999, Table A-12, p. 52. Unlike the Census figures quoted earlier, these numbers include government payments in kind, such as housing allowances and food stamps.

52. *Social Security Bulletin* 62, no. 4 (1999), inside back cover, and "Fact Sheet on the Old-Age, Survivors', and Disability Insurance Program," Office of the Chief Actuary, Social Security Administration, Baltimore, December 31, 1999.

53. "Social Security and Poverty among the Elderly," Table 6, p. 20.

54. Ibid., Table 9, p. 22.

CHAPTER 3

1. Although some payments for damages are service connected in that they attempt to restore what one had earned previously or to make up for what one is prevented from earning in the future, others are in excess of the loss and are in the nature of a penalty against the one who committed the injury. Still others are made in consideration of suffering. Both of these latter types are the result of legal rights, but they are not earned rights. The distribution of income through inheritance also is something of an exception. Inheritance seems partly an unearned right and partly a gratuity. Except for the interest of a spouse in real property, inheritance as a right really exists only in the absence of clear direction from the deceased. He or she has given it as desired, and the rights of even the closest members of the family are very limited indeed. However, insofar as it is a gratuity, our attitude toward an inheritance and other gratuities is very different. Perhaps this is partly the result of our special consideration for payments from one member of a family to another and partly the result of the one who inherits being released from some of the obligations, emotional and other, that go with many gifts bestowed by living relatives. Veterans' benefits are properly classified as service connected, even though the service is not an economic one. Gambling is "getting something for nothing," and our moral disapproval of it is based on this fact. Businesses in which there is a large speculative element are at great pains to show that they perform economic functions and are not gambling. The speculative trader in agricultural commodities, for example, justifies the activity on the grounds that he or she relieves the grower of a portion of the risk, and the trader in stocks is given

the function of providing a continuous market for securities and thereby facilitating investment.

2. Karl de Schweinitz, "People and Process in Social Security," American Council on Education, Washington, D.C., 1948.

3. See Leslie Lipson, "The New Zealand Means Test: An Appraisal," *Public Administration* 22 (Winter 1944–45): 131–36.

4. This is not meant to imply that workers should be indefinitely guaranteed against a reduction in living standards but only that they should become eligible for benefits under these circumstances. In unemployment insurance it is proper that one should be required to accept a job even though it means a reduction in living standards after the full opportunity to seek employment at one's appropriate skill level has been granted without producing results.

5. Lewis Meriam, *Relief and Social Security* (Washington, D.C.: Brookings Institution, 1946), p. 867.

6. George E. Bigge, "Looking Ahead in Public Assistance," *Social Security Bulletin* (December 1944): 4.

CHAPTER 4

1. U.S. Department of Health and Human Services, *Income of the Population 55 or Older, 1998* (Washington, D.C.: Government Printing Office, 2000).

2. U.S. Department of Labor, Social Security Administration, U.S. Small Business Administration, and Pension Benefit Guaranty Corporation, *Pension and Health Benefits of American Workers: New Findings from the April 1993 Current Population Survey* (Washington, D.C.: Government Printing Office, 1994).

3. About a fourth of all state and local employees, the only major group not covered by Social Security in the entire U.S. workforce, are covered only by their own plans. Of the 14 million full-time state and local employees, 3.7 million are not covered by Social Security (estimate by Office of the Actuary, Social Security Administration).

4. Social Security contribution rates are currently 7.65 percent of earnings (6.2 percent for Old-Age, Survivors, and Disability Insurance, plus 1.45 percent for Medicare), with the employee's contribution matched by the employer. In point of fact, most economists hold that workers are contributing the full 15.3 percent since the employer share actually comes out of what would otherwise be available for higher wages or other forms of employee compensation.

5. Coverage of this group can be gradually extended by first covering the newly hired. This approach, which was used when coverage was extended to federal employees, allows the employing entity gradually to absorb any

increasing cost. Setting an effective date a year or two after enactment would provide time to work out the integration of Social Security with the state and local retirement systems and either to reduce or eliminate any new cost to the employer while maintaining the desired level of protection for employees.

6. Stephen C. Goss, deputy chief actuary, Social Security Administration, memorandum to Harry Ballantyne, chief actuary, Social Security Administration, August 4, 2000.

7. Of the 0.55 percent, 0.35 percent would take the place of the tax on benefits now going to Hospital Insurance, Part A of Medicare. It is a peculiarity of present law that the proceeds from the taxes on OASDI benefits imposed by the 1993 amendments went into the HI fund. This came about because it would have required 60 votes in the Senate to increase income for OASDI, whereas this was not the case for HI. This change should not be made until, say, 2026, when it may be assumed that there will need to be changes in Medicare financing in any event.

8. "Fact Sheet on the Old Age Survivors and Disability Insurance Program," Office of the Actuary, Social Security Administration, June 30, 2000.

9. Stephen C. Goss, supervisory actuary, Social Security Administration, "Analysis of Relationship Between Mortality and Income Levels," memorandum to Harry Ballantyne, chief actuary, Social Security Administration, March 9, 1995.

10. Estimates by the Office of the Actuary, Social Security Administration.

11. Frank Ackerman, *Hazardous to Our Wealth: Economic Policies in the 1980s* (Boston: South End Press, 1984).

12. *Averting the Old Age Crisis: Policies to Protect the Old and Promote Growth* (Washington, D.C.: World Bank, 1994).

13. Personal communication with Stephen C. Goss, supervisory actuary, Social Security Administration, May 9, 1995.

14. The Kerrey proposal discussed here is the 1996 proposal. Since then, Senator Kerrey has made modifications in the details but not in the broad approach.

15. The Primary Insurance Amount (PIA) is the monthly benefit payable to a person who retires at the age of first eligibility for full retirement benefits. All other benefit amounts, such as those for a surviving spouse and dependents, are based on the PIA and are calculated as a percentage of it.

16. Indeed, it is hard to exaggerate the importance of the COLA. To illustrate, consider this example, using a working couple who are relatively well-off. One is earning the average wage—$24,825 in 1995—and one is earning a wage halfway between the average and the maximum covered under Social Security, which would work out to be $43,013 in 1995. They plan to retire in 2010, when one will be 62 and the other 65. They figure that in order to maintain about the same level of living in retirement they had while working, they will require an income that is about 70 percent of their combined

earnings. In current dollars, their Social Security benefits will be $38,676 a year, and they are counting on private pensions and income from savings amounting to $49,538 to give them the 70 percent they want. Thus, when they start out in retirement their Social Security benefits account for 43.8 percent of their income. But since Social Security is indexed to prices after retirement and private pensions and savings are not, Social Security plays an increasingly important role during retirement. When they are 72 and 75, their Social Security benefits will be $61,977, assuming an average inflation rate of 3 percent, but their other income will still be $49,538. After 20 years in retirement, Social Security will represent not 43.8 but 58.5 percent of their total income ($69,853 in current dollars). Social Security benefits will have maintained their value, in contrast to the private pension income that they were counting on to meet their overall goal.

17. Peter A. Diamond, "Social Security Reform in Chile: An Economist's Perspective," in *Social Security: What Role for the Future?*, ed. Peter A. Diamond, David C. Lindeman, and Howard Young (Washington, D.C.: National Academy of Social Insurance, 1996).

CHAPTER 14

1. Robert M. Ball, Martha E. Keys, Lane Kirkland, Daniel Patrick Moynihan, and Claude Pepper. Kirkland dissented from the proposal to cover new federal employees and instead proposed taxing the entire employer payroll.

2. Bill Archer, William Armstrong, Robert A. Beck, Barber Conable, Mary Falvey Fuller, Alan Greenspan, Alexander B. Trowbridge, and Joe D. Waggoner.

3. As previously noted, Kirkland is not joining in the recommendation to extend coverage to federal employees.

CHAPTER 15

1. These include not only the 50 states but Puerto Rico, Guam, American Samoa, the Virgin Islands, and Americans living abroad.

CHAPTER 17

1. The contributions collected must be somewhat in excess of the survivors benefits paid out, in order to meet the deferred cost of paying benefits to widows at age 65x. There are some increases in annual costs in the survivors part of the program, but these are small in comparison with the increasing costs in the old-age part.

2. *Committee on Economic Security, Report to the President, 1935*, pp. 31–32.

3. William Beveridge, *Social Insurance and Allied Services* (New York: The Macmillan Co., 1942), pp. 177–78.

4. Advisory Council on Social Security of 1947–48, *Recommendations for Social Security Legislation* (Washington, D.C.: Government Printing Office, 1948). The major recommendations for old-age and survivors insurance included benefit increases, which in the next few years would result in average benefits more than double the 1948 average, practically universal coverage, substantial liberalization of the eligibility requirements for older workers, reduction in the qualifying age to 60 for women, abolition of the retirement test at age 70 and liberalization of the test between age 65 and 70, increase in the wage and contribution base from $3,000 to $4,200 per year, raising the minimum and maximum benefits, and increasing the protection of survivors.

5. Throughout this paper the contribution rate selected has been the midpoint between a high-cost and a low-cost estimate based on level wage assumptions. Such a rate may need revision from time to time since actual experience may indicate that costs are not at the midpoint but closer to either the low-cost or high-cost estimate. The estimates are based on the Social Security Administration's Actuarial Study no. 28, *Long-range Cost Estimates for Expanded Coverage and Liberalized Benefits Proposed to the Old-Age and Survivors Insurance System by H. R. 2893*, and the cost estimates in the advisory council's report. The higher long-run costs of the administration plan result largely from the provision for an increase of 1 percent in the basic benefit amount for each year in which the worker is paid $200 or more in covered employment.

6. It is unrealistic to expect this deficit to be made up by a lump-sum appropriation to the trust funds at the beginning of the program. In the absence of such appropriation, however, a government contribution is needed in perpetuity to make up for the loss of interest that would otherwise be earned by such a lump sum.

7. This statement assumes that the qualifying retirement age for women workers is reduced to age 60. Since, by and large, women workers do not have dependents who are protected by the program, many of them would otherwise overpay. Those self-employed persons who have relatively high earnings would overpay if they are charged as much as one and a half times the employee rate.

8. Charging the actuarial rate from the beginning of the program also would be deflationary at first, although considerably less so than charging the level-premium rate. Partly for this reason it is suggested later in this paper that the imposition of the full actuarial rate be postponed until the amount being paid out in benefits is greatly increased.

9. All the plans discussed in this paper are based on the assumption that the system will continue to be supported in large part by equal contributions from employers and employees. No attempt is made to explore radically different methods of financing, such as complete support from general revenues or from general revenues and either the employee or employer contribution alone, or support from special taxes on transactions or income, earmarked but, from the viewpoint of the one who pays the tax, completely unrelated to the value of the protection afforded.

10. Advisory Council on Social Security fo 1937–38, *Recommendations for Social Security Legislation,* pp. 46–47.

11. If permanent and total disability protection is added to the program, an additional contribution to cover the cost of these benefits on a level-premium basis might well be introduced immediately. The level-premium rate for a relatively generous program would not exceed 1 percent for employers and employees combined and would probably be in the neighborhood of 0.75 percent.

12. It would, of course, be at least theoretically possible to introduce the government contribution sooner and thus to keep down its ultimate size. An appropriation to the trust funds from general revenues at a time when income from employer and employee contributions exceeds current costs would have the effect of increasing the earning reserve and would substitute future interest payments for part of the government contribution. There is no real saving to the government, however, in this procedure. Its general fiscal position is the same whether the general revenues are used to reduce the national debt or prevent further increases in the debt or are appropriated to the trust funds. Whichever of these courses is followed, the amount of the federal debt held in private hands will be smaller than it would otherwise be by the amount of taxes in question, and consequently any one of the alternatives saves an equal amount of interest for the government.

13. The Social Security Administration proposal for basing benefits on an average of the five consecutive years of coverage in which the individual's wages were the highest rather than on the average over a working lifetime is designed partly to meet this problem in the benefit structure. Even under this formula, however, if wages rise, average benefits will be a lower percentage of average wages than if wage levels were to remain constant.

14. Advisory Council on Social Security fo 1937–38, *Recommendations for Social Security Legislation.*

CHAPTER 18

1. Arthur J. Altmeyer, *The Formative Years of Social Security* (Madison: University of Wisconsin Press, 1968), p. 5.

2. J. Douglas Brown, *An American Philosophy of Social Security* (Princeton, N.J.: Princeton University Press, 1971), pp. 97–99.

3. Altmeyer, *Formative Years of Social Security*, p. 5.

4. Ibid., p. 89.

CHAPTER 19

1. In connection with this change in policy it also would be desirable to change, over time, the way Social Security is accounted for in the finances of the federal government. Social Security income and expenditure should not be included in the budget used in determining the balance of federal obligations and income. The budget is a device for allocating government income among programs during the budget period, while Social Security, with its benefit commitments and fiduciary provisions spread over decades, requires a long-range framework. After all, people are paying today for benefits that may not be payable until 40 or 50 years from now. Social Security, like the retirement systems of the states, should be outside the allocation goals of the short-term budget cycle (while remaining subject to review, of course, as part of the government's long-range planning).

The validity of this argument has been recognized by the Congress, which by law has placed the income and outgo of Social Security "off-budget." Yet, in reporting on the budget, the various executive branch and congressional agencies concerned with budgeting have continued to include Social Security in a "unified budget," which is the one used in budget negotiations. This creates confusion about the nature of the program and can result in unsatisfactory policy decisions affecting not only Social Security but other programs as well.

The discipline of Social Security is in the long-range balance of income and expenditure (as illustrated by the fact that, working within a 75-year time frame, we are currently concerned with an imbalance that does not arise until some 30 to 35 years from now). In contrast, the discipline of the general budget is undermined by continuing to treat balances in Social Security, which by law may be used only to pay Social Security benefits and to meet related expenses, as though these funds are available for other purposes. With Social Security off-budget in actual practice, we would see more clearly the challenge of finding ways to pay for what the nation needs, and it would be easier to ensure that the buildup in Social Security assets is saved.

2. Forty percent is not intended to be taken as some sort of magic point above which the risks of investing Social Security funds in private equities are thought to become unacceptable. An analysis conducted for the advisory council, using stochastic modeling, showed almost no increase in risk as

higher proportions of the trust funds were invested in equities. Regardless of the percentage of funds chosen for private investment, with the approach that we recommend—investment year in and year out and indexed to virtually all of the U.S. industry—the investment risks are kept low, especially in comparison to the risks of individual investments and to the individual investor's risk of having to buy or sell at unfavorable times. In short, this approach protects Social Security funds against all but the risk of another full-blown depression—that is, a very long-term decline affecting the entire economy. Moreover, in a defined-benefit plan, if actual income were less than anticipated, policymakers would have to make new choices between additional financing and benefit cuts. In a defined-contribution plan, lower than expected investment income is accepted as one of the risks of the plan.

3. Francis X. Cavanaugh, *The Truth About the National Debt: Five Myths and One Reality* (Cambridge, Mass.: Harvard Business School Press, 1996).

4. Under the proposal for personal savings accounts offered by other advisory council members, initially only workers under 55 would have such accounts—about 127 million people in 1998, the year the plan was proposed to go into effect—but eventually the entire labor force would be involved and at risk.

CHAPTER 21

1. Young disabled persons, in particular, would lose. With wages reduced or eliminated by disability, they could not expect to put much into the compulsory savings plan, but, as the overall program developed, Social Security benefits for the disabled would still be reduced by 30 percent on average.

2. Op-ed, *Wall Street Journal*, February 5, 1997.

CHAPTER 22

1. See, for example, Joseph Pechman, speaking of Social Security financing in *International Trends in the Distribution of Tax Burdens: Implications for Tax Policy* (Washington, D.C.: Brookings Institution, 1974), p. 7: "Perhaps the most puzzling feature of modern tax systems is the continued acceptance of regressive payroll taxation as a major source of revenue."

2. There are many examples of this in recent history. In one area, students' benefits, the Ford administration in the fiscal year 1978 budget proposed that students' benefits be dropped, and the Carter administration proposed that they be limited to the amount payable under the Basic Educational Opportunity Grant Program for needy students ($1,400 in fiscal year 1978). This would have created a situation in which contributory

Social Security benefits would be related to the loss of parental support for young people through age 17 but would be reduced arbitrarily by a ceiling borrowed from another program at age 18. In the Carter budget for fiscal year 1979, the student benefit proposal was renewed; it also was proposed that retroactive benefits be limited to three months instead of twelve months as under previous law, that the minimum benefit in Social Security be dropped altogether for newly eligible people (rather than frozen at the December 1978 level as under previous law), that people already receiving the minimum be denied future, automatic cost-of-living increases that they have had a right to, and that the age of first eligibility for retirement benefits be postponed a month. It is inconceivable that such proposals would have been made were it not for the unified budget procedure that makes it appear that savings from such changes can be used for general government purposes and can help balance the budget.

3. This formulation of a goal for retirement income policy was adopted in 1977 by the National Planning Association Joint Planning Committee on Private Pensions, of which I was a member.

INDEX

Aaron, Henry J., 93, 200, 243
Account statements, Social Security, 76, 263
Ackerman, Frank, 75
Ackley, Gardner, 200
Actuarial balance. *See* Balance in Social Security
Actuarial rate, 213–214, 228; advantages of, 220; and government contribution, 214, 219, 222; implementation of, 220–222; recommendation for, 223–224
Administration of individual accounts, challenges in, 264–270
Administration of Social Security, 233–234; by bipartisan board, 28; by independent board, recommendation for, 275; quality of, importance of, 118; success of, 123–124; *See also* Social Security Administration
Administrative costs: of individual investments, 239–240; of investment of Social Security funds, 236–237, 240; of privatization schemes, 85; of Social Security, 71, 106, 139
Administrator, role of, 97–99
Advanced age: improved services for, need for, 287–288; increase in benefits in, recommendation for, 288–289; *See also* Elderly

Adverse selection problem, in annuities, 87
Advisory Councils on Social Security: 1936-37, 17–18, 296*n*26; 1937-38, recommendations of, 18–20; 1947-49, 21–22, 23; 1948, 201–202, 213, 218, 303*n*4; 1965, introduction to report of, 142–143; 1978-79, 200–201, 202–206; 1994-96, 175–176, 233, 234–241, 258, 270–271; reaffirmation of original understanding by, 14–15; *See also* Greenspan Commission
African Americans: poverty rates among, 30, 135, 185; in Social Security Administration, 125–127, 130
Age of first eligibility: benefit reduction prior to, 151; changes in, 16, 23–24; gradual increase in, 155; options in, 172; original, 16; raising, adverse impact of, 64, 172, 283; raising, proposal of some Greenspan Commission members for, 158–159
Altmeyer, Arthur J., 17, 196, 228, 231
Amendments to Social Security Act: 1939, 296*n*35; 1950, 22–23, 296*n*35; 1972, 25–26, 252; 1977, 26; 1983, 23, 26, 252. *See also* Greenspan Commission

---

Note: Page numbers followed by letters *n* and *t* refer to notes and tables, respectively.